# INTO THE DEEP

## The Hidden Confession
## of Natalee's Killer

*by*

Andrew G. Hodges, M.D.

INDIAN PRAIRIE PUBLIC LIBRARY
401 Plainfield Rd., Darien, IL
www.indianprairielibrary.org

**Into the Deep**
**The Hidden Confession of Natalee's Killer**

© 2007 by Andrew G. Hodges, M.D.
Published by Village House Publishers
Birmingham, AL

Cover design by Scott Fuller
Cover art by Ray Watkins

Author's Website: www.forensicthoughtprints.com

ISBN-13: 978-1-9617255-3-9
ISBN-10: 1-9617255-3-3

Scripture quotations are taken from
The New King James Version (NKJV), copyright 1979, 1980, 1982, 1992
Thomas Nelson, Inc., Publishers.

Library of Congress Cataloging-in-Publication Data

Hodges, Andrew G.
Into the Deep
Summary: An analysis of the Natalee Holloway case

1. True Crime   2. Psychology (Unconscious Mind)   3. Criminology
4. Forensic Profiling   5. Psycholinguistics

Printed in the United States of America

# Dedication

*To Robert Langs, M.D.*

The discoverer of the deeper intelligence who enabled
this paradigm shift to be applied to forensic science.

Without question the greatest genius the field of psychiatry
has ever produced. Freud, however limited, was the first pioneer
who discovered that the unconscious mind had a language all its own.
Langs was the man who truly broke the code to that language.

# Acknowledgments

For all those people who helped me on the journey to seeing this book to its completion. This includes my friend and publicist Joyce Farrell, my wife Dorothy who has always believed in me, and my brother Greg for his usual significant creative contributions. I appreciate others concerned for justice, including those professionals mentioned in the endorsements along with John Taylor, who runs his own homeland security firm and as an investigative consultant in the case encouraged my profile. I don't want to overlook other justice seekers who played an important role—in particular "Wonder Woman," Betty, and Rhonda Jordan, along with several parents of Mountain Brook students on the trip (and some of the students themselves). I am also greatly indebted to Russ Tarby and Michael Christopher, two fine editors who helped shape this book and provided the emotional support only an editor can.

# Contents

# Foreword

Dr. Andrew Hodges' investigation of forensic documents and police interviews in the Natalee Holloway case suggests very strongly that his "thoughtprint" decoding—his "reading between the lines" profiling method—has now become a major law enforcement tool and could be used in countless future cases by criminal investigators. Thoughtprint decoding focuses on unconscious communication, dramatically differentiating it from other profiling methods. Based on extensive clinical research into the unconscious mind, this approach is an extension of psychiatrist Robert Langs' discovery of "super-intelligence" in his patients' unconscious, which both perceived and communicated subliminally in an encoded language.

Hodges refers to these unconsciously patterned messages as "thoughtprints." He continues to make the case that thoughtprints reveal unconscious minds far more perceptive than our conscious minds, and incredibly honest. In short, Hodges contends that whenever a criminal offender communicates he cannot prevent himself from telling the truth unconsciously, between the lines, in encoded messages. Deep down, all perpetrators have a need to confess no matter how hardened they might appear to be at the conscious level. Indeed, Hodges has demonstrated that criminal offenders speak through deeper encoded messages, either in their written or verbal communications, revealing their guilt, motives, and true identities.

I have followed Hodges' work for some time, beginning with his decoding of the crucial ransom note in the JonBenét Ramsey case. Impressively, he made the case that the ransom note was an *unconscious confession* and should have been the central evidence in that instance. In the note the writer identified the murderers and explained powerful motives, yet it was overlooked by authorities who had not yet come to appreciate its true value. Forensic authorities' use of the ransom note was restricted exclusively to fingerprint and handwriting analysis, even though thoughtprint decoding opened up an entirely new world of a deeper verbal language straight from the unconscious mind of the killer(s).

In the BTK case, Hodges decoded fresh but limited communication thoughtprints from the taunting serial killer, written immediately before his capture, and warned that BTK was unconsciously informing authorities that he was on the verge of killing again, *an issue no other profiler had raised.* Out of concern for any number of potential victims, Hodges went public with his profile. Shortly after his capture, BTK revealed that Hodges was right: he had already begun stalking his next victim. This serves as a well-validated example of the potential thought-print decoding offers.

Judging from his prior work and his current work in the Holloway case, Hodges' in-depth analysis of verbal and written communication is indeed becoming the cutting edge of forensic science.

Steven A. Egger, Ph.D.
Associate Professor of Criminology
University of Houston-Clear Lake
Houston, Texas

# Preface

The forensic profile contained in this book is my expert, professional opinion based on extensive research and experience.

I developed this profile by using a new form of profiling, called "thoughtprint decoding." Thoughtprint decoding was developed as a result of extensive clinical research and experience with the unconscious mind and unconscious communication. It is applied to forensic documents and oral interrogations to identify the unconscious content built-in to such communications.

The unconscious mind, meaning the so-called "other 90 percent," which I have called the deeper intelligence has been clinically proven to be the most capable and most honest part of the mind. It can be repressed but it cannot be fooled. Thus this deeper intelligence brilliantly analyzes motives that are fully understood only at its own unconscious level, and then does everything it can to communicate those motives in a vivid, hidden "thoughtprint language" all its own.

To achieve a smoother narrative flow in this book I am reporting my forensic conclusions step-by-step, not necessarily in the order in which they revealed themselves to me or even as they relate to the various sections of the documents in this book. Thus, when you read this profile you may ask yourself whether the unconscious human mind is really this organized, this capable, and this insistent on describing its own deepest motives in such an intricate, detailed way.

The unequivocal answer is yes. The human mind is capable of weaving together a powerful story, utterly true yet remaining completely below the conscious level. Typically, such stories use every word, every item of punctuation, and every spacing and organizing technique in rich, intentional-yet-subconscious ways that utterly contradict what the owner of the mind in question might be saying at the conscious level.

What we commonly call cover stories are exactly that, except that no cover story can truly cover up the truth any more than a bed sheet can cover up a mattress. Once the sheet is pulled back the mattress is revealed.

Beyond all that, after years of listening to brilliant deeper minds communicate, hour after hour in case after case, I can tell you that we all, indeed, possess extraordinary minds! Nowhere is this more true—

and *nowhere does the impetus to tell the truth become more compelling*—than when we have committed a crime and harmed one of our fellow human beings.

The case before us amply demonstrates this simple, irrefutable truth. If you stick around for the story—even if some aspects make you uncomfortable on a physical level and perhaps even violated or angry on a psychological level—you will experience sheer amazement at what you might learn about the minds we possess.

I continually deal with the same amazement almost every day, and I've been there hundreds of times before. Our minds desperately yearn to show us and tell us what they know to be true. This book reveals how one such mind and one such yearning led a guilty young man to tell the truth—despite his own best efforts to suppress it—about a lovely, innocent girl whose life was taken away in the twinkling of an eye.

My hope is that this book will cause other eyes to open.

# Introduction

*If I take the wings of the morning,*
*And dwell in the uttermost parts of the sea,*
*Even there Your hand shall lead me,*
*And Your right hand shall hold me.*
(PSALM 139:9–10 NKJV)

I am an experienced psychiatrist and forensic psycholinguist. In my practice as a psychiatrist I see patients in therapy. As a forensic psycholinguist, I study the written or spoken words of suspects to analyze the inner workings of the criminal mind.

Within the last 12 years—and owing much to the work of one pioneering specialist in my field—I have developed a new form of psychological profiling now known as "thoughtprint decoding."

The process is not simple but I'll state it as simply as I can. I am able to read between the lines of what suspects in criminal cases say in spontaneous oral and written communications. I specialize in *unconscious communication*. I use the perpetrator's own unconscious mind as my primary source of information, because the unconscious mind always wants to tell the truth. And, of course, it's always the *one unimpeachable source of truth about what its owner actually saw and did.*

More than twenty-five years of experience have convinced me that the unconscious mind never lies. Literally, it can't. The challenge for my profession is to learn how to understand exactly what the unconscious mind is saying. I have dedicated a major portion of my career to furthering this understanding.

Coincidentally, I live in Birmingham, Alabama, where my daughter once attended the same high school as Natalee Holloway, the 18-year-old honors student who disappeared from a post-graduation party on the Caribbean island of Aruba on May 30, 2005. After vacationing for five days, Natalee went off alone with three young guys she barely knew. That was her last night in "paradise"—a night that suddenly erupted into her own personal hell.

Whatever Natalee's high school classmates say about what happened that night, and whatever momentary impulse precipitated Natalee's decision to get into a car in a foreign country with three young men—all strangers to her—is really not important. The friends who speculate on her unhappy fate were not with her during her final hours. The three guys were. And so far, more than two years after the fact, except for those three islanders ranging in age from 17 to 21, few witnesses have come forward. None have shed significant light on her fate. Meanwhile, two of the three young men have spoken publicly, and all three are admitted liars.

Likewise, no FBI agents were with Natalee that night, nor were any Aruban police officers. Even so, all these investigators continue to ignore the single most crucial clue, an email written soon after the crime by one of the three prime suspects. But I have examined it in detail. In this book I reveal its often shocking content by probing the suspect's own words and reading the messages he delivers between the lines.

The story that emerges from that email echoes the beliefs of Natalee's mother and father, who have strongly suspected that their daughter's disappearance was caused by a date rape gone bad—real bad. That same story was supported by my earliest forensic profile of the case, pulled together from verbatim interviews long before I had the email. But the email reveals vivid details of Natalee's final night that no one else knows except the three suspects.

All of this is the story I will tell you now: how that witness came forward, what pressured him to do so, and how he happened to be at the crime scene that night. Most important, I will tell you what he said happened.

Such a witness is the only person who could possibly answer the questions that have hung over Aruba like a pall for the last two years. It's his story that I reveal here. Luckily for us, this witness was especially observant, insightful, and capable of delivering a rock-solid narrative that verifies itself and describes in excruciating detail something that will horrify most of us, but which still cries out to be understood.

The only remaining question is whether the three perpetrators will ever be officially punished for committing such a hellish crime in a supposed island paradise. And I use that word "officially" on purpose, for as this book makes clear, at least one of those young men continues to be punished unmercifully, within his own mind, for the brutal crime committed by all three.

# I
# Unforgettable Meeting, Unforgettable Promise

Deepak Kalpoe and Joran van der Sloot will never forget the moment, about 4 am on the morning of May 31, 2005, when they walked up to Beth Twitty, Natalee Holloway's mother. Beth sat in her rental van next to the Holiday Inn SunSpree Resort on Palm Beach, a few miles north of Oranjestad, the biggest city in Aruba. Aruba is an island with a population of about 100,000 people, most of whom rely on a constant influx of tourist dollars. Almost exactly twenty-four hours earlier, Deepak and Joran claimed, they'd left her daughter, an innocent tourist, alive and well at that same Holiday Inn.

## The Basic Sequence

Eighteen-year-old Natalee Holloway had last been seen on the previous night, with Joran, then 17, Deepak, 21, and Deepak's younger brother, Satish, 18, as she was leaving the popular Oranjestad nightspot *Carlos'n Charlie's* at closing time around 1 am on May 30, 2005. Joran, a Dutch citizen, was a tall, high school tennis player with fair features, short-cropped dark hair, and an eye for the ladies. Deepak and Satish were natives of Surinam, a country located southeast of Guyana on the eastern shore of South America, heavily populated by dark-skinned people of East Indian descent such as the Kalpoes.

The next morning Natalee failed to appear at Aruba's Queen Beatrix International Airport, and thus she failed to board the plane that took the rest of her recently graduated high school classmates back home to Alabama. As soon as they knew she was missing, which didn't take long—the plane landed just a few hours later in Birmingham—Beth and Jug Twitty (Natalee's mother and stepfather at the time) flew to Aruba in a private jet supplied by friends. Shortly after their arrival, late in the evening of the same day, May 30, through local contacts at the Holiday Inn and elsewhere, the Twittys discovered the name and address of Joran (pronounced YOUR-ahn) van der Sloot, the guy with whom Natalee was last spotted. In minutes they were on their way to Joran's house in the Oranjestad suburb of Noord, with an entourage of friends and a few key locals they had engaged in the process.

When the Twittys and their friends arrived at Joran's house around 1 am, Joran's father, Paulus van der Sloot, did not respond to efforts to get him to come to the door. However, two Aruban eyewitnesses in the group peered over the fence surrounding the property and spotted what later turned out to be Deepak Kalpoe's silver-gray Honda sedan parked near the house. The Twitty group left to find the local police and eventually ended up back at the van der Sloot home around 3 am, where Paulus this time took fifteen minutes to come to the door. Appearing perplexed, he claimed that his son was out with friends. Then he reached Joran by cell phone. Supposedly, a mix-up then occurred, with Paulus sending everyone on a wild goose chase to the Wyndham Hotel, looking for Joran and Deepak. Meanwhile, Joran had heard the message that he was to return home, which he did, easily beating the police—who had accompanied the Twitty entourage to the Wyndham—back to his house.

With Beth still in the van, Jug Twitty and several of his Alabama friends then confronted the two boys as a police officer stood nearby. Joran and Deepak maintained their innocence, claiming they hadn't seen Natalee since dropping her off at the Holiday Inn the previous night. At that point, according to Deepak, Jug Twitty blew up.

*"She disappeared because after she went with you assholes she lost,"* was how Deepak recalled what the stepfather said.

Joran's own father, Paulus van der Sloot, was also present at that confrontation and—again according to Deepak—he jumped in to defend the boys, insisting that Aruba was not the United States and that Jug and his friends were out of their jurisdiction.

"I want you people out of my yard. I know the law!" At the time, Paulus van der Sloot was connected to the local court system as a kind of "judge-in-training" in Aruba, a constituent nation of the Kingdom of the Netherlands.

As Deepak remembers it, one of Jug's friends stepped in to break up the tension, suggesting that they all go to the Holiday Inn to see if Joran and Deepak could identify the security guard with whom they reportedly had left Natalee. The police agreed and the group proceeded to the hotel, but—in Deepak's own words—*"We went there there was no suck security working there as we described."*

At that moment, Deepak and Joran noticed Beth Twitty sitting nearby in her car, in the hotel parking lot. She was crying. For some reason they felt compelled to speak to her. Having just experienced "bad cop" Jug Twitty's harsh treatment, perhaps they hoped to find "good cop" Beth Twitty more understanding. After walking over to Natalee's grieving mother, Deepak states that he and Joran said, *"Ma'am, you have to believe us! We did not do anything with you [sic] daughter."*

The two boys were completely unprepared for what came next. Beth Twitty—looking them both in the eye—immediately responded, *"I don't believe you two. I promise you I will make you [sic] life a living hell because of this."*

As we will see, those words from the worried mother, as recounted by Deepak himself, shook the two boys to their cores. Though hoping for relief, the two suspects felt red-hot coals heaped on their heads, so searing that one of the boys would crack under the heat. Deepak— young, frightened, and in much farther over his head than he ever imagined in his worst *"nightmare"*—his own word which he repeats twice— did not hold out long before he broke.

Exactly five days after encountering Beth Twitty, Deepak told us virtually the entire story of Natalee Holloway's final hours on earth. He revealed the gory details, making it plain that she did indeed die. He confessed that he and his two companions, Joran and his own brother, Satish, had engineered the entire escapade, and he answered most of the important questions the police and the parents had been asking. In his own rambling recollections, Deepak told a graphic, X-rated story of sex and violence.

## How I Know This Story

As I write this, two years after Natalee disappeared, Deepak's written confession remains the most accurate body of information in this entire case. In a moment I'll explain how I came to possess it, and how I then became involved in decoding it. But first you need to know a little more about how and why I'm able to fully understand it.

I am a clinical psychiatrist with a specialty in forensic profiling. In other words, I am a "mind detective," a comparatively new type of profiler who examines the written words and statements of suspects in criminal cases. To coin a phrase, I "read between the lines" of messages delivered by such people.

In short, when I have verbatim communication from a suspect, either oral or written, I can read secret messages. And interestingly enough, *guilty perpetrators prefer to use written communications to unconsciously confess*.

By the time written communications from suspects reach my hands they are known as *forensic documents*. They can be letters, emails, journal writings, ransom notes, or taunting letters from serial killers. My profiling methods can be equally effective, however, in virtually all such cases. As a result, I've emerged as a new type of forensic document examiner, and also as an analyst of psycholinguistics in oral communications.

Reading the deeper meanings contained in forensic documents can be just as valuable as the work of skilled interrogations in breaking down a suspect's alibis and getting at the truth. In fact, as I will demonstrate, written documents offer unique advantages. Such unintentional confessions allow perpetrators to communicate in even clearer ways, as though they had personally painted a picture of the crime scene.

Writing's visual component also adds another element that simply is not available for analysis in oral interrogations. It offers vivid insights that can be studied over and over, providing an unparalleled, never-goes-away look into a perpetrator's mind at the moment of his crime. And invariably, that's where he takes you. The crime scene, as we will see, is indelibly etched in a perpetrator's mind. And naturally enough, the sooner the writing sample is written after the crime the fresher the crime scene will be in the writer's mind.

Beyond that, my work with the deeper intelligence has taught me that no matter how hardened a sociopath may seem on the surface, inside it's an entirely different story. In fact, another of the major contributions thoughtprint decoding brings to forensic science is an enhanced understanding of the criminal mind. The common misperception is that a hardened criminal has a so-called "Swiss cheese" conscience and harbors no secret urges whatsoever to get caught. That would essentially mean that he had no conscience at all, when in reality, deep down, virtually every perpetrator desperately wants to confess—unconsciously. And they often do so, secretly.

All of this leads directly into the evidence available to me in the Holloway case. *The most damning and revealing forensic document in this case is a lengthy email written by Deepak Kalpoe just a few days after the crime.* He wrote it as a direct reaction to his encounters with Beth and Jug Twitty. In it, Deepak revealed how vivid the crime scene remained in his mind's eye, as he went over and over the key moments of mayhem that he was unable to erase from his memory. He undoubtedly retains these same memories in the same place, in much of the same lucid detail, even today.

The bottom line here is quite simple. Verbatim communications from a suspect, the more spontaneous the better, are extremely valuable. And if Deepak Kalpoe was anything in this communication, he was intensely spontaneous, almost running off at the mouth.

In addition, Joran and Deepak also spoke spontaneously with the police, with Jug and his friends and with a few other people as well. This was also quite fortunate for us, because—as I will explain in the next chapter—spontaneous comments from a suspect are often far superior to comments laboriously "drawn out" in police interviews. Such unsolicited comments, whether spoken or written, can provide all kinds of clues, all of which the suspect reveals unconsciously.

## Personal Involvement

My house in Birmingham is not far from the brick split-level home where Natalee lived, which is close to Mountain Brook High School. Twelve years before Natalee Holloway flew away on her senior trip to the Caribbean, my youngest daughter took a similar graduation trip from the same school. Different place and different time, but the same idea— the senior trip was a traditional celebration, a rite of passage foreshadowing plans to leave home for college two months later. It's the type of trip taken every year by thousands of graduating high school seniors.

Looking back I shudder. What happened to Natalee Holloway could just as easily have happened to my own daughter. Natalee had been a member of the same high school dance club, *The Dorians*, and the same girl's Bible study group. Natalee sat for the same style of senior picture in the black V-necked dress, and she was the same good student. She was an 18-year-old girl with the same vulnerabilities as my daughter, and she was going to a seemingly safe, carefree, warm and sunny island resort with a group of girls, close friends who knew each other well and would look after one another.

Truly—Natalee could have been anybody's daughter, and almost every parent of a high school senior knows it. That is why this case has received so much attention. Natalee is every parent's ideal daughter, going off to take on the world; the child blossoming into a young woman. Though she's maturing more quickly than we ever anticipated, she's still our child and she carries all our hopes and dreams as we finally turn her over to herself and to a big, bad world we all know is out there. We all share that hollow feeling that parents know well, the one that originates in the backs of our minds every time our daughters go out with friends and are late coming home. Or when she goes off on an overnight trip.

In particular, Natalee represents that first child that we turn loose, the one we've always been most anxious about because we simply haven't been there before, and we know she hasn't either. But even if she's your fifth child she's still your little girl, and she still has to take on the world. There is something special about girls, a certain softness and vulnerability, and parents feel that deeply in their own hearts. When that vulnerability is violated it amounts to your worst nightmare coming true. That's why we all feel the pain now being endured by Beth Twitty and Dave Holloway, Natalee's natural father.

## I Wanted to Help

So here I was, living in Natalee's own neighborhood, having developed a new criminal-profiling technique, and I was more than willing to help. I also knew that if any suspects talked, and if they were guilty, they would reveal their involvement, wittingly or not. But I knew of no forensic documents from the suspects, and I had no access to their police interviews.

Early on, however, I was fortunate to receive verbatim communication from eyewitnesses who had traveled to Aruba with the Twittys, people who had talked to Deepak and Joran and had also watched his father, Paulus van der Sloot, in action that first night after Natalee's disappearance. On a few occasions I also spoke directly with Jug Twitty.

I had also gleaned information from Dave Holloway, who had spoken at length to Paulus. In addition, I interviewed numerous students who took the post-graduation trip with Natalee, and I talked with several Aruban journalists who provided background information on the suspects. I soon became involved with some of the family's own investigators, and they also shared information with me.

Eventually I developed an early profile based on various verbatim interviews, and I included information from reported leaks of police interviews. When I sent the preliminary profile to the family's investigative team and to Natalee's parents, one of the consultants hired by the Twittys quickly caught on to what I was doing. His name was John Taylor, and as a senior analyst for his client (Layered Voice Analysis, or LVA) he introduced their innovative voice-analysis technology into the case. He was impressed with my cutting-edge approach. (Later, and not surprisingly, LVA's analysis of Joran van der Sloot's various television interviews in the US in March of 2006 would reveal a high probability of deceit.)

Then, through the efforts of the family's investigators, my profile eventually ended up in the hands of Aruban authorities, including prosecutor Karin Janssen. I discussed this with Vinda De Sousa, one of the family's initial attorneys in Aruba, who discussed the case every day with Janssen. Vinda told me that both she and Karin were impressed with my profile.

"How did you get it so right?" she asked. "It's exactly what we're thinking."

## Dave Holloway

I also discussed my original profile with Dave Holloway who later mentioned my work in his April 2006 book, *Aruba: The Tragic Untold Story of Natalee Holloway and Corruption in Paradise*. At that point Dave had some doubts about my report. He believed that an interview with the suspects would have been more helpful, but as I told him, spontaneous comments from the suspects obtained from eyewitnesses could often be even *more* helpful.

Now that I have Deepak's confession, my early profile proves quite valid and contains important information the suspects have struggled to conceal. However, some of my original profile was based on speculative police reports that I couldn't verify. And, I agreed with Dave that an interview—or more verbatim communication from one of the suspects—would be even more valuable.

I also knew that if I could access police reports of interviews with the three suspects, the information there, even though it would be riddled with lies, would contain hidden messages that I could unlock by using my method. Police don't fully understand how the mind works, especially the unconscious mind where the soul lives, and I do.

No matter how the suspects shaped their lies they would also be revealing the truth. I knew that at the exact moment when Joran and Deepak spoke to police investigators they would be trying their "left-brained" best to cover up what their "right-brained" consciences would be saying, loudly and clearly enough for me to hear. (As I will explain later, symbolic right-brain communication is the key to this case, as opposed to literal left-brain lies.) I wasn't able to get the reports I wanted, so I bided my time—which just proves, perhaps that good things sometimes come to those who wait.

## Deepak's Email

I'll never forget the day when I obtained the email written by Deepak Kalpoe, which almost literally blows the case wide open. This four-page email was written on June 4, 2005, exactly six days after Natalee's disappearance. Deepak used it to reiterate his version of the story in devastating detail. The email eventually made its way to the Internet and was posted within the month. How I gained access to this email—and how I verified it—is a fascinating story in itself and is told in the next chapter.

I was not the first person to see the email, but as a profiler I was the first one to see its full value. And I'm the only investigator who has verified its authenticity. The forensic document containing Deepak's hidden confession is a personal correspondence written to a friend. She is a surrogate grandmother figure named Betty, an engaging, older Chicago woman who unofficially adopted Deepak after meeting him in an Internet café at which he was employed in Oranjestad. She had gone to the café with her friend, coincidentally named Natalie, while they were vacationing together a few years ago. On two separate vacations Betty had contact with Deepak at the café where he worked.

Betty and Deepak had also corresponded by email for a few years prior to Natalee's disappearance. Deepak's decision to confide in Betty, and the timing of when he wrote her, are major keys to solving this case, as Deepak himself will make clear to us.

## Verification

I have spoken with Betty and I have discussed her relationship with Deepak at length. I have also seen original copies of the email, and have seen proof that Deepak wrote it, along with two other emails to Betty that he sent shortly afterward.

Betty also shared other correspondence between the two of them. For the record, Betty believes that Deepak is innocent, although she has considered briefly that he might have been involved. She acknowledges that people in general—and young people in particular—are certainly capable of unacceptable behaviors. But she's still not convinced that Deepak participated in Natalee Holloway's death.

# 2
# Seeking Justice

Criminologist Vernon Geberth, a former New York City detective and the author of *Practical Homicide Investigation*, had it right when he instructed all of us to expect great opposition to justice. The greater the crime, he noted, the greater the opposition would be, particularly if the perpetrator has the motive and the means to avoid prosecution. That's why Geberth so strongly worded his timeless advice about investigating homicides:

> Death investigation constitutes a heavy responsibility . . . let no person deter you from the truth . . . to see that justice is done . . . and remember 'you're working for God.'"

Deepak Kalpoe will himself show us just how much he agrees with Geberth. There's a corollary to Geberth's dictum, one with which I'm sure he would agree: The strength needed to pursue justice requires a determined team. Never has this been more true than in the Natalee Holloway case.

## Parents, Friends, and Surprise Helpers

Shortly after midnight on Monday night, May 31, 2005—twenty-four hours after Natalee went missing—Paulus van der Sloot was shocked to find the Twittys knocking on his door in Aruba, asking to speak to his son about their daughter. He might have expected such a scene at some point, but not this soon.

Eyewitnesses on the scene testify that the elder van der Sloot at some point expressed surprise that the Twittys had arrived so quickly, commenting, "How did you get here? There are no flights into Aruba until Thursday!" He never imagined that Beth and Jug would fly immediately to Aruba on a friend's corporate jet.

Several of their other friends also joined the Twittys aboard the jet, then helped them begin their search for Natalee in Oranjestad. Some of these friends were Jug's hunting buddies and others whose daughters had been on the trip with Natalee. As the night progressed, they suddenly found themselves standing beside Jug in front of Joran's house, even out-shouting the desperate stepfather: "Where is Natalee?!"

One of them nearly came to blows with Paulus van der Sloot. These were successful businessmen from the states, and they weren't used to being pushed around. More than that, losing Natalee reminded them of how easily they could have lost their own daughters.

The next morning, two of Jug's and Beth's friends walked into Joran's school, spoke with the principal about him, and asked to see him. They also taped flyers on school bulletin boards, about Joran and their search for Natalee. These same flyers made a deep impression on Deepak, as he points out in his email. In fact, one of these flyers became the most overtly striking message in it, demonstrating how important was the entire "friendship team" in stirring things up and motivating Deepak to confess.

The Twittys and their friends rented cars and quickly assembled a team of locals who knew their way around the island. Using their own cash to loosen lips, they began tracking down every rumor involving Natalee's whereabouts. They knocked on the doors of crack houses, barged into drug dens, showed the girl's picture to nightclub patrons, and established numerous contacts within Aruba's seamy underworld. Searching day and night, they pressured Aruba as it had never been pressured before, and Deepak makes it plain that he felt that pressure. Down the road they would continue to keep the heat on. Several of the Twitty's Birmingham supporters have made repeated trips to the island to carry on the search.

Then there was Beth, the mother tiger whose restless energy spurred the media to action and captured the hearts of the American people. An attractive and articulate woman in her mid-40s, Beth made a memorable impression on television interviewers and viewers alike. With flaxen hair framing her face, her dark eyes burned with an unyielding resolve. Despite criticism at times that she was the "ugly American," Beth was doing what any caring parent would do, keeping the case alive any way she could. Likewise, Dave Holloway quickly entered the picture as the concerned father searching relentlessly for his lost daughter.

The three Aruban boys had taken advantage of an American. They looked upon the tourist girls who flocked to their sunny island paradise as theirs for the picking. But this time they'd picked an American teenager to whom thousands of American parents could easily relate, a young, vulnerable girl who symbolized all of our daughters. The media kept Natalee's story alive for many months, but the news people never could have done so unless the American people were responding. The media's viewers, listeners, and readers did respond, however, assuring the case a high public profile across the United States and around the world.

Because Joran, Deepak, and Satish had preyed upon a girl with strong parents who had strong friends, the suspects found themselves in deep water. The Twitty/Holloway team—justice-seekers all—was in place. And soon the team would get much larger.

While we will soon see how Deepak unconsciously joined the team within a few days, it also appears that Joran's unconscious mind was pushing him to help as well. An Aruban who witnessed the tension-filled encounter between the Twitty team and the van der Sloots in the early morning hours of May 31, 2005, at Joran's house, described to me how badly Joran wanted to join the team in his own way. But as Joran was being pressured by Jug and his friends to reveal information about Natalee's whereabouts, Paulus interrupted his son four times to prevent him from speaking.

Each time Joran told his father, "I must speak to them. I will help in any way I can." Of course Joran had no conscious intention to help the Twittys and aid the investigation. His conscious mind was working overtime to obfuscate, rationalize, and avoid being blamed for Natalee's fate. Nevertheless, his actions and words reveal that, like Deepak, Joran unconsciously wanted to confess. In fact, later on, in several public interviews Joran actually did confess between the lines.

This is why I was convinced from the beginning that the police interviews contained helpful information from Joran that the police ultimately overlooked. In fact, Beth Twitty recalls having the distinct impression that Joran was trying to confess that very same night when he approached her, beating on his chest and repeating "What do you want me to do now?"—as though telling her Natalee was dead and there was nothing he could do.

Later Deepak will tell us that, indeed, Joran secretly wants to confess, and Deepak will also join the justice seekers when he makes a huge promise to help, a promise that he ultimately fulfills.

## Wonder Woman

In late-June 2005, three weeks after Natalee's disappearance, an Internet blogger/poster known as "Wonder Woman" placed three emails allegedly written by Deepak Kalpoe on an Internet discussion site dedicated to the Holloway case. The emails had been sent by Deepak to a woman named Betty, whom we have already identified. The most extensive email, the first of the three, was dated June 4, 2005, just five days after Natalee's disappearance during the early hours of May 30.

Wonder Woman had a connection to a good friend of Betty's. She said she'd gotten the emails from Betty herself, who told her all about Deepak. Wonder Woman explained the circumstances, which seemed preposterous on the surface. She reported that Deepak had written three emails— in particular the rambling email about his involvement with the 18-year-old blonde who had disappeared—to an American lady from Chicago, a grandmother whom he had previously met in Aruba. It seemed like such a stretch that Wonder Woman, who posted the emails three weeks after they were written, was widely ridiculed. One critic after another found reason to doubt their accuracy, yet Wonder Woman stuck to her guns.

By mid-summer, I had already begun profiling the case by using information provided by eyewitnesses who had interviewed Joran and Deepak. I still hoped to get a look at the police interviews or at some verbatim communication from the suspects, such as a media interview. Little did I know that Deepak's email would far surpass my grandest wish. Dan Riehl, who hosts an Internet discussion site (Riehl World View) and with whom I had discussed the case, suggested at the time that I look over the emails to at least verify their validity. Also, a mother of one of the Mountain Brook graduates on the trip knew of my work on the case. She too advised me to review the emails, and I am indebted to both of them.

The first time I read the emails—almost two months after Wonder Woman had posted them—I was immediately impressed. There was no reason to think they were phony. In fact, what they revealed strongly suggested that they were authentic. They contained certain details which eyewitnesses had related to me but which were not widely known at the time the emails were written. Plus, they had all the earmarks of an unconscious confession. The sheer length of the June 4 email made that fact clear.

This told me that the communicator was under a lot of pressure to talk, and talk a lot. Surely it fit a young and naïve Deepak Kalpoe if he were involved in this crime, which was already my impression from my early profile. I had to get in touch with Wonder Woman before investing the countless hours I knew I'd have to spend profiling the emails, using my new method.

I inquired if Wonder Woman would speak with me privately. If she would do that, I believed I could make her understand how valuable these emails were. To her everlasting credit, Wonder Woman both spoke to me and verified the emails' authenticity by sending me the original emails she had obtained, and by putting me in touch with Betty.

Betty was a successful antique retailer who told me of how she'd first come to know Deepak. In 2003, when they met in Deepak's Internet café, he deeply missed his grandmother with whom he had lived in his native Surinam, and the friendly, effervescent Betty was the perfect sub- stitute. Deepak—polite, soft-spoken and helpful—related well to her. For Betty it was as though he were the grandson she herself had helped to raise. The two of them hit it off and developed a pleasant relationship when Betty visited his café several times on her vacation—and renewed it a year later under similar circumstances.

Over the next two years they corresponded via email, several of which Betty sent me. Little did Betty know when she received Deepak's June 4, 2005 email, however, that it contained the entire story of the case, revealing Natalee's fate. But unquestionably, after talking with her and receiving copies from her of all the emails, I had no doubt that she knew Deepak, and I was certain I now had in my possession a valuable forensic document. Clearly it would establish either Deepak's guilt or his innocence.

Wonder Woman had indeed proven to be a wonder! She intuitively knew the emails had significance. And when I came along she instinc- tively realized that I was the person to whom she should give them. At the time, I told her that they'd likely prove to be the most valuable information in the case, because they allowed us to look deeply into the mind of a major suspect immediately after a major crime. Already there were strong indications of Deepak's involvement in Natalee's disappearance.

It's my understanding that since then Wonder Woman has progres- sively shifted into Deepak's corner, but that's not really surprising given her connection to Betty. As much as both women wanted to believe Deepak was innocent, to their credit they freely shared his emails with me, knowing I was a profiler. I believe they unconsciously suspected something and were acting on the side of justice. Why else would they do what they did? Easily, those emails might never have come to light. To this day I correspond with Betty, who continues to hope I'm wrong but, as she told me, "I believe in helping people out when they are in desperate circumstances." Did she ever help!

As I studied the email it became clear that suspect Deepak Kalpoe was so troubled and so burdened that, six days after Natalee's disappearance and only five days after a powerful face-to-face meeting with Natalee's mother, he had to set the record straight. Responding to an irresistible urge to confess, Deepak's unconscious mind did what his conscious mind couldn't do.

In this moment of torment, who better for Deepak Kalpoe to write to than his grandmother-confessor figure, Betty? Or was she? To whom did he really need to confess? The email itself will show that, while Deepak Kalpoe sent his June 4 email to Betty, he was clearly writing to another person as well—in particular, the person who most needed to know what really happened that horrific night when Natalee Holloway lost her life. And we will see that, indirectly, Deepak was also writing one other key person. Stay tuned.

## The Profiling Journey Begins

When I first got Deepak's email I had no idea that I was beginning a nearly two-year journey that would take me to the verge of a new search for Natalee's body in August 2007. Little did I know that one day the profile I developed would encourage Dave Holloway to renew his efforts to pursue that search. And little did I know that Deepak, in this very email, would provide specific instructions on how to find the body.

However, from the very beginning I knew I had my work cut out for me. Deepak's email was four pages long and contained 2,400 words, with many of those words having at least one additional, deeper meaning, not including special, creative communications embedded in the punctuation. It was six times longer than the 400-word ransom note in the JonBenét Ramsey case, which I had spent months studying and on which I eventually wrote two books. In other words, I knew how long profiling could take because I knew the process well.

Parenthetically, looking back on the Ramsey case, I should have anticipated that Deepak would give us remarkably detailed instructions about finding the body, because that's precisely what the writer of that ransom note did. That writer directed the police to JonBenét's body in the home where John Ramsey later "discovered" it. But my analysis in that case came after-the-fact, while in the Holloway case, as I decoded Deepak's email, the body still remained "out there."

My profile of Deepak's email then unfolded over the course of the next year. For various reasons, including my work as a practicing psychiatrist, I could move only so fast. Profiling is a terribly exciting process—it involves trying to solve a mystery by decoding hidden messages, and tracking the thoughtprints from an utterly brilliant mind (more on this in chapter 3). Still, you can't hurry the profiling process—it has to be done right or not at all.

Gradually, the hidden messages in whatever the document (email, ransom note, letter, personal journal, taunting serial killer letter) becomes clear, step-by-step. You look and read and think; at first you see a little bit here and a little bit there; you recognize how this idea/ thoughtprint fits with that one; and slowly the puzzle comes together until suddenly—boom!—a major part of the case opens up to you in a flash, crystal clear. You see exactly what the writer's confessing. Each answer then takes you back to a previous answer, which you now see in an even deeper way.

You never know in advance where the mind of the perpetrator is going to take you, but you can bet it will be one exciting, mind-boggling insight after another. You will see the case like you could never imagine it in advance. For example, the killer might tell you exactly what happened, how it happened, the order of events, and the like. It's a remarkable process to experience. And yet, in the end, no matter how horrific the crime, you always end up with a strange admiration for the perpetrator's unconscious mind. You know you're looking at a brilliant communicator, even though you're also looking at a guilty soul.

Deepak's email was no exception. Early on I could see that it was a confirmation that Natalee was dead, and that the three boys were completely responsible. In due time the specific details emerged in remarkable depth just as I anticipated, largely because of the phenomenal length of the email. Deepak's obsessive personality shone through to such an extent that he almost went overboard in describing specific details. But you could see why, because of the tremendous unconscious guilt driving him to confess. Eventually I saw that he was leading us to the body, first revealing that it was in the ocean and then becoming more and more specific. Unquestionably Deepak was countering Paulus van der Sloot's widely reported advice to the three suspects, "No body, no case," with counsel of his own: "Find body, solve case."

With my completed profile in hand, I then had to decide what to do with it. This was now more than a year after the crime. Numerous searches had already been made, raising false hopes in a hundred different ways, but nothing definitive had turned up. In the meantime the three suspects had gone on with their lives: Deepak returned to his

Internet café and Joran went to college in Holland. Eventually the Dutch took over the investigation, and as recently as May 2007 they were digging into the grounds around both Joran's and the Kalpoes' houses, apparently on a tip. But as of this writing, nothing has been revealed about those renewed efforts.

Meanwhile, as I was completing my profile, I had contact with Beth Twitty through an associate. Beth had never seen Deepak's email and she asked me for a copy. She then took it to John Q. Kelly, an attorney jointly retained by Beth and her ex-husband, Dave Holloway. I had requested a chance to explain the profile I had on the email myself, but circumstances got in the way. Everyone was preoccupied with legal maneuverings, first to bring a wrongful death suit against Joran's parents, and then to bring a countersuit against Deepak Kalpoe who was suing the *Dr. Phil Show* because of a report from his investigator, Jamie Skeeters, that pointed toward Deepak's guilt. In fact, a limited sea-search for Natalee's body had been called off in favor of investing in legal efforts. At the time, Tim Miller's Texas EquuSearch operation had only searched out about a mile from the Aruban shore.

It was always clear to me that, apart from the rare possibility of turning up DNA evidence linking the suspects to the crime, Paulus was right. Finding the body was the only hope for justice. And I knew where it was because I had absolutely no doubt whatsoever that Deepak had told us where it was. So at this point, in January 2007, I again contacted Dave Holloway with my profile to see where he was with respect to renewing the ocean search.

## Back to Dave Holloway

I didn't bother with the FBI because I had learned from an impeccable source within the Bureau that Aruba didn't want its help. I was told that the FBI's original offer to put 150 to 200 agents on the ground in Aruba immediately after Natalee's disappearance had been roundly rejected. Also, the FBI special agent at Quantico, most interested in my work, had retired, and her successors were too busy to learn about a new type of profiler, believing they had plenty of their own profilers in-house. Still, several retired FBI agents embraced my work and specifically validated my new profile in the Holloway case.

So, as I approached Dave again I was confident that I now had the information he was looking for, and more. First I informed him about Deepak's extensive email and, like Beth Twitty, he had never heard about it. We talked again about how, in my experience, a spontaneous communication that came only five days after the crime was superior to any police interview. I also told Dave that my profile of police interviews from all three suspects and other key people—having by then been made available—matched my profile of Deepak's email to a "T."

Dave was open-minded. Having had some education in psychology, he was familiar with dreams and the symbolic language of the unconscious mind. He was willing to consider between-the-lines messages from Deepak's email. By this time Dave was also certain that Natalee was no longer alive, and he had come to the same conclusion about her body being in the ocean, for reasons of his own.

He reviewed with me how, early in the Aruban investigation after Natalee went missing, an assistant prosecutor, Amalin Flanegan, told him she felt certain the body was in the water. Flanegan resigned a short time later, over inadequate police investigation of suspects. Somewhat later than that, Aruban Deputy Police Chief Gerald Dompig suggested the same thing. Thus the consensus among the Aruban police, Dave knew, was that Natalee's body was indeed in the ocean in a large, heavy crab cage that had gone missing the very week of her disappearance from the Fisherman's Huts area, where local fishermen kept their gear.

Dave also told me how Joran and Deepak were spotted on several occasions that same week, repeatedly driving around the somewhat isolated Fisherman's Huts area of the beach, as if they were looking for something. Dave believed this was where Natalee's body had been loaded into a boat before being dropped into the sea. To both of us the most logical reason for Joran and Deepak's behavior was that they were double-checking the Fisherman's Huts shoreline in case Natalee's body washed up. In fact, as I will describe later, Dave even believed the body was located generally where Deepak suggested it was. Another striking observation by the police suggested that the body was in the ocean, for whenever they searched for Natalee's body on the land the suspects seemed to relax, but when ocean searches occurred the three would become noticeably anxious.

In addition, Dave believed Natalee had been sexually assaulted, which led to her death, because Joran had described her panties in exact detail (another hidden confession on his part). Dave took comfort in knowing that I had arrived at my conclusion in an entirely different way, by letting Deepak's unconscious mind tell me. We discussed how the ocean search had been postponed, and he informed me that there were tentative plans, again with Tim Miller of Texas EquuSearch, to resume the effort in April 2007. He expressed a strong intent to pursue the sea-search and establish a definite plan with Tim. I sent Dave a partial profile, which he then asked me to send to Tim Miller.

Since then, Dave and I have continued to talk on a regular basis. As he shared with me several times, his worst nightmare was that the search would never take place. And, indeed, the planned search for April 2007 was moved back to August. The good news, however, was that by then Texas EquuSearch had vastly upgraded its equipment for underwater searches, including a new type of magnetometer that reportedly could find anything substantial made of metal. And the fishermen informed Dave that the approximately 60-pound crab cage in which Natalee's body had probably been placed would not move from its place on the ocean floor where it was originally dropped. My profile reveals that Deepak's unconscious mind believes the same thing. The body is staying put in its watery grave.

I was greatly encouraged by Dave's persistence. He did everything possible to inspire Tim, including attending a fund-raiser in Houston for Texas EquuSearch. He kept Beth Twitty apprised of the plans, and she offered her help in getting Tim Miller's team situated in Aruba when the time came. Dave was every bit as determined as the higher-profile Beth had been much earlier in the case, as chronicled in the media. My admiration for him continued to grow.

Finally, as I reviewed the brutal specifics of my profile with Dave, he showed great courage in listening to it. It was hard for him to take it all in, and he told me he often felt like two people. Sometimes he could view the case with some distance, focusing on the details and searching for the body, always seeking justice for Natalee. At other times the memories of Natalee would come flowing back into his mind, and then the tears would come.

With Dave Holloway, what you see is what you get—good-natured, extremely likeable, seemingly without guile, but plenty smart—he was the quintessential "Southern boy" as we like to say, and I mean that in every positive way. Dave is definitely down to earth, but he's also worldly wise. As we went over the disturbing details of Deepak's email, Dave displayed a remarkable capacity to read through the suspect's blatant denials of culpability. I took delight in that, but there was no way a father could take in Deepak's violent story except slowly and solemnly. After all, Deepak was describing the death of Dave's precious daughter.

## Beth Twitty

Shortly before the second anniversary of Natalee's disappearance, Joran released his book, *The Natalee Holloway Case*, in Holland. The book provides even more material for profiling, on which I'll comment later in this book.

However, on that sad anniversary, I met Beth Twitty on the night of May 30, 2007, at a television studio in Birmingham where we were both being interviewed about the case on different national news programs. I reminded Beth of my note to her several months before, after she'd requested a copy of Deepak's email. In the note I'd told her that she was responsible for Deepak's almost immediate confession. In person, I told her again that when she looked Deepak in the eye twenty-four hours after Natalee's disappearance, when she told him that he was lying through his teeth and promised to make his life a living hell, she had crushed him so badly he couldn't contain himself.

In that TV studio Beth momentarily lost her composure. With tears in her eyes she recalled that exact moment, when she confronted two of the three suspects in Aruba. She then reminded me how she had shortly thereafter gone to Deepak's Internet café to speak to him again. He refused to look at her, she recalled, never once raising his head. Speaking as a former teacher and now a mother, she told me, "I know all about eye contact" and how Deepak's refusal to look her in the eye spoke volumes. Surely he recalled that unsettling experience at the Holiday Inn the last time he had looked Natalee's mother in the eye, and couldn't bear to do it again.

Sometimes looks or no looks are worth a thousand words. In fact, in his email Deepak will indeed return over and over to his own eyes— about what he saw the night Natalee died and how he can't erase those images from his mind.

Meanwhile, as this book goes to press the ocean search for Natalee Holloway's body is imminent. Will it be successful? I fully expect it to be.

On the other hand, suppose we do find the body where Deepak tells us it is. Will they say I was right? I believe that some will ignore this book and say: "Oh, we knew it was there all along." And what will the three suspects then do? We can be sure they will immediately lawyer up and deny once more that they had anything to do with it, continuing to blame a phantom kidnapper—anyone besides themselves. But this email is now in the public record, unmistakably linking all three suspects to the body and Deepak Kalpoe put it there.

## No Body?

Suppose the search fails, and Natalee's body remains missing. Dave Holloway dreads that thought but he and I realize it's possible. While Beth certainly wishes for a successful search and supports it, it seemed to me in my brief conversation with her that she couldn't allow herself to believe it would succeed. Likely Beth is simply beyond hope that the body will be discovered

Certainly it's a big ocean and underwater currents can be very strong. Perhaps the cage has moved or has broken apart. What if searchers don't go out far enough?

But one thing is for sure. Deepak Kalpoe's unconscious mind is clearly telling us the body was discoverable in the ocean at the time they supposedly dropped Natalee at the hotel. Given perpetrators' guilt-driven tendency to make mistakes that get them caught, combined with Deepak's unconscious instructions for finding the body, I believe the search will indeed be successful. If the fishermen's instincts are right and the heavy crab cage remains on the ocean floor, the chances for accomplishing this mission dramatically increase. Sometimes, too, justice catches a break, such as the search equipment having reportedly improved dramatically in the last year.

But suppose the worst-case scenario unfolds — "no body, no case." This is where the prison of the mind comes into play, because deep down each and every one of the three suspects will continue to self-sabotage. Joran has already adopted such behavior, reportedly smoking heavily after publicly announcing his opposition to habitual tobacco use. And we're guaranteed to see something of the same from Deepak and Satish.

It's no coincidence that Joran, of all people, actually predicted this case's outcome in May 2007 when he said that those responsible for Natalee's disappearance will eventually break. In the end neither Joran nor Deepak nor Satish can outrun their own deeper intelligence, their souls. As Deepak noted, each of their lives will continue to be a living hell.

Now for the rest of the story.

# 3
# Thoughtprint Decoding

To appreciate my analysis of Deepak Kalpoe's revealing email, you must understand how a profiler of forensic documents decodes messages from the deeper mind. The foundation of my thoughtprint decoding method is built on the understanding that the human mind is at all times working simultaneously on two levels, the conscious and unconscious.

For convenience I call the conscious mind "L-1" (for Level 1), and the unconscious mind "L-2" (for Level 2). Breakthrough research in which I participated has shown that the unconscious mind, L-2, is truly a deeper intelligence far superior to the L-1 conscious mind. L-2 is commonly known as "the other ninety percent" of our minds, which we have only recently learned how to actually access immediately. Equally important, we are now learning how to understand its own unique special language, which speaks with detailed precision.

This work came about because of a true genius, psychiatrist Robert J. Langs, who first established that our unconscious intelligence functions far beyond anything we had previously believed. After years of therapy experience with his patients, Dr. Langs learned to decode L-2 messages in a practical, hands-on setting. He discovered that his therapy patients—using disguised L-2 communications—were secretly trying to guide him to new understandings of themselves. And, they were simultaneously correcting subtle defects in his therapy to make him a more effective therapist. Deep down, his patients knew exactly what they needed to face to begin healing their wounds, and they dramatically improved when Dr. Langs listened and responded to their L-2 corrections.

Langs is a psychoanalyst by training, based in New York City, who has now authored more than 50 books. He was the first clinician to *fully* tap into unconscious communication—the first man to truly understand how a patient's unconscious L-2 mind structured its messages in patterns designed to reveal what it alone perceived, to thereby guide the therapist in his efforts to help.

As Langs' research unfolded, all the other clinical researchers working with him (including myself) were frequently amazed and astounded by L-2's remarkable abilities. At L-2, the mind observes what's going on at a much deeper level. It then expresses itself with extreme honesty, and it accurately communicates its secret observations between the lines of its own unique language.

Obviously, then, the key to unlocking a whole new world of knowledge lies in understanding how the L-2 mind communicates. Basically, Langs' research has demonstrated that L-2 tells stories are filled with disguised symbolic messages—the identical language of dreams. In a nutshell, the unconscious mind speaks in symbolic code. Therefore, as a profiler my basic job is to read code, to decode otherwise "hidden" messages from the most fantastic computer imaginable, the human mind.

To put it another way, the unconscious L-2 mind communicates *symbolically* while the conscious mind communicates *literally*. The familiar idea that left-brain communication is literal ("just the facts") and right-brain communication is symbolic (think "images") will also help clarify the difference in conscious and unconscious communication. In my model, by analogy the conscious mind speaks "left brain" and the unconscious mind speaks "right brain," which further helps to explain how both can speak *simultaneously*. For example, a person might be talking about a moment when Natalee literally saw a shark—but symbolically he might be telling us that *he* was the shark Natalee encountered.

## Therapy Example

A quick example from therapy, where L-2's abilities were first discovered, also demonstrates the difference between how L-1 and L-2 communicate. A patient announces he's ready to stop therapy, but his L-2 mind then guides him to "casually" tell several stories featuring unfinished business. To cite just two examples, he mentions that his daughter needs to continue her college education even though she wants to drop out. Then he talks about the addition onto his house, which he's been working on for months but hasn't yet finished.

What he's really saying in these two examples—and what he might even repeat in other stories, over and over again—is that he knows unconsciously that he needs to continue therapy, no matter how much his conscious mind wants him to stop. A therapist keyed into L-2 can read the repetitive "unfinished business" code to help the person stay in therapy.

In such a secret "repeat-the-matching-story" pattern, L-2 can communicate virtually any message it wants to, in code. (And, as Deepak will show us, a perpetrator's L-2 mind, which thrives on integrity, insists—*insists*—on communicating.) In forensic work I have called these symbolic story-messages "thoughtprints," all of which tell the same story in different ways, further allowing L-2 to present important details. A thoughtprint, then, is a *symbolic* idea as opposed to a *literal* idea.

Forensic documents such as those I have already identified—in a nutshell—tell secret stories. The L-2 mind of a perpetrator strings together a number of secretly matching symbolic thoughts and ideas to form a "thoughtprint code"—or, in actuality, a series of thoughtprint codes.

In fact, in forensic documents we usually find several main codes or stories within the larger story: what happened, who was involved, often what were their motives, and how police can bring them to justice. In other words, the L-2 mind tells a cohesive hidden story of the case, from beginning to end, by repeatedly answering each important question in code, step-by-step, until it leaves no doubt about the answer to that particular question.

And always, the L-2 mind is far ahead of investigators, anticipating virtually every important question. Thus a profiler's job—and the authorities' job as well—is to sit back and listen, then follow the guidance of the L-2 mind exactly as a psychoanalyst allows a patient's deeper intelligence to guide his therapy. Without exception, when perpetrators communicate in forensic documents, their L-2 minds are far and away the best detectives on the case.

As a profiler examining forensic documents, I track down these thoughtprints and read the code, looking for matches in confirming thoughtprints, all the while knowing that I am watching a genius mind working overtime to help me. Put more simply, I look for a series of codes answering logical questions, starting with a "This is a confession" code with the implied message, "I'm going to guide you through it—pay close attention."

I then move to a "What happened?" code. (In Natalee's case that question was obviously "Is she dead or alive?") That answer, of course, will come with its own unique code of thoughtprints. Then, after I discover that a crime has been committed, I began searching for the next logical code that answers the question, "How did it take place and who was involved?"

In this way I listen to a perpetrator answer a number of different questions, each one separately in code, until I find a cohesive rational story explaining the entire case. Believe me, perpetrators unconsciously tell their hidden stories in remarkable detail. As we will see, Deepak begins his email with the striking promise that between the lines he will tell us the real story of the three primary suspects' last night with Natalee, and will confess that his cover-up version is a lie. That was one of the first signs that this email was indeed a forensic document containing his confession.

To summarize, the bottom line is that every word in a forensic document always has two meanings—one literal and one symbolic. So, Deepak's June 4 email is really a twofer, one message overt and the other message hidden. As we will see, because of its enormous length, it's filled with secret stories. Deepak's L-2 wanted to leave no doubt that this was a full confession.

To put it another way, think of a spy who is sending headquarters a "spy letter" in code. On the surface he is communicating one story, but underneath he is sending an entirely different encoded message. In the same way, Deepak's email is really two emails, but with one huge caveat. Consciously he remains completely unaware that his L-2 deeper intelligence both *exists* and *is spying* on him. His left hand/brain has no idea what his right hand/brain is doing. Zero; zip; nada; nothing! Two totally different systems of the mind, which is just what we often experience every night when we're totally asleep and our L-2 mind produces elaborate dreams featuring "symbology." This explains how a perpetrator's L-2 unconscious mind confesses while L-1 remains in the dark, thinking it's strongly defending himself.

## The U-CAVE Method

Coincidentally, my profiling approach, though far more advanced, has striking similarities to the CAVE (Content Analysis Verbatim Explanation) method used by the creative attorney Bob Beattie to help capture Wichita's serial killer, BTK. He analyzed verbatim messages for conscious (L-1) content. On the other hand, I read verbatim messages for unconscious (L-2) content, for deeper content and symbolic messages. Such exact messages are absolutely crucial to my method, because they provide the only way of obtaining thoughtprints.

Thoughtprint decoding is really a deeper CAVE method. Indeed, it could be called "U-CAVE" for "Unconscious Content Analysis of

Verbatim Explanation." Think of CAVE as exploring obvious land-based caves, whereas U-CAVE explores underwater caves, unconscious caves that exist below the radar of our conscious minds.

## Deepak Joins the Team and Points to the Evidence

Remembering that virtually every single communication is really two, we find that a compelling comment in Deepak's email jumps out immediately. After describing his unforgettable, soul-shaking encounter with Beth Twitty, who had just promised Deepak a literal hell on earth, he continues expressing sympathy to Beth and tells her, *"We will help in anyway possible."*

You can read that two ways. On the L-1 level he's simply expressing sympathy. Or, you can read it as Deepak Code in which—because he's overwhelmed with guilt—his L-2 mind is promising that he will indeed be of great help "in any way" to Beth Twitty, by making a detailed confession.

When I hear a suspect in a forensic document say that he wants to "help" I know that the perpetrator is ready to point us toward new, important truths. In fact, in the next chapter I will show how such key communications are *message markers* designed to guide the reader and help him recognize especially important messages. That's why, on the heels of such a promise, we should expect an especially crucial communication from Deepak. This is how the L-2 decoding process works—promises made, promises fulfilled. While L-1 often obfuscates, dodges, and misleads, L-2 invariably tells the truth.

In this case, Deepak delivers on this specific promise by revealing details so specific that he literally points us to the body in an even stronger fashion. He removes any doubt as to what happened to Natalee Holloway, and he makes it very clear that the three suspects were all deeply involved.

Also, as we decode his message you will see how Deepak's profile could well lead us to important evidence—specifically, to Natalee Holloway's body. The circumstantial evidence gathered in this case to date is strong, certainly strong enough for indictments and possibly strong enough to get a criminal conviction in the United States, but we need something more to get a conviction in the Never Never Land of Aruba.

Think of how important it would be to discover Natalee's body. What if Deepak's L-2 mind were capable of leading us to the body, no matter how hard he tried to prevent it? Wouldn't law enforcement personnel and others searching for Natalee's body want to take advantage of it?

## Deepak's L-2: The Final Word

Deepak Kalpoe himself will make the case that his L-2 word is, indeed, the final word, a complete accounting of Natalee Holloway's final hours, because he was there. Unknowingly, through his L-2 mind he's looking at his own deeper motives. He's looking at his soul and his conscience. He knows how badly he behaved, and he knows better than anyone what he deserves. And, of course, he also knows exactly who else was involved.

As we will also see in chapter 5, when we begin to examine his profile in-depth, Deepak insists on how definite he is about the story he tells. You can read it for yourself. I'm sure that readers who quickly catch on to L-2 communication will even see unique messages that have been overlooked. This is one reason thoughtprint decoding is such exciting forensic work. The L-2 mind is so brilliant there are always more messages to discover, which makes forensic documents so vital to solving cases— often including cold cases.

Meanwhile, in chapter 4 we'll examine in more detail another major concept—how Deepak guides the listener in how to listen to his confession—before we can get on with the actual decoding.

# 4
# From the Large to the Small

By the time you've finished this book you'll realize that current law enforcement and forensic science—in the main—have little understanding of unconscious communication. Investigators profile the physical minutiae of crime scenes remarkably well, but they never fully profile a suspect's written or spoken communications.

For example, in the JonBenét Ramsey case the body was found inside, clothed, obviously discoverable, and covered by a blanket. Profilers would typically read that as indicating that the perpetrator was protective of, and probably personally involved with, the victim. This image would be opposed to that of an uninvolved, sadistic murderer who would have taken the body and dumped it—possibly nude and uncovered—in some barren repository, hoping it wouldn't be discovered.

Even though professional investigators routinely read crime scenes for symbolic behavioral communications and clues—including what's known as "staging," which amounts to "efforts to mislead"—they rarely read written or verbal communications symbolically. They just need to take the next step and read symbolic right-brain messages in written documents or interrogations. Otherwise, law enforcement's exclusively left-brain focus can cause investigators to miss virtually all unconscious communication from perpetrators, which can sometimes amount to hundreds of vital messages in a single case! Because, most authorities are simply unaware of how urgently virtually all perpetrators want to confess.

Again even the most hardened sociopaths unconsciously harbor strong urges to confess, and they often do so. But law enforcement personnel are simply not trained to understand the machinations of the unconscious mind, or its special language. That expertise must come from clinical researchers (i.e., therapists such as myself) who study the unconscious mind on a daily basis.

Unfortunately, given the territorial nature of conscientious, hard-driving investigators and experts in any field, we would expect law enforcement largely to resist a breakthrough to right-brain communication—and they do. They are all human beings with natural skepticisms, and they are trained to adhere to the status quo. That's why, if law enforcement is going to catch on, investigators must change their understanding of the human mind.

Specifically, they must learn how it communicates. They must become willing to see left-brain and right-brain messages simultaneously. They must move from a simple view to a far more complicated understanding of the human mind. And this, of course, will be extremely challenging, but in the long run it will also be even more rewarding.

I have worked with a few investigators who have actually listened and embraced unconscious communication, so I know it can be done. In any field, the path to the future is found by riding the right waves and recognizing when a big one comes along.

Former L.A. Police Detective Mark Fuhrman partially demonstrated the kind of thinking police must adopt. Early in the Holloway case, he decoded a popular rumor, supposedly culled from police interviews, to the effect that the three suspects had reported that Natalee had suffered a head injury. His take was that the three perpetrators were *consciously* setting up an excuse for blunt trauma. To his credit, Fuhrman decoded a communication symbolically, but he also needed to appreciate how the unconscious mind, not the conscious mind, communicates symbolically. Not so coincidentally, Deepak himself will make that same suggestion of a type of head injury in an unconscious slip.

## Noticing the Bigger Things: A Perfect Example

Clearly, this case could have been solved a long time ago by using key information provided by Deepak, one of the three main suspects. Aruban authorities could have used it to compare with thoughtprints delivered by the suspects in their police interviews. After I formulated my original profile regarding Deepak's clear and chilling "hidden" confession, the police interviews suddenly surfaced. This provided a tremendous opportunity to validate the profile—or not.

What unfolded in police interviews was a charade in which three suspects initially told two different versions of the story on which they had all agreed. When version one didn't fly they went to plan B. But then, proving once again that there is no honor among thieves, they began playing a brutal blame game among themselves, at which point the boys changed their stories yet a third time. Without the benefit of understanding thoughtprint messages, either in the interviews or from Deepak's invaluable email, police found this far too confusing. They knew that they had three liars on their hands, yet they had to pick and choose among the lies, operating entirely on instinct and trying to figure out who or what to believe, which never allowed them to develop a solid case.

But now, since we can decipher thoughtprints, we need to check and see if—unbeknownst to them all—the suspects' thoughtprints tell the same story. Do all three confess to the real truth? Do their unconscious admissions offer more detail than ever? Will the hidden details from one boy's story match the hidden details from the next story? Will their right-brain "truth telling" symbolism trump their left-brain cover-ups?

## Deepak's Unconscious: A Brilliant Film Director

We will soon begin the actual process of decoding Deepak's email, line-by-line and sometimes word-by-word. But first, a final warning.

For those encountering this process for the first time, the specifics can sometimes seem a bit overwhelming. Even so, we dare not take a single thing for granted. In addition to noting every individual word we must pay careful attention to every single linguistic and formatting feature in the forensic document. These include punctuation (commas, periods, colons, capital letters, etc.), spacing issues, and the writer's tendency to repeat certain words. Word location itself is always extremely important as well.

But most of all we must appreciate how the unconscious L-2 mind tells the truth by utilizing images. We must understand its rich, powerful language, a language utterly unique to the individual, a language of images that always illuminate the major facts of the case in question.

As we read Deepak's thoughtprints we gradually begin to see how they fit together. At times Deepak's story unfolds in strictly chronological order, but at other times his story is characterized by obsessive repetition and the retelling of various parts of the story without concern for sequential narrative. He does this unconsciously, reassuring himself that he's telling a consistent story—and also to add more details.

We can think of these moments as what a movie director does when he repeatedly "flashes back" to a scene from the past at key moments. It's also a lot like putting a crossword puzzle together, as we find matching images and ideas scattered in key places throughout his story. At times he will overtly define the meaning of a repetitive keyword at one particular place. Indeed, the experience of tracking down and discovering matching thoughtprints is precisely a key way in which thoughtprint decoding verifies deeper L-2 messages.

Eventually his underlying story takes shape. Deepak, of course, like every writer of a forensic document, makes certain "slips," or "tells," that jump off the page once the groundwork has been laid. But certainly these cannot be fully appreciated until we get to them and consider them in context.

Above all, make no mistake: Deepak is the producer/director for a story, a "homemade movie" of his own creation, telling a powerful tale. Thus he takes us through a number of scenes, and with every scene he chooses to emphasize this or downplay that, exactly as a film director does.

In fact, as everyone knows, movie directors often tell their stories on two levels at once, attempting to create vivid scenes filled with symbolic meaning designed to affect the viewer in powerful ways. For example, the classical western movie with the good guys in white hats fighting the rustlers in black hats appeals to the universal good-versus-evil struggle within each person and within our culture. The lone western hero standing against the forces of evil—be it Gary Cooper in *High Noon* or Marshall Dillon in *Gunsmoke*—speaks to our deep-seated need to overcome a sense of powerlessness in our lives, and to the injustice we see all around us. A detective solving a crime, or a lawyer overcoming injustice for his client, are part and parcel of the same underlying dynamic.

For example, movie buffs can never forget Gary Cooper at the peak moment in the Academy Award-winning classic I mentioned above, *High Noon*. There he is, standing tall, sheriff's badge on his chest, six-shooter in his holster, the bright midday sun beating down, cowboy hat shading his dark eyes, bandanna around his neck. Now he walks slowly, utterly alone, down a long, dusty street in the heart of a western town on the brink of disaster. His eyes glance about, ever on the alert, ready for the troublemakers no one else would confront.

Meanwhile, they scurry in the shadows preparing to ambush him. The showdown draws closer. The big clock on the bank in the center of town ticks down to 12 o'clock noon as he walks on, step-by-step, glancing about, willing to look death squarely in the eye to do his job.

As the tension mounts you feel the heat, taste the dust and even sense the hair standing up on the back of his neck. All of this occurs just as the director intended, the good-versus-evil dichotomy perfectly depicted in black and white. The director had carefully chosen every single symbol.

## Deepak Carefully Chooses His Own Images

In the story you are about to read, Deepak Kalpoe will set a number of scenes in much the same way. In so doing he will chose his symbols very carefully. However, unlike a conventional movie director, he will do so unconsciously. On the surface Deepak seems to be casually running through an explanation so quickly he can barely pause to take a breath. But it's a false cover story, underneath which he is brilliantly piecing together an entirely different story that tells the truth about what happened to Natalee Holloway.

Like a conventional movie director, Deepak will use what we call *message markers*. They are always communication images—either striking images like "lighthouse" or "alarm" or "flyers" or more mundane images such as "talk" or "school" (implying verbal teaching) or "confirmed"—and Deepak uses all of these as I will explain in detail shortly.

## Key Images: *'lighthouse'* and *'sharks'*

Let's begin with some of the key images that Deepak will use in the story ahead. For example, in a key scene Deepak will use a "lighthouse" image five different times. Just think for a moment what that image suggests: (1) a strong light shining in the darkness; (2) a warning about impending danger, such as storms and shipwrecks; (3) boats, safety, the ocean; (4) the land on the edge of the ocean; (5) something permanent that can withstand the storm; (6) the ability to see above the storm; (7) trust on the part of the sea captain; and the like.

Deepak did not choose that image by accident. Unconsciously he is trying to shed light on the case, to tell us something valuable, something crucial. Likewise, his five-fold usage makes lighthouse a keyword and a crucial element in his story, clearly conveying several of the meanings suggested above.

The word "lighthouse" also qualifies as a *message marker*—a communication image as briefly defined above. By using it, Deepak is telling us to remain alert for the information on which its light will soon be shed.

In Deepak's lighthouse scene he will also use the image "sharks," which just for starters suggests predator, danger, victim consumed, silent, sudden attack, death in the ocean, deep in the ocean, fast-moving, terrifying, huge, and overwhelming terror. The word "shark" is also frequently applied to the business world, where it suggests someone who is ruthless, shrewd, self-centered, manipulative, destructive, and likely to take advantage of you in half-a-second.

Taking the sharks metaphor a step farther into the social scene, we find the term often used in singles' bars to refer to males on the prowl, looking for sex. Not coincidentally, perhaps, a large, garishly painted shark adorns the entrance to Carlos'n Charlie's in Oranjestad, where Natalee was seen leaving alone with Joran, Deepak's buddy, early on the morning of May 30, 2005. And, the locals in Aruba routinely warn young girls to beware of "the sharks" at Carlos'n Charlie's.

Because this case deals with Natalee's fate—with what happened if she died, and where her body might be—we can see that these two images might provide some answers. Deepak's use of "sharks" itself might suggest what happened, and even where her body is. That possibility becomes even more likely when "sharks" is taken in combination with lighthouse, one of the two most important images in the entire email.

## Deepak Guides Scene-by-Scene

Murder cases often turn on the smallest of clues, the slightest of perpetrators' mistakes. Creating a written document is one of those mistakes, often prompted by a perpetrator's deep need to confess, a far more urgent need than law enforcement has ever imagined. When murderers leave behind written communications they virtually shout out loud a thousand hidden hints, until their confessions become a cacophony of guilty pleas.

For example, Deepak's lengthy email of June 4 not only shouts out to us but blatantly admits his criminal involvement, behind such a paper-thin disguise you can almost hear him consciously confessing. Indeed, the sheer length of his email tells us that he has something enormous to get off his chest.

Such a massive document can be a daunting challenge, even for a profiler. Yet Deepak unconsciously organizes the story for us, as if he were outlining chapters in a book. His unconscious mind knew that such a long and detailed recounting of his crime needed to be well organized so it could be better understood. Therefore, to highlight his central messages, Deepak's L-2 mind used the most basic, straightforward element of punctuation: periods.

He will also organize the letter to describe his encounter with Natalee in scene-by-scene fashion, including . . .

1. Her first meeting with Joran at the Holiday Inn

2. The encounter at Carlos'n Charlie's

3. The ride home with Joran and Natalee in the backseat

4. Dropping Natalee off at the Holiday Inn (except, of course, that they didn't!)

5. Meeting with the family one night later

6. Undergoing the police interrogation

7. Dealing with the reactions of Natalee's family and friends, and . . .

8. Everything in between.

At times he will also use the keyword "so" to indicate shifts in the action.

Deepak's scene-by-scene method first creates for us a dynamic, moving story, demonstrating the brilliance of his vastly superior L-2 unconscious mind, which gradually unfolds the case in a believable, understandable fashion. In so doing he also answers every major question; indeed, we can see the enormous potential in setting up answers to major questions with matching scenes.

For example, when he describes the three boys getting Natalee alone for the first time—in the backseat of his own car, no less—we would expect Deepak to reveal between the lines what really did happen in that particular circumstance. Likewise, when he describes the last time the three suspects saw Natalee, dropping her off at her hotel, we would expect his L-2 unconscious mind to tell us where her body is now. Indeed, in his email Deepak is directing a brilliant creative production.

Now we must consider another key way he leads the profiler/reader, very much like a director setting up major clues.

[Note: For interested readers, a more detailed explanation of message markers and how they guide the profiler can be found in Appendix A.]

## Message Markers: Nonverbal and Verbal

To properly profile forensic documents we must keep our eyes peeled for signposts pointing to the truth. These again are called *message markers,* and they amount to hidden signals, within the document, that point the way through a maze of information. Or, put another way, they are thoughtprints specifically designed to highlight L-2 communications. They are guides that point like signposts to the truth—ways of saying "Pay special attention here!" And there are two types: nonverbal and verbal.

Deepak's email uses such nonverbal message markers as *punctuation* and *spacing, capital letters,* and *quotes* and *parentheses* to point us to important L-2 messages that he wants delivered. And when he quotes someone directly—especially Natalee—we must take special notice.

Deepak uses periods, a nonverbal punctuation marker, in striking ways to guide the profiling, and these deserve a special heads-up. First he uses them (often in very brief sentences) to establish major points, as if he's saying, "This is a definite—a conclusion you can take to the bank." Conversely, he also writes extremely lengthy sentences with no periods at all. This shows us he's so utterly desperate to confess that he does so without slowing down. By failing to put periods in a number of run-on sentences, Deepak highlights various parts of his confession that would otherwise be hidden, by encouraging the reader to combine phrases and sentences in different ways.

Nonverbal markers work hand-in-hand with *verbal* message markers to guide the profiler to a perpetrator's confession, and that's what happens in Deepak's email. Verbal message markers are thoughtprints that primarily refer to communication per se—communication images. These include everyday words such as "called," "talked," "said," "questioned," and "answered." Such words become even more important when connected to powerful qualifiers, such as "police questioned." Such references to communication are red flags, indicating that key messages are being delivered. In these ways the writer says, "I'm telling you—or I'm about to tell you—something really important."

Many times a writer will use more dramatic message markers for emphasis. We can think of these as *different types of "messaging"* similar to text-messaging on cell phones. Here are some other common yet specialized types of verbal L-2 message markers that Deepak uses:

1. *Elite "flashing light"* markers are references to vivid, attention-getting types of communication, such as a lighthouse, an alarm going off, a traffic light, screamed, news, and police questioned.

2. *Education "school zone"* markers, which include Deepak's references to school, classes, scholars, learning, telling a story, and "why we did this," all of which urge the profiler to "go to school here."

3. *Keyword* or *repeat messaging* occurs when a writer uses the same word two or more times, thus suggesting "don't miss this." Deepak repeats several keywords, including "Betty," "natalee," and "Holiday Inn."

4. *Denial messaging*, or "thou doth protest too much" (for example "I didn't do this crime") all suggest exactly the opposite message. They function like spontaneous red flags, signaling that a person's deeper intelligence is pressuring him to tell the truth. Deepak resorts to this device time and time again, particularly at one of the three moments when he puts in all caps the word "NEVER."

5. *"Slips"* or *"slip messaging"* includes misspellings or omissions that the L-1 mind overlooks, which describe what the perpetrator has done. The L-2 mind briefly takes over and says, in effect, "Let me say it directly and unmistakably so you'll be sure to read the message."

6. *"Blatant phrases"* are special slips that Deepak makes—an overlooked "blatant phrase" which tells the real story. As an example Deepak puts a blatant phrase *"last day"* in quotes and speaks for his victim.

7. *"Sounds like"* messaging is similar to the way the parlor game Charades is played.

8. *"Linkage messaging"* is a technique in which he unknowingly links two key ideas together, to show they're related.

## Three Unique Messages Summarize the Crime

In another vivid example from his email, Deepak's film director subconscious did something else quite striking. He strongly emphasized certain words/images in three places, by putting them in all-caps, which in Internet language implies that he's shouting the messages. These were: (1) describing Natalee right before leaving Carlos'n Charlie's with them as "VERY *drunk*," (2) reporting a flyer placed at Joran's school after Natalee's disappearance, "GIRL KIDNAPPED ASK JORAN VANDER SLOOT," which Deepak insists isn't true, (3) declaring his innocence in *"we promise i[sic] would NEVER hurt anyone in anyway . . . I would take a bullet to save her."*

Notice the powerful images: (1) missing girl extremely intoxicated, (2) girl kidnapped linked to a particular name on a flyer (a striking image itself), accompanied by an emphatic denial, and (3) hurting (implying severely) another person, who happens to be the missing girl, also accompanied by another emphatic denial and followed by a brutal, self-punishing image (taking a bullet to save her).

We might ask, "Why did Deepak's brilliant subconscious movie director choose to emphasize only three words when he could have chosen six or eight or ten images instead?" In the end, we'll find that he actually did so, because these three all-caps messages tell the entire story of Natalee's disappearance in a nutshell—three extremely brief messages were all he needed. And a film director knows there's great power in brevity, exactly as Gary Cooper's character in *High Noon* was a man of few words—yet you never forgot what they were.

## Will the Real 'Betty' Please Stand Up?

Before we begin the profile, there is one last symbol that Deepak emphasized, and that is "a person named Betty" to whom he wrote his lengthy email. This is a bit tricky because, when it comes to a person's name, we're inclined to think literally. But every single person we know or read about also symbolizes something to us. For example, *"Betty"* was literally a distant but likeable acquaintance with whom Deepak had struck up a conversation when, as a tourist in Aruba, she visited the Internet café where he worked. Obviously then, *"Betty"* was both a real person to Deepak but also much more of a symbolic grandmother figure. She reminded Deepak of his nurturing grandmother from Surinam, to whom he was utterly devoted. He missed her greatly.

So why would Deepak choose to write to an American grandmother he barely knew, whom he had met only briefly twice in his life and with whom he had exchanged only occasional emails? Why would he send her an extensive email about a possible crime that was suddenly attracting worldwide attention, in which he found himself a major suspect? And also, why was he compelled to write to his supposed friend a story full of lies even before waiting for the smoke to clear to see if his original cover-up story held up?

We can be sure the American grandmother acquaintance is not the real *"Betty"* in Deepak's deeper story. He doesn't have the emotional investment in her that he personally has with another *"Betty."* On the contrary, the film director in his deeper mind unconsciously selected the perfect symbolic person to write for his own reasons—to tell the truth. It's standard operating procedure.

To whom might Deepak really be writing symbolically? Considering that we will see a hidden, unconscious confession with all the gory details, we might think that Deepak was secretly confessing to his own grandmother, whom *"Betty"* represented. But she's not the main person. To identify that person we have to think like a guilty criminal who has an almost desperate, unconscious need to bare his soul. To whom would he want to confess, besides the authorities? Whom might a judge allow to look Deepak in the eye at his sentencing, after a confession, to tell him about the devastating effects his actions had on that person's life?

Initially we can think of only two possibilities, above all others. But when we think of "Betty" as representing an American grandmother or an American mother—who are one and the same symbolically—we can quickly surmise to whom Deepak is unconsciously speaking. In fact, when that person is mentioned in his email (she had, in fact just looked him in the eye and let him know how much he had hurt her), then we have our person. Beyond a shadow of doubt we know who the real *"Betty"* is. But even so, I will let Deepak tell you that himself as he takes us through his confession. It won't take long for him to do so.

We might think of this as similar to what happened on the popular television quiz show, *To Tell the Truth,* from several years ago. Three contestants, all claiming to be the same person, would appear before a panel whose job was to determine which of the three was the real person. After each contestant would say convincingly, "I am Bill Johnson," for instance, the host would give the panel a brief thumbnail sketch of Bill's life and vocation and the panelists would question each contestant. Then the panelists would vote separately as to which person they thought was really "Bill." Finally the host would declare, "Would the real Bill Johnson please stand up." At that point one of the imposters would often feign a step forward before "Bill" himself actually rose to his feet.

So now we want to know: "Will the real Betty please stand up?"

## Lies Conceal the Truth

We must also ask, what purpose would lies serve in a forensic document such as Deepak's email? The best answer comes in two parts.

1. Lies allow the deeper mind to operate unrestricted. Paradoxically, it can create any lie, any image, to tell the truth with rich imagery

and powerful thoughtprints. Two good examples are Deepak's insistence that Natalee was *"VERY drunk"* and that they dropped her off at the *"Holiday Inn,"* both of which are major keys to the case. Also, if Deepak had not thought of lying to his friend, Betty, we would never have had a confession; in particular, a confession made to the real Betty.

2. The deeper mind also unconsciously encourages a person to consciously lie because such lies paint that person in a corner when the real truth is discovered. This is precisely what happened in the case of all three suspects, who quickly admitted lying to police in a cover-up story.

A similar thing also happened in the JonBenét Ramsey case when the crucial ransom note, implying a kidnapping, proved to be total fiction. I call it the case of the "non-kidnap kidnapping" because the body was later discovered by the father in the home, and no kidnapper ever telephoned. Yet, between the lines, the ransom note revealed the killer.

## How L-2 Validates Its Messages

The unconscious/L-2 mind repeatedly uses a basic two-step method to validate its messages, involving (1) prediction and (2) prediction fulfilled. Over and over a message marker of one type or another will suggest "important message coming up," and then that message will be delivered in detail.

Let's take one precise moment at which Deepak makes a hidden prediction and then dramatically fulfills it, something he does repeatedly. Early in his email he uses an extremely valuable message marker in forensic work, *"started talking,"* followed by one of the most blatant sentences also speaking first person for Natalee: *"Today is the last day I will be,"* which says it all. In no uncertain terms, Deepak is confessing that Natalee died that night in the presence of all three suspects.

Sadly, there are many people who totally deny the existence of the unconscious mind, of unconscious communication with its rich, right-brain language. Certainly it takes time and patience to understand unconscious communication, and we all have a natural reluctance to entertain the possibility. But, if you hang with Deepak Kalpoe you will be rewarded with a memorable glimpse inside the unconscious mind of a criminal. You'll see both how it covers up and how badly it wants to confess. And, as you move from being a left-brain reader to a right-brain reader, the story will become plainer and plainer.

Finally, before we look at Deepak's email self-portrait, a profile offered up by his brilliant, all-seeing, all-knowing producer/director L-2 mind, we still have just a few more things to consider.

## The Prevailing Theory: Deepak's Staging Overlooked

Briefly I must address the theory prevailing here in mid-2007, among those who closely follow the Holloway case. A growing number of these observers focus exclusively on Joran, leaving Deepak and Satish largely out of the mix. We must see through the Kalpoes' only defense or many people will continue to buy into it—and will fail to recognize Deepak's June 4 email as his hidden confession.

People studying the case have noted that Deepak (and Satish) have seemingly established that they were at their parents' home in Hooiberg, about seven miles east of the Holiday Inn and the Marriott, by 2:30 am on May 30, 2005, the night Natalee disappeared. They point to computer and cell phone records as evidence. As a result many observers believe that the Kalpoes were unlikely to be involved in Natalee's disappearance and were thought to be telling the truth. Joran arrived home later—again as "verified" by computer records—and he admitted to having been alone with Natalee on the beach where they became sexually involved. Given that scenario, Joran was the much more likely suspect.

Without question Deepak's computer records remain his and his brother's chief defense. In fact, however, there are many indicators powerfully pointing toward Deepak's involvement in Natalee's disappearance.

## Brief Summary of Deepak's Involvement

First Deepak has every reason—despite those who think otherwise—to continue lying since, if guilty, he faces serious criminal charges. Meanwhile, he's simply relieved that public opinion, especially as expressed on Internet sites, blogs, and the media, is pinning the blame squarely on Joran. Secondly, Deepak is an admitted liar and repeatedly lied in police interviews. He has constantly backtracked and offered widely varying accounts of witnessing sexual activity in his car's backseat, noticing Natalee being drunk/impaired, and personally participating in sexual activity with Natalee. He has even turned the tables on his old friend, Joran, once praising van der Sloot's upright character and later labeling him a rapist.

On the night Natalee disappeared, Deepak apparently sent an email to his friend, John Croes, an email that supposedly established Deepak's innocence because it was transmitted from his personal computer in Hooiberg at 2:30 am on May 30, 2005. In that email, Deepak bragged to Croes that Natalee had "put her hands down his pants." Deepak has also said he saw extensive sexual activity earlier that night between Joran and Natalee in the backseat of his Honda. Deepak and Satish have also admitted their own past history of group sex with tourist girls.

What has been largely overlooked is that, from that very time, at 2:30 am on May 30, Deepak and the other two suspects were again seemingly busy establishing alibis by utilizing Internet communications, cell phones, and cell-phone text messages. The three young men attempted to establish hard evidence that seemed to show Deepak on his computer by 2:30 am, some thirty minutes after the time of Natalee's death according to Deepak's June 4 email to Betty.

## 'Hotel' Story/3-on-1 vs. 'Beach' Story/1-on-1

Using their techno-toys, the three guys concocted the "beach story" in which Joran went to the beach alone with Natalee—a "one-on-one" version—and left her there unharmed about 3 am By the time the Twittys showed up twenty-four hours later, strangely enough, the boys had adopted the far weaker "hotel story," which portrayed a three-on-one situation in which they dropped Natalee off at the Holiday Inn at 2 am. Deepak attempted to manufacture a false eyewitness (his friend, Steve Croes), but the hotel story quickly collapsed when surveillance cameras proved no drop-off had ever occurred.

The false hotel story showed three things: (1) the boys were liars; (2) they all were likely sexually involved with Natalee; and (3) they would readily resort to staging or establishing false alibis. Most important, Deepak's email explains why the three suspects went with the hotel story even though there was no real evidence to support it, instead of using the beach story which had the "hard evidence" of an apparent computer timeline: *the compulsion to confess.*

In truth, the three-on-one hotel story revealed the real truth— a three-way sexual assault upon Natalee that resulted in her death. And, indeed, the three boys as we shall see dropped her body off at another

"Holiday Inn," the *Holloway end,* the ocean. By emphasizing the hotel story at the heart of his June 4 email, Deepak unconsciously revealed that the investigators then would hold the key to determining the location of Natalee's body once they understand that "Holiday Inn" was code for where the boys really left the body . His email clarifies this code extensively, as his deeper intelligence in essence guides us to find the body.

It is possible that Paulus van der Sloot, who was almost certainly involved in the cover-up that first night, didn't like the risk of depicting his son at the center of the beach story all by himself, thus making Joran the prime suspect. Yet he probably didn't immediately see any other cover-up story that might offer a logical explanation of what happened to Natalee. Certainly she would never have gone to the beach alone with either Deepak or Satish—and the boys had to come up with a somewhat credible story as to how they parted with Natalee.

Paulus also was likely called within the first fifteen minutes of Natalee's death and, with the gears spinning in his lawyer's mind, immediately grasped the importance of the three suspects quickly appearing to split up. It's less likely that the three boys on their own could have devised the idea of Deepak—or someone else using his computer and cell phone—immediately establishing an alibi that could also work, at least partially, for all three.

Sometime in the twenty or so hours before the Twittys showed up, Paulus might have considered floating the hotel story, hoping Deepak could come through with an eyewitness willing to testify to the Holiday Inn drop-off. Deepak had the entire following day to establish that "fact." Indeed, it took five days before his friend did come forward, apparently not wanting to appear too anxious to do so. However, in any case, they all decided to present the flawed hotel story first, even while knowing they had a stronger fall-back position with the computer/cell phone timeline in place.

Tellingly, no witness ever emerged who saw any of the three suspects, or Natalee, anywhere near the beach on the night she disappeared, because it was a total fiction. Yet the beach story had significant advantages: (1) it took the focus off a three-on-one situation, moving it to a one-on-one; (2) it enabled the suspects—at least potentially—to blame one another. Deepak could claim Joran harmed Natalee, and vice versa. In fact, some ten days later after the suspects' hotel story had fallen apart, and the beach story then emerged, both Joran and Deepak immediately blamed the other for Natalee's death, depicting a sexual assault gone bad.

Unfortunately, for the most part the media and the police have embraced the beach story, mainly because they don't know how to read between the lines of Deepak's communications. They haven't done so either in analyzing his police interviews or in reading his June 4 email, which tells the entire story of the crime scene-by-scene.

In addition, Deepak's "hard computer evidence" establishing a secure timeline raises specific questions. Having thoroughly reviewed all relevant computer and cell phone records, police have thrown up their hands and admitted that the truth remains elusive. As Gerald Dompig put it in his *Vanity Fair* interview (published in January 2006), "Nobody knows what time he (Joran) got home. Nor is it clear how he got there." Dompig strongly doubted that Joran walked the two miles from the Marriott beach to his home in Noord, without shoes no less. Certainly, all this makes Deepak's email "communication" that night highly suspect.

So, in probing the beach story, investigators don't know when or how Joran arrived home. Meanwhile, because establishing (1) that Joran was on his way home and (2) what time he got there was the dual purpose of Deepak's "computer evidence," this strongly implies police doubt the accuracy of Deepak's computer communication. Time records on computers can be manipulated by experienced hackers such as Deepak, who has worked for years at an Internet café in Oranjestad. Ultimately, only the server can verify time. Plus, computers can be accessed from cell phones.

Also, the police haven't publicly mentioned this possibility but it's entirely possible that someone else could substitute for another person on a computer. Online and/or on a certain cell phone, Satish could appear to be Deepak or Paulus could appear to be Joran. Perhaps most strikingly, thoughtprint analysis of Deepak's computer and cell phone communications (the "hard evidence") suggests that their staging *included an excessive effort to make it appear that Joran was "going home"* while Deepak was already at the Kalpoe home.

Other factors undermine the beach story cover-up. There's no logical reason to believe that Natalee would resist returning to her hotel room after Joran left, and would instead choose to remain on the beach alone. Late at night, on a foreign island, away from all her friends, a girl who was always with somebody—it doesn't fit at all.

## Deepak's Unconscious Tells the Truth: 'Beach/Hotel Story'

In the final analysis, Deepak's June 4 email shows his deeper intelligence deftly connecting the two cover-up stories. First, the hotel story confirms that Natalee's death is the sad ending of the story of a three-on-one assault. And second, the beach story also reveals not only what led to Natalee's death but where the body was taken. Both stories, properly decoded, strongly confirm the body's location and how it can be discovered. In other words, Deepak's L-2 story—in essence the "Beach-Hotel Story"—reveals the real truth while providing striking details.

When we let Deepak speak in his email he will tell us the entire story, answering virtually every question about the cover-up. In the end his own mind will leave his thinly constructed alibi—his computer/cell phone timeline—hanging out to dry like a lone sheet flapping in a high wind.

## Additional Triggers for Deepak's Hidden Confession

On top of the soul-shaking confrontation with Beth Twitty five days earlier, when she invoked the idea of God's law and a sentence to hell as the consequence of that law's violation, Deepak had two other powerful encounters with another kind of "law" just before he wrote his lengthy confession to Betty. On Friday, June 3, while Deepak was visiting Joran at the van der Sloot home and was discussing their situation with Joran's father, Paulus told the boys in no uncertain terms that they were in trouble. He then informed Deepak that he had hired attorney Anthony Carlo for Joran, and had asked another attorney, Dennis Oomen, to represent the Kalpoe brothers.

At that point Joran reportedly asked his father what was the worst that could happen to them. Pulling out one of his law books, Paulus reviewed the investigative process. He went over what they could expect step-by-step: they would be arrested, handcuffed, and taken to police headquarters. They would then be interrogated, after being told of their right to remain silent until they had spoken to an attorney. This is what Paulus instructed them to do. Remain silent! Do not tell the police anything! Then he gave Deepak the attorney's number.

The following morning, June 4, Deepak and his family met with his new attorney, Dennis Oomen. Interestingly Joran and his parents were also present. At Oomen's request, the boys then reviewed their hotel story. After listening intently the lawyer told them that this was a serious matter, and that they could be arrested.

After the meeting Deepak went home with his family and did not see Joran for the rest of that day. Then, at about 8 pm he called Joran, he said, because he'd planned to spend the night with him in Noord, but Deepak's mother suggested otherwise so Deepak stayed home in Hooiberg.

Soon after hanging up the telephone, alone in his parents' house as the sun set on the sandy island outside, almost exactly five days after meeting Beth Twitty and six days after watching Natalee take her last breath, Deepak couldn't stand it anymore. He figuratively picked up "paper and pen" and wrote Betty his unforgettable email.

The email was transmitted at 7:33 pm (CST) on June 4. The unconscious law of the conscience had forced Deepak to confess between the lines, even as he reiterated the hotel story and other aspects of the cover-up. He was also spurred on by the laws of God and country with which Beth Twitty, Paulus van der Sloot and his new attorney had all confronted him. These laws so impressed Deepak that he referred to them repeatedly in his email.

Ironically, similar concerns regarding the law would soon distress Paulus van der Sloot as well.

## Surprise Visit: Beth Pressures Paulus

Beth Twitty spent most of July and August 2005 in Aruba, passing out prayer cards and pictures of Natalee. One afternoon, according to *Vanity Fair*, she was walking through Noord accompanied by Greta Van Susteren, a commentator for Fox News Channel, when she realized that they were near the van der Sloot compound. Proceeding there to leave a card at the gate, Beth ran into Paulus out in his yard. One thing then led to another, and Joran's parents invited Beth in for what turned out to be a tension-packed, hour-and-a-half discussion.

After spending some time listening to Joran's parents defend him, Beth pressured Paulus by telling him that he was "responsible for Aruba being trapped in hell." *Vanity Fair* writer Bryan Burroughs reported that Beth told Paulus that, "until he came forward (with the truth) . . . his country would be trapped in perpetual hell." Despite claiming he could remember little of what happened the night Natalee disappeared, Paulus then started sweating profusely. "Beads of sweat were rolling down from his head onto the kitchen table, pooling on the table" according to Beth. Paulus' physical discomfort was so noticeable that his wife, Anita, fetched a kitchen towel to pat him down.

We can easily read through Paulus' claim that he knew very little about Natalee's last night to understand that he did, indeed, know a *great deal* about it, as Deepak's email will show. In Paulus' mid-summer, 2005 encounter with the tenacious Beth Twitty, we can also see his body speaking volumes about his lingering guilt.

## Deepak and Joran Speak through Disguised Stories: Dogs and Ants

In the same way that sweat poured out of Paulus, Deepak's guilt and non-stop confession comes pouring out of his email as though he, too, had suddenly turned on a spigot. It was Deepak's misguided effort to look Beth Twitty in the eye on May 31 that first opened his confessional floodgates. But two months later, on Aug. 8, when Beth looked him up at his Internet café to look him in the eye, Deepak couldn't face her. He couldn't even make eye contact with her because he'd never consciously owned his confession.

Beth told me personally how she stared at him in silence for fifteen minutes, but he never raised his head once. Deepak looked down almost the entire time Beth was there. Though a tad less soggy than Paulus' reaction to Beth, Deepak's behavior in the café clearly mirrored the older man's nervousness. Finally, as *Vanity Fair* reported, Deepak looked up and said, "The media has never seen this side of you." Beth responded immediately, "I've been saving it for you, Deepak."

We can be sure Deepak has never forgotten those words from Beth either, the second time that she knocked him out with a simple, direct statement. In response to Beth's conscience-breaking blow we must not miss Deepak's second confession—the decoded version—which perfectly matches his email: "the media has never seen *this side of me.*"

Indeed they haven't. Nobody could look this deeply into Deepak's actions and misgivings except one witness, his own deeper intelligence, his soul. Take your pick—Freud, who talked about projection, or Jesus, who said that the speck you think you see in your neighbor's eye is often the log in your own eye. Deepak Kalpoe's email reveals his other side, the savage side that lashed out at Natalee Holloway in the early morning of May 30, 2005.

Deepak was also addressing the media, telling the newspeople to look deeper because they'd missed the real story. Well, here's their opportunity, and no one can say it gets any better. We are about to gaze deeply into a criminal's other side, his shadow side, where he tries to dissemble with all his conscious might even as his unconscious inevitably unleashes the truth.

His surface L-1 mind is no match at all for his deeper L-2 mind. If he was overmatched in his two face-to-face battles with Beth Twitty, Deepak's now in another league altogether, consciously trying to match wits with his own unconscious genius, a part of his mind that's a thousand times brighter than his L-1. Two basic examples in this case—one from Deepak and one from Joran—will show you I'm not exaggerating when we see each suspect's unconscious mind respond immediately to a cover-up. They each provide sterling illustrations of how to listen to the unconscious mind, and how the L-2 mind tells the truth in the face of a blatant cover-up/lie.

## Deepak and Joran: Key Confessions Following Denial

The most basic principle of profiling via thoughtprint decoding is understanding denial, because we must look beyond denial to comprehend symbolic thoughtprints. As a profiler, I count on the fact that denial takes two forms:

1. First, the perpetrator's conscious denial of a crime, which he intentionally covers up.

2. Second, his denial of his unconscious mind because he has no idea that his deeper mind constantly communicates the truth.

Now let's look at how Joran's L-2 mind took over in one situation. When he broke during police interrogation and revealed that the hotel story—the three guys' first cover-up effort—was a hoax, he then told the beach story, which can basically be reduced to "I left her alone at the beach unharmed." But his unconscious wouldn't let him stop there. Fortunately for us, Joran proceeded to embellish that beach story, shifting into the symbolic language of the unconscious mind.

Practically without a pause, Joran offers the following story. First, he speculates that Deepak returned to the beach, raped and murdered Natalee, and buried her body. To spice up his lie, he adds the detail that when Deepak came back to the beach he brought his two dogs with him.

See the thoughtprint? The true assailant who sexually assaulted and killed Natalee had two other beings accompanying him, beings Joran calls "dogs."

Thus Joran's deeper mind is telling us that Natalee's death involved three beings on one being, or a three-on-one. This is not difficult decoding—Natalee was attacked by three dogs named Deepak, Joran, and Satish, facts that Joran was attempting to bury. Dogs bite, and a pack of wild dogs can destroy. Joran thus confesses that they were all predator dogs, even as he specifically introduces the idea of rape and murder in a group assault. In a nutshell he takes us right back to his "hotel" story of "three guys and one girl," only this time he provides specific details of a group rape. He also confesses that the three-on-one assault led to Natalee's death and disposing of her body.

Ironically, at the very moment when Joran is trying to lie through his teeth, he has no idea that his brilliant story-telling mind is telling the truth through symbolic stories that must be decoded. His L-2 mind quickly takes over and says, "Now let me tell you the real story, and listen between the lines because I'm going to be real plain. All three of us were involved in a brutal gang rape, and in the end we consumed Natalee, destroyed her. Don't fall for this one-on-one story about the beach." In a flash Joran has totally discounted his cover-up beach story and provided striking details of a group assault in just a few sentences. The listening equation is: Read past the denial and read symbolically, being particularly attuned to other stories.

In his June 4 email Deepak gives us the same opportunity—*denial followed by a key story revealing the real truth*. The very next day, during a police interview after Joran broke and claimed the beach story was, in fact, what really happened, Deepak agrees. But Deepak denies ever setting foot on the beach and states his belief that Joran raped her and something happened causing Natalee to die. Just as Joran did, without prompting, Deepak suddenly introduced the concepts of rape and death.

Later in the same interview, Deepak spontaneously related an invaluable and revealing story. After first choosing to lie about cleaning his car after Natalee disappeared (even though eyewitnesses verified that he'd done so) he did admit to cleaning his car beforehand. Deepak then described ants in his car, and claims he told Satish they should clean the car because "If there were going to be girls in the car there (sic) were going to be bitten by ants too."

Notice the subtle picture: another predator, "ants," which would surely bite a girl who might get in his car. Decode ants symbolically:

small black creatures which slip up on you in great numbers and bite you, as in a sneak attack in a car, no less! Without question, "ants" is not as powerful a predator image as a "pack of wild dogs" but it enables Deepak to describe other details of the attack, including how the boys, two of whom were black, suddenly and unexpectedly turned on Natalee in a violent group rape, indeed biting her, which led to her demise. In his email Deepak will ratchet up his predator images to maximum violence.

But for now, simply appreciate how both boys, using symbolically coded stories, have confirmed the same story, unconsciously letting us in on the real one. Despite their surface efforts at obfuscation, they make clear that their second effort at cover-up, the beach story, is not to be believed.

At the same time, the police have also demonstrated how important it is to understand the symbolic language of the mind in their failure to do so. They wasted much time and effort searching for the "real" story by trying to force the suspects into overt confessions when, right before their eyes and ears, both suspects had already admitted that it was a group assault.

In other words, if they comprehended the messages delivered by the suspect's deeper intelligence, police interrogators would know exactly how to pressure the boys. Certainly, after decoding the L-2's symbolic language, authorities would have no reason to believe their beach story. But without such decoding, investigators unwittingly continue to give credence to that false, one-on-one scenario.

In another development that also speaks a message of its own, again the moment they began telling their new beach story, Deepak and Joran turned on each other. Such finger-pointing itself reinforces the idea all were in on it from the beginning. And, it also helps explain why they first agreed to tell the hotel story, in which no one would be blamed for being alone with Natalee.

By putting both Joran's and Deepak's stories together we can see how suspects give up the real story *bit by bit*, which underscores the value of stories culled from police interviews and stories from Joran's recently published book. Throughout this book we will see how stories from these two additional sources corroborate Deepak's email, and how Joran and Satish add their own hidden confessions in the process. Some of these stories provide dramatic details about exactly what happened to Natalee Holloway.

Finally, as we turn at last to Deepak's June 4 email, I want to empha-size one more time that we must keep one basic principle in mind. *The unconscious mind speaks symbolically between the lines, often in seemingly unrelated stories. It cannot be stopped.*

And, indeed, as he starts his email Deepak makes an unconscious promise, giving us solid evidence that he intends to tell the whole truth and nothing but the truth, so help him God.

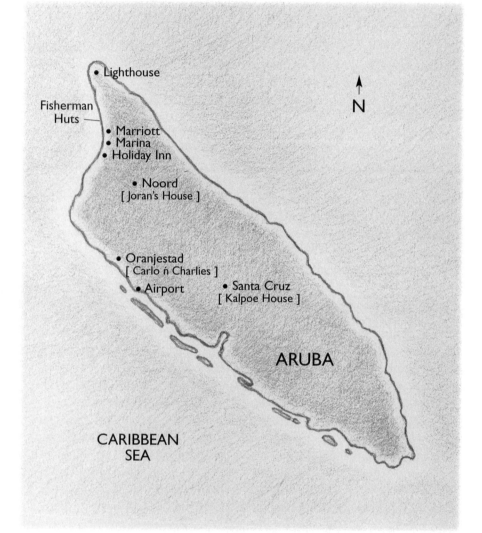

• Lighthouse

Fisherman
Huts

• Marriott
• Marina
• Holiday Inn

• Noord
[ Joran's House ]

• Oranjestad
[ Carlo ń Charlies ]
• Airport

• Santa Cruz
[ Kalpoe House ]

N

ARUBA

CARIBBEAN
SEA

# 5
# The Profile Begins

Before we begin the actual profile, to give you an overall sense of what we're working with, here is a scrupulously accurate facsimile of the email itself, followed immediately by the beginning of my profile/analysis.

*From: Deepak Kalpoe 6/4/05*
*To: Betty*
*In a message dated 6/4/2005 7:33:34 pm Central Standard Time,*
*deepakkalpoe@_____ com writes:*

*Hi betty :*

*How are you i hope you and your family is fine.*
*Betty is better i tell you the truth , before it will be a shock for you later, but*
*i think it will be a shock for you rightnow.*
*The missing girl natalee hollaway,I spoke to her , sunday she left with me ,*
*mybrother and a friend from carlos n' charlies , it was my car like the news*
*said she got in to,  I am one of the persons of intrest , i am one the the  students*
*they've questioned and released as they claimed in the news .*
*Let see where to start i don't even know where to begin these last days where*
*so crazy for me i'm very tired haven't slept good in days : The story starts*
*Sunday night when a friend of mine was playing poker at a local casino*
*(in the holiday inn) after he won the poker at the fourth place he decided to*
*get up and play some blackjack so he went to the blackjack table and there*
*was natalee (they were a lil drunk ) so my friend started playing blackjack*
*and he was winning quite good , so then natalee approached him and*
*introduced herself and said to him" your a lucky guy , can you help me win*
*some of my money back i lost $ 360 , of my fathers money" so my friend said*
*ok , why not . so he started playing and he won 100 $ for her back and he said*
*hey thats the best i can do for you because i doubt it I can win more money for*
*you so its better i quit so she said ok but at least let me buy you a drink so they*
*went to the bar (in the casino ). so they took a drink and started talking etc.*
*about school, the vacation etc.etc.afterwards my friend had to go and she said*

63

that "today is my last day i will be in carlos n' charlies will you be there" and my friend said well i have school tomorrow i don't think so . well she begged him and he still said yes i'll be there.So that was in the casino i was not present , i was at work so my friend called me and said hey i met some girls in the casino and her friends and they want us to meet them in carlos tonight do you have to work tomorrow morning i said no , so he said pick me up later then i said ok. so i got off my shift at 10 pm and went home took a bath had to fix something and then me and my younger brother went to pick up my friend was around 12.10 am so i came to his home and was talked for like 15 min and then left to go to carlos (we all went out without or parents knew) so we arrived like 12.30 am in carlos (carlos is closing 1 pm ) and headed straight for the bar and bought 3 drinks my friend paid for them, so besides the bar there is a stage and people were dancing and there was natalee dancing too (thats the first time i saw her ) ad she was calling my friend to get on the stage and dance with her  my friend laughed and refused so after the song was finished she came up to my friend and asked why he won't dance with her , i only heared that part because i was talking to someone else so i don't know what he responded(by then natalee was VERY drunk)so as i said i was talking to someone when i turned i had lost my brother , natalee and my friend. well they were announced that they were closing soon so i thought well maybe they' re waiting for me by the car its better i go there so i went to my car and nobody was there so i started playing music and was waiting on my brother and my friend.i waited for like 10 min and then i saw my brother stepping in the car and my friend who was with natalee. so i was surprised but anyways i started the engine and my brother was besides me and my friend and natalee were in the backseet so i started cruising in the area and asked my friend whats going on so natalee responded to me "hey its no prob let us just drive around and have fun its my last night , she said you can drop me off later at holiday inn anyways right" i said sure why not so as i was drove out of the carlos road and got on the mainroad there were natalees friends and she , pushed het head out of the window and screamed something i can't recall.so i was driving very slow to make a left to get in the next road and then one of natalees friend screamed for her to get out of the car , and she refused so then i stopped my car and i said natalee if your friends want you to go with them its better you go listen to them and go with them , she said no i will stay with you guys i will get a lift from you anways later, so she said bye to her friends and i drove away, so then we were just talking etc, in the car and then she said she wanted to see sharks ,it was by the lighthouse she saw them before that can we go , my friend said ok ,deepak lets go. so on my my to the lighthouse there was music playing and noone talking for a while when i looked in the backmirror my friend and natalee were kissing and touching (his hands etc was in her blouse but nothing nude or

*against natalees will ) so my brother siad just leave them for a while untill we get
to the lighthouse, when i arrived at the lighthouse i said well here is the lighthouse
they did not pay attention to me , so my brother said lets return (i did not stop
anywhere not for a min only trafficlights) so after like 10 min my friend is telling me
that natalee fell asleep i said you kidding just wake her up and tell ask her if its
holiday inn for sure she is staying so my friend woke her up and confirmed with
natalee she was staying at the holiday inn, so i drove to the lobby driveway of
holiday inn  and then we woke her up, she got out of the car and fell on the floor
my friend said damn she fell and then rushed out of the same door natalee came
out and picked her up immediately, after she stood up she pushed my friend and
said leave me alone or something like that i can't recall , my friend offered to help
het to her room she said no. she he stepped in the car and while i was driving
away i saw natalee walking towards the lobby and a gentleman with a walkie
talkie and black clothes approached her and i think they were talking and i had
never seen natalee again sinds.(holiday inn has no cameras in the driveway or
lobby) it was around 2.15 am .monday  i came to work normally 4- 11 pm
after  work i called my friend i said whats up he said ok i'm at the raddison casino
meet me there , i said ok  so i went there we played poker , we had some drinks
and chat and then we had enough and decided that this casino was booring lets
go to whyndham hotel casino . so i drove to whyndham and as i was parking my
friends dad called him and said the police is at his home with some family
members its about the girl you guys went out with yesterday , so my friend said
wait there i be there, so we rushed at my friends home and there was the police
and nataless family and it was a nightmare sinds then. the police asked us if we
knew this girl showed us a picture we said yes thats her , they said she was
missing and eyewitness say she was the last seen with you guys . so they asked
a few more questions and we said we don't understand we left her at holiday inn
lobby drive way how could she dissapear and then natalees stepfather jumped and
said "yes thats because after she went with you assholes she lost" and then my
friends father jumped and said thats enough you can't talk to the kids like that this
is not the us your out of you juristiction this is not the way i want you people out
of my yard i know the law (my friends father is e judge) so afterwards another
family member of natalee suggested to the police if we can id the security gard we
said ok. we went there there was no suck security working there as we discribed.
so then we were just standing in the lobby there were questions etc. asked by
other members , and then me and my friend walked to the car natalees mom was
sitting and we said mam you have to believe us we did not do anything with you
daughter, she was crying and said i don't believe you 2 , i promise you i will make
you life a living hell because of this . anwyas we said we were sorry again ans that
we will help in any way possible.i went home 7 pm tuesday, i was then called 2*

pm by the police for questioning i went gave a statement they said i was a witness no suspect the same went for my brother and my friend they were questionded and had to sign their statement also , the checked my car and i was clear to go , wednesday i was called again to show them how i drove the route that day ( i could refuse was my right i still decided to go , as did my brother and friend ) the drove us one by one and then we were free to go again. Thursday morning my friend called me (he goes to aruba international school and his mother is a teacher there and he is a straight A student ) in panic and said there a re family members here at school and they are sharing flyers and the flyers said : GIRL KIDNAPPED ASK JORAN VANDER SLOOT (thats my friends name ) the principle asked them to leave ad they did .so thats my part of the story yesterday and today it was quiet no treathen phoncalls what we got before and I won't mention the crazythings the newspapers etc. writes about us its to much to mention. at home my mom is losing it she is cryimg constantly , my dad bloodpressure got high also his hands are red , my friends home is a disaster also ,his mom is crying constantly also his dad is pretty cool he calmes us down and talks to us also not to worry , my brother is preety cool but on his face you see he is worried , my friend is pretty worried also. i'm pretty worried also , we have 2 lawyers one for my friend and one for me in case we get arrested and charched with something his dad can't defend hin he is a judge and he is too emotional attached .my friend has his graduation this thursday he has to go to the states in july he has a full scholarship. i had to go to vacation also end of this month.many politicians find we should be locked up rightnow. We heard a lot of false alarms that she was dead , she was seen with 2 guys , her hair is cut and is red now ,she was in a crackhouse etc, we were arrested and , my car is by the police we confessed to murder and rape,  she went in a restaurant to buy food but none of those were true. So betty that was my part of the story what i said here is the same in my statement,people are saying they are bad guys lock them up , the family is going thru a lot righnow , but what they don't know how the other families feel and how they also have a reputation and carreers etc. because when this all is over they will still be talks that were the 3 guys that had something to do with the kidnap of natalee its a small island.they don't understand the pressure we are having also, if this girl turns up dead we have a problem we were the last seen with her . I lost a lot of friends who think we had to do something with this, many of my friends supported us also brought food etc. for us at home and know we are innocent, we are innocent also we promise i would NEVER hurt anyone in anyway, i would do every everything to help find her thats what we told eveyone also , i would take a bullet to save her and bring her back to her family if i had to so would my friend also.i would never never hurt anyone i'm a very happy and social person who likes to make  friends with people and not hurting them

*So betty i will say goodbye now hope you believe me and i pray to god that they find natalee soon and find her well so that this nightmare ends  for all of us and they  we prove we had nothing  to do with this, i hope you pray for all of us say hi to everyone there hope to hear from you soon and  may god bless.........*

*bye bye*

*Deepak*

## Scene 1: "Hi Betty"

*Hi betty :*

*How are you i hope you and your family is* **fine**.
***Betty*** *is better i tell you the truth , before it will be a shock for you later, but i think it will be a shock for you* **rightnow**. *The missing girl natalee hollaway,I spoke to her , sunday she left with me with me , my brother and a friend from carlos n' charlies ,"*

The email opens with "*Hi betty :*" Immediately, Deepak draws our attention to "Betty" in three distinct ways.

First, he places her name on a line all its own, and there "Betty" sits at the absolute top of the page, with extra spacing below it setting it well above the body of the letter. In forensic document terms these are prime "key location" and "spacing" issues.

Second, to make sure we don't take the seemingly simple greeting for granted, Deepak immediately elevates "Betty" to far more importance. He repeats her name, thus making it a keyword. And then he positions it at the most prominent place in the second line, the left margin.

Finally, to make triple sure we don't miss it, this time he capitalizes "Betty," which is very unusual for Deepak. Typically he writes everything in lowercase letters—in fact, over the course of this entire email Deepak will capitalize only three names: Betty, Joran, and Deepak. And despite referring to Natalee numerous times he will never once capitalize her name.

We must not overlook the obvious. By placing Betty's name in the greeting, Deepak is telling us that everything in the email will have something to do with her. This is called "linkage messaging."

Now, at first blush this can seem trivial but it's not. For example, in the famous JonBenét Ramsey ransom note, the killer first wrote a practice note to "*Mr. and Mrs. Ramsey*" but then changed it to "*Mr. Ramsey*," which turned out to be of crucial importance. The writer of the note not only linked everything in the note to John Ramsey, she clearly differentiated John from Patsy in order to place the blame on John, where the writer felt it belonged.

Deepak's way of introducing Betty might seem to be one more minor communication, but don't be fooled. Never forget that Deepak's L-2 mind is a brilliant communicator and knows exactly where he's going with this story. Thus it's no surprise—knowing that punctuation often contains unique messages on its own (called "punctuation messaging")—that we observe Deepak using a very unusual "colon" or "double period" after his greeting: "*Hi betty :*" This, in turn, was set apart from her name with extra spacing.

First of all, letter-writers don't normally use a colon in a greeting to a friend. A colon suggests something more formal, such as a report or a business letter. Later Deepak plainly admits that this email is indeed a secret forensic report, and the colon is a sure sign that he's getting down to business. For a profiler this is a positive sign, an indication that important information will soon be forthcoming. It suggests, early on, that we're about to receive a "police report" from Officer Deepak Kalpoe, cast by his inner director in the role of principal investigator.

In fact, when a perpetrator confesses his conscience actually functions as a secret policeman, speaking on behalf of the victim. The JonBenét ransom note-writer precisely demonstrated that approach when she made several overt references to the "police" even as she was secretly talking about herself, her inner policewoman. In the same way, Deepak will refer to the police several times in his email, all the while secretly referring to himself.

We also know that even simple periods carry important messages, implying, for example, a conclusion, the culmination of a definite event. Deepak will clearly use periods in an extremely creative way—very sparingly, to mark key events and to help the reader organize this lengthy communication. At the very end of his email he'll even sign off with a string of periods, to underscore the importance of this punctuation signal. For the moment we can also read the colon after Betty's name as telling us that something doubly important and extremely final (remember, a period means "conclusion") has happened to "*Betty*," whomever she ultimately represents to Deepak.

In other words, right off the bat Deepak uses a multitude of message markers to suggest that *"Betty"* is of extreme importance. This will serve as an immediate test for validating our thoughtprint decoding. At first glance we might wonder why in the world Deepak is emphasizing *"Betty"* to this degree. But knowing that his unconscious L-2 mind is way ahead of us, we proceed with full assurance that Deepak has something special for us and that it definitely involves *"Betty."* Deepak suggests that understanding the identity represented by the word *"Betty"* is a major key to unlocking the Deepak Code.

## Betty's Family

So who is Betty? Deepak doesn't take long to answer our question. The first thing on his mind is Betty's family and their well-being. This suggests the possibility that someone in Betty's family is not fine. The fact that Deepak puts a period here, instead of a question mark, suggests that he has definite concern about someone in Betty's family. He expresses this concern in an abruptly short sentence on the very first line—all by itself no less—to further highlight the ominous possibility. Such short sentences communicate important messages very concisely.

Next, the grammatical slip "is fine" instead of "are fine" suggests that Deepak has *one person* in mind whom he's concerned about, either Betty or someone in her family. The possibility that some particular person in Betty's family is not fine is clearly hinted at and doubly suggested by punctuation messaging, with the first period immediately after "fine." Deepak indicates he's under enormous pressure to make this point by his absence of punctuation and his inability to properly stop his first sentence with "How are you?"

## Who 'Betty' Represents—'B.TTy.'

> *Hi betty* (**beth twitty**) *:How are you i hope you and **your family is fine**. Betty (**Beth twitty**) is better i tell you the truth , before it will be a shock for you later, but i think it will be a shock for you rightnow. The missing girl natalee hollaway,I spoke to her , sunday she left with me with me , my brother and a friend from carlos n' charlies ,*

We can be certain that, in the grand scheme of things, especially as he awaits the knock of the police on his door, a casual acquaintance in America is not all that important to Deepak Kalpoe. So we should start wondering exactly who Betty represents to him, not simply who she literally is. She's certainly someone important: he capitalized her name in the sentence in which he claims to want to tell the truth, but he rarely capitalizes any other names. And he didn't capitalize "Betty" the first time he used it, suggesting he is writing to two "Bettys"– one on the surface who is not nearly as important as the second Betty, to whom he promises the truth. We will shortly see that the shock Deepak has in store for "Betty" does not fit his surrogate grandmother figure to whom he allegedly wrote (see below), but it does indeed fit someone else perfectly—**Beth Twitty**. "Betty" is a perfect combination of "**Beth**" and "**Twitty**." And of course "Betty" and "Beth" both derive from "Elizabeth."

Just five nights before he sat down to write this email, Deepak had a dramatic encounter with Natalee's mother, one he describes later in the email, a description that specifically validates this email as his deeper communication to the worried parent. As it unfolds it will become apparent that this entire email was unconsciously written to Beth Twitty, and we have abundant evidence telling us why.

Of all the people on his mind, even more than the police, Deepak knew that he had to answer first of all to Beth Twitty, the worried mother. As he introduces his email with the words *"hope you and your family is fine"* Deepak reveals how deeply he knew that, which is precisely what his L-2 did. Betty, the grandmother to whom he wrote, also symbolized Deepak's own beloved natural grandmother. He turned to Betty, the surrogate grandmother, for comfort, but simultaneously he also confessed to his real grandmother, letting her know how badly he had failed. In essence he secretly wrote Beth Twitty and "copied" his real grandmother.

Also, by mentioning Betty's or Beth's family and asking after them, Deepak shows that he's also confessing to everyone else in Natalee's family, including her natural father, Dave Holloway, and her stepfather, Jug Twitty, whom Deepak mentions later in the email.

But first, the striking similarity in their names—Betty and Beth— leaps off the page. As he writes to the most motherly American he knows, in reality Deepak is writing a confession to Beth Twitty, an American mother desperately searching for her missing daughter. Deepak wants her to hear from him what really happened that night.

## Deepak in His "Own Voice"

Deepak's thoughtprints are so clear it's almost as though we can hear his deeper intelligence actually speaking to us as he explains the purpose of this lengthy email:

Dear Beth Twitty –

Please understand that this entire email was written to you. I'm constantly speaking to you indirectly, in code—the only way my soul can speak, the only way I can tell the truth because part of me still wants to cover up. So pay attention—I'm going to show you how I get my secret messages between the lines.

For example, check out how well 'Betty' condenses 'Beth Twitty,' even at first sounding like 'Bet–th,' then rhyming with 'Beth Twitty.' Have you ever played Charades, where you have to get someone to understand a word by suggesting a word that sounds like it? That's just one of the ways my deeper mind communicates. Please understand that I'm using 'Betty' to get the message to you—and I came as close as I could without my conscious mind catching on. My above-the-surface, conscious mind wants to cover up, of course. In fact, every waking moment is dedicated to crawling out from under this awful cloud of suspicion. But here in this email to you, Beth, everything's out on the table. The whole terrible truth.

Right away I point to my reason for writing to you by inquiring about your family and their well-being. Maybe everything's not so well, eh? And then I hint about one person in particular—you know, when I wrote 'is' instead of 'are'! Is that person OK? Might not be, so I drop a few hints and then I'm ready to really talk. I'm ready to start making my hidden confession to you, Beth. And, to make sure you 'get it' I'm going to repeat the same idea in different ways. Over and over again. But it's stuff you want to know. I'm going to tell you who Natalee was with and what she was doing—where she went, who went with her, and what they did.

You may not want to hear it but you really want to know! You **need** to know! You need to hear what I'm really telling you. After all, you're the one who looked right into my eyes and asked me to confess.

Beth, you must do what law enforcement must do. Stop pretending to be an expert and just listen to me! Because of what I'm about to tell you, though, it's going to be much harder for you than for them. The picture I've got to paint for you is not pretty, and because it involves your own precious daughter it's sure to overwhelm you at moments. It will be incredibly painful but I still have to tell the story. I have to say it and you need to hear it. It's the only way you'll ever know the truth because—at least for now—only my deeper intelligence can tell it.

## The Shocking Truth for Beth

*"Betty is better i tell you the* **truth** *, before it will be a* **shock** *for you later, but i think it will be a* **shock** *for you rightnow."*

Next Deepak personally promises Beth *"is better I tell you the truth."* He vows to tell the truth to Beth, the authorities, and the world. That phrase, featuring the word "truth," is as powerful a message marker as you could find, one that points toward a hidden confession. He further promises not only the truth but the *shocking* truth—doubly emphasizing the word "shock." Deepak is about to tell Beth Twitty something traumatic. We should expect a powerful, graphic email filled with disturbing news about her daughter.

Indeed, delivered between the lines, the hidden narrative will relate a particularly detailed and personal story answering the questions Beth would naturally have about what happened to Natalee. Closing this brief sentence with a period/punctuation marker suggests a definite, unmistakable conclusion. Thoughtprint by thoughtprint, the evidence continues to build that Deepak is unquestionably addressing Beth Twitty. And, thoughtprint by thoughtprint we continue to find every indication of a hidden confession. He has expressed concern about her family's well-being and now promises to shock her with the absolute truth.

Once more we hear Deepak's deeper intelligence at work:

Please look at all the messages I'm delivering—quick and concise—and see what I'm promising to tell you with those two magic words *"the truth."* See how I quickly repeated your name, Beth—how I capitalized it this time and located it in a prominent place—left margin, beginning of a sentence—so you wouldn't miss it. As you're reading you might also notice that I capitalize only three persons' names in this letter—yours, mine and Joran's. Oh sure, I mention Natalee's name lots of times—okay, 24 times to be exact! But never once do I capitalize it. What does that tell you? And don't forget to pay attention because, like all experienced emailers, I use 'caps' for important messages that I want to shout out to you.

Why you, Beth? Well, no other living person on this planet makes me feel my guilt like you do. I'll never forget that look in your eye. Confronting you was the dumbest thing we ever could have done. Joran and I tried to put one over on you, and instead we heard about our guilt straight from your mouth. But to tell you the truth, our consciences were already bothering us so badly that we were looking for ways to punish ourselves, and secretly hoping to be pushed into a hidden confession. Yeah, that was the real reason we approached you. I was so tortured by my guilt—that's why I said it was '*better for me*' to tell you the truth. Joran was feeling the pressure too, even though he tries to be slick about hiding it.

( . . . *before it will be a* **shock** *for you later, but i think it will be a* **shock** *for you rightnow.*)

Do you think a person, a real person, can take a life and simply walk away? Let me tell you it was a shock for me to learn that I couldn't. That's why I repeated the word 'shock' twice in that sentence.

And like I said, I deliver two messages at the same time. By repeating 'shock' I was also telling you that the truth is going to be an incredible shock for you. As I warned you, I have some shocking news for you *"rightnow"* and much more *"later."* Prepare yourself for both. And I merged two words into one *"rightnow"'* because I was so desperate to confess. When I do something like that, the very next thing I tell you is going to be crucial. Like I said, Beth, pay attention!

## 'The News'—Another Keyword

"*The missing girl natalee hollaway,I spoke to her , sunday she left with me , my brother and a friend from carlos n' charlies , it was my car like* **the news** *said she got in to, I am one of the persons of intrest , i am one* the the *students they've* questioned and released *as they claimed in* **the news** *. Let see where to start i don't even know where to begin*"

Before we see the specific message Deepak delivers next, we must appreciate the flashing-light message marker, *"the news,"* underscored as a keyword by triple repetition. This suggests that Deepak is indeed telling us the "news" and reporting on this very case. This is one of the most crucial and hopeful message markers in the entire email. It comes on the heels of his promise to tell Beth the shocking truth, and its placement so early in the email further underscores its own validity as a powerful hidden confession.

Clearly, Deepak appears to be shouting out a confession—the news that he was involved in this crime. Because of these early thoughtprints, we should expect all the disturbing details about Natalee's disappearance to show up soon, because shocking news reports deal in such facts. Since Deepak has informed Beth that the truth will be terribly shocking for her, it's likely that Natalee is dead.

In "the News" Deepak promises that he will function like a reporter who delivers all the important parts of the story. Indeed—as he instructs—we should read the entire email, every word and every message in it, as if we were listening to the best reporter in the world reveal the inside story.

## Prediction: Followed by News Flash—'*Hollaway*'—Natalee is Dead

As we think logically of what we would want to know, the first thing would be whether Deepak knows what happened to Natalee and, if so, what exactly *did* happen. The most basic news we need is whether Natalee is alive. If Deepak begins here we can be sure that he was involved, which we would also expect his L-2 to admit.

Deepak immediately fulfills his promise to deliver the most shocking news Beth could imagine. *"The missing girl natalee hollaway,(I spoke to her)"* informs Beth that, without question, Natalee is missing, that she is not present and that she is probably dead. The news flash that he had for Beth was that Natalee was "missing."

Next comes *"hollaway"*— "Holl-**away**" (instead of Holloway)—one of the most blatant slips in the email, further reflecting the identical thoughtprint that Natalee has "gone away." Deepak makes the surface suggestion that Natalee is "simply" missing and perhaps has been taken away to another place, but his thoughtprints tell us otherwise: Natalee has died.

Here we again hear Deepak's deeper mind speaking to Beth Twitty:

Yes, Natalee is missing. She has gone away. I can't say it any more strongly than "missing." Remember, I promised you immediate, shocking news. Then I just happened to write "Hollaway"—and this is the only time I used her last name at all. I could just as easily have used 'Natalee.' But you need to know she's gone away. Away. So that's how I wrote the last name. You can understand it clearly. It truly was her very last name. She went away. It was the last thing she did.

Now notice, *"The missing girl natalee hollaway,I spoke to her , sunday she left."* That's right, *"she left."* What more do you need? In less than two sentences I've given you four clear indications that she's gone. Read it like this: 'On Sunday Natalee was not well. Then she was missing—left for good, and went far away. She died.'

Remember, I have to find secret ways to communicate since there's that one awful part of me that always wants to cover up what we did. There's a battle going on between my good-natured soul and the devil part of me, and that battle rages through this whole email. Of course I'll make it more explicit that Natalee has died—believe me, I'll do that—but first things first. I want you to know that your daughter is dead and gone.

## Hopeful News: Slip Suggests Body Can Be Found

"*Hollaway*" also suggests "Holloway is away, holed away in a secret hole or hollow somewhere." Later Deepak tells us exactly where her body now rests, a location that will fit with a "hollow" or even a "hole." As it happens, "*Hollaway*" also suggests something even more specific— that her body could possibly be found inside some type of container with holes in it.

Once again Deepak's conscience speaks to Beth:

You want to know where she is, right? I know you do. Just look at "*Hollaway*" and figure it out yourself. You'll find her stowed away deep in a hole somewhere. This shouldn't surprise you at all—if I'm going to tell you how Natalee died I might as well tell you where the body is, too. Just pay attention. We have a long way to go and I have a lot more to say.

## Summary of Scene 1

- Deepak immediately indicates signs of a hidden confession.

- Right off, Deepak is unconsciously confessing to Betty—aka Beth Twitty.

- Three powerful message markers reveal Deepak's plan to tell us *"the truth," "the shocking truth,"* and *"the news."*

- Deepak immediately answers the first major question: she is indeed missing and not well—something is wrong with Natalee, suggesting she has died.

- Deepak's major slip and powerful image *"Hollaway"* likewise suggests Natalee has died—and that her body is discoverable "away in a hole"

## Scene 2: More Signs of Confession

## More News: Sexual Innuendos Emerge

*"The missing girl natalee **hollaway,I** spoke to her"*

Now we move to more subtle clues. First, by neglecting the proper spacing and thus merging himself with Natalee (*"natalee hollaway,I"*), Deepak suggests that, at the instant of her death—exactly when Natalee went away—he was enmeshed with her, probably via a sexual assault. Simultaneously, he emphasizes this with another striking punctuation message in which he puts "I" in caps for one of only three times in the entire email. All his other uses of the first-person singular come in lower-case i's. First, the capitalized "I" shouts at us Deepak's responsibility.

Second, a capitalized "I" as opposed to a lowercase "i" is also the most obvious phallic symbol in the entire alphabet. Of course these thoughtprints are subtle at this point, but nevertheless we have an early hypothesis about what Deepak is trying to tell us.

Again, it's as though we hear Deepak's soul speaking to Beth:

Every detail tells a story, Beth. I know how to punctuate. I know how to use capital letters. And so, when I wrote *"The missing girl natalee **hollaway,I**"* that shows how close I got to her. When she died I was that close, because I was having sex with her. That's what happened to your daughter. Okay? And look how responsible I feel—that's why the capitalized 'I' linked with the first time I mention her name. Later you will see exactly why I feel so guilty, even more than Satish and Joran.

Likewise, when I want to separate myself from something I put lots of spaces in between. Sometimes those spaces should remind you of the distances between places. Sometimes like at the very end of my email they just remind me that I'm lost. Ever since this happened I've been lost—from my family, from myself, from God—and I don't know if I'm ever going to find myself again.

## The News: 'I speak for Natalee'

"*I spoke to her* ," is Deepak's very first phrase after suggesting twice that Natalee has died and that sexual contact had something to do with it. We can hear Deepak's deeper intelligence speaking symbolically, explaining this seemingly benign comment to Beth, and the explanation comes at a key moment, immediately following his prediction of "shocking news."

Yes, Beth, 'I spoke to her.' Sounds innocent, doesn't it? Don't be fooled. I've carefully chosen every comment to convey the shocking news. What I'm really saying here is not only that 'I spoke to Natalee' but that 'I spoke *for* Natalee.' I'm speaking for her now, telling the identical story she'd tell you if she could. Don't miss my message. She can't talk so I'm talking for her. Can you hear me? Can you hear her?

Whatever you do, don't let my surface voice drown out Natalee's voice as it speaks through me. My surface voice claims I'm not guilty and keeps working overtime on the cover-up. You decide which voice is telling the truth.

Both of Deepak's first two deeper messages in "*I spoke*" fit perfectly with the recent discovery of the deeper intelligence in therapy, and its striking capability to speak the truth in a totally separate and deeper L-2 voice. Because I was trained to hear this voice in therapy—a voice that insisted on telling the truth in the speaker's best interest—I was able to listen for that same voice in a perpetrator's (or suspect's) communication.

In another vivid example, the murderers of JonBenét Ramsey opened the ransom note with *"we represent a **small** foreign faction,"* telling us they were speaking for the dead child. "Unconsciously, we represent the little foreign entity/girl with the French name, JonBenét, whose life we have just taken. We must speak for her because she can no longer speak." They then proceeded to do exactly that, even as Deepak Kalpoe suggests he is doing the same thing in this case.

## The News: Double Entendres Grow Stronger (Spoke, Poke, Probe)

Deepak's sexual-innuendo code will continually grow stronger and stronger. In this chapter he begins to introduce a series of phallic symbols, starting with a *"spoke"* followed by more blatant images shortly, including "poke" and "probe."

Deepak continues to speak between the lines:

Beth, look at *"The missing girl natalee hollaway,I **spoke** to her"* again and see how close this is to '*The missing girl natalee hollaway,**I poke her**.'* The sexual message is plain. Look at 'spoke' another way, too. If you turn 'spoke' from a verb into a noun, what do you get? What's a spoke? Yeah, I hate to tell you this—I spoked her. Like a driving wheel, I was one of the spokes and she was the shiny hub cap. To be blunt, I entered her. I spoked her and poked her. We all did.

See what I mean about symbolism? Very visual. So is my spacing. I even leave an empty open space after *"I spoke to her ,"* suggesting that I entered her open space, her vagina. Furthermore, this suggests that after I raped her she was gone—keep that idea in mind. And even the sounds of the words and all their connotations help me tell my—yes, I know—"crude shocking story." So listen closely.

*"The missing girl natalee hollaway,I spoke to her , sunday she left with me , my brother and a friend from carlos n' charlies "*

Also, remember when I said, *"I spoke to her"*? I didn't describe any return communication from her, did I? Well maybe that's because, at some point Natalee wasn't able to speak with me. Or maybe I wasn't listening. Maybe that's when something went way wrong, horribly wrong.

## The News: Three Guys Involved; More Sexual Innuendos— 'I Got Into Her'

> *"sunday she left with me , my brother and a friend from carlos n' charlies , it was my car like the **news** said **she got in to,** I am one of the persons of intrest , i am one **the the** students they've questioned"*

As the story continues to unfold, Deepak makes it plain that all three guys were involved in Natalee's disappearance, and that something important happened at Carlos'n Charlie's that led to her being gone. Deepak will later complete this part of the news, but we must logically raise the possibility that Natalee had been drugged, because all her friends strongly suggest she never would have gone off with three strange guys no matter how much alcohol she might had had. Without question, Deepak's automobile is also a key part of the story: *"it was my car like the news said."* Step-by-step he appears to be fulfilling his promise to provide valuable information.

> Beth, notice how quickly I link all three of us to Natalee's disappearance: *"The missing girl . . . .she left with me, my brother, and a friend from carlos n' charlies."* Translation: we were all involved in her leaving, her death. Right off the bat I'm hinting also that someone inside the nightclub assisted Joran to leave with Natalee. Instead of calling Joran by name I called him *"a friend from carlos n' charlies"* which can be taken two ways as secretly referring to both.

We must not overlook another sexual innuendo. Deepak appears to be bending over backwards to draw our attention to a sexual assault. Looking closely we find the blatant phrase **"(it was my car like) The news said, 'She got into I.'"**
Deepak's deeper intelligence explains:

> Yeah, I could have written, 'the news reported she got into my car, I am . . . ' But to tell the truth I precisely arranged the awkward phrase, *"it was my car like **the news** said she got in to, I."* Why? Because the real news is that '**she got into I.**' or you could say, '**I got into she/her,**' if you know what I mean. And, yes, it all happened in my car. Detect any subtle sexual symbolism there, Beth? On top of that, doesn't a car often represent power to a man? I mean, a car is the ultimate phallic symbol!

What about a woman's car? By mentioning how Natalee got into my car, I'm suggesting how we got into her car, her container. You'll see that I'm fond of female imagery, Beth—containers, vessels and vehicles that represent a woman, just as knives and pens and cigars represent a man. So a car can represent manly power or a womanly container.

Because she carries babies, a woman is the ultimate sacred container, starting with her vagina container before her uterus container. But beyond the lust, it's really all about love and nurturing, holding someone as only a woman can. A woman is a holder, a container. Maybe that's why I'm pouring my heart out to you, Beth, because you're a mom, a hurting mom who will never be able to nurture your girl again.

I suppose you might be glad to know that your girl didn't give it up easily. Try another way of reading the sentence, *"it was my car like the news said she got in to (it)."* The sentence begs for the missing word "it," as in 'getting into it' with someone, like a fight. Yeah, Natalee resisted when we started touching her in the car, when it was three against one. But remember, this is 'The News.' If I'm going to tell you what we did, I'm going to have to describe Natalee's response.

## "The The Studs"

*"I am one of the persons of intrest , i am one* **the the stud[ents]** *they've* <u>questioned</u> *and* <u>released</u> *as they claimed in* **the news** *.[period]"*

Beth, I want to jump ahead just briefly. Pay attention when I use the word 'students' I'm advising you to 'really go to school here.' And what's next? Yikes! The police! That's the last thing I want to have to deal with—being questioned by police! But both of those references should alert you that I'm ready and willing to talk, between the lines. Back-to-back, they shout out important news about the case.

Now when I say, *"I am one* **the the** *students they've questioned"* that suggests two students connected (*"the the students"*). You have the first message, 'I am one of the students that was merged with another student,' and you know who I'm talking about. And you know what I mean by merged—I raped her. But notice my much stronger sexual innuendo—'I am one the the **studs**.' And take it a step further 'stud–ent' suggesting "stud enter" her. But notice how specific my mind gets, it's ***'the the studs'*** meaning two identical studs behaving in the same fashion. That would be me and my brother, Satish—and I'm telling you we didn't waste any time, one followed the other. Stay tuned and I will give you the exact order of the assaults because I'm admitting to you here that all three of us did this to your Natalee, and two of us were brothers.

## More News: Held Then Released—Bondage and the Moment of Death

But Beth, what about 'a student' being held and then released 'by them'? Think symbolically. Natalee fought us, so we had to control her with something around her neck, tightening and loosening it, *"as they claimed in the news."* This is the secret news here—that as she struggled the three of us used a type of bondage to control her, a loose, chokehold kind of thing around her neck. And that had a lot to do with why she died—her final release, her last day. At the moment Natalee died she was bound, being held down. That's the story. Period. See how I confirm the message again with a space and a period in "*as they claimed in **the news** .[period]"* The empty space suggests 'something missing' as in Natalee's missing as a result of our group rape, and I confirm the message with my typical punctuation message period.

Now, I've not only told you about the group rape but about how we controlled her, which led to her major problem. And by connecting 'studs' to the police, indirectly I'm telling you how guilty I really am. Whenever you see me refer to the police, understand that's a major part of my confession, because my 'inner policeman'—my soul—is driving this confession. Looking back, you can also appreciate how significant my double entendre *"spoke"* was, and you'll also be prepared to hear another revealing slip.

Deepak follows up immediately with another strong suggestion of sexual assault.

## Another Important Slip: *'persons of intrest'*

*"I am one of the persons of **intrest**"*

I'm not through telling you about the sexual assault yet. After all, "*I am one of the persons of intrest."* Read my slip *"intrest"* first as 'in rest' or 'rest in.' I guess you could say that I'm one of the persons who 'rested in' Natalee, entered her, went into her. So did Joran and Satish.

And there's more. You know *"intrest"* sounds like 'in dress' or 'undress' along with 'in tryst'—all sexual suggestions. I'm telling you that I am one of the guys who was in her dress; one of those who undressed her and initiated an involuntary tryst with her. You know Natalee was wearing a skirt. You know how Joran described her panties in detail. No matter what my cover-up voice says, Natalee was nude in the backseat of my Honda as I will describe later in my email. All three of us took turns with her.

## *"intrest"* Suggests Lying 'In rest'

So yeah, we were trysting and she was twisting, resisting. We should have seen it coming. In a way, *'intrest'* says it all. And it's also another not-so-subtle hint that Natalee is lying 'in rest'—that she died, yes, during this 'tryst.'

And next, if you've digested that, listen to this. I'm using 'in rest' to hint at where her body is, where she lies in rest. You can see the slip that 'in-trest' suggests 'and–the rest' or 'the rest of the story.' I fully intend to tell  the whole story. My deeper mind totally means business.

## The News: Carlos'n Charlie's—Keyword Used Six Times

*"The missing girl natalee hollaway ( , I spoke to her , sunday she left with me , my brother and a friend from* **carlos n' charlies** *,)"*

Beth, notice how quickly I bring Carlos'n Charlie's into the picture. It really starts the whole episode involving Natalee. And I go on to mention the name of this popular Aruban nightspot *six times,* making it an exceptional keyword. Important stuff happened in this place, something involving a person you don't know about, someone who works at the bar who was instrumental in Natalee's decision to go off with us three guys. And usually it's no big deal. We've all done this before with other girls. After it's over they don't squawk—they're too embarrassed. It's just good times on the faraway fantasy island, unless something goes wrong.

When that happens, it's good to have connections. It's good to know people who know how things work in Aruba. And, yes, there is at least one other person of interest who helped put Natalee to rest. We couldn't have dumped the body without him, but more on that later.

## Joran's Book: Chapter 3—'Going Out at Carlos 'n Charlie's'

In his book, *The Natalee Holloway Case*, published in Holland in May 2007, Joran describes Carlos'n Charlie's as a wild nightclub where people drink belly shots from the navel of prone persons lying on the bar. He devoted an entire chapter to Carlos'n Charlie's, which became his regular hangout. Joran could scarcely contain himself as he detailed his nocturnal revelries at the bar. He vividly recalled his first night there at age 16, characterizing it as a coming-out party. Joran depicted the dancing as wild and sexy, and reported that the competition was heavy for "players" to score chicks. The girls in Aruba, he wrote, were sexually uninhibited and primed for action. Waiters would use fans to blow girls skirts up while they were dancing, revealing thong underwear or nothing at all. In addition Joran was routinely admitted free and was so tall that no one questioned his age, although the legal drinking age in Aruba is 18.

Joran characterized Carlos'n Charlie's as a perfect place to pick up tourist girls. He boldly revealed his secret for success with young, unsuspecting ladies—tell them you're also a tourist but claim you have a vacation home in Aruba, which explains why you know the hottest nightspots and also differentiates you from the local beach bums.

Carlos'n Charlie's is well-known as a meeting place for those interested in casual sex. As Aruban police authorities told Dave Holloway, girls have described their drinks being spiked there, and customers have observed bartenders—particularly at the back bar—pouring an unknown liquid into only one of two drinks, in all likelihood the girl's drink.

## Police Interviews

So the subject of sexual contact between Natalee and the three guys has been quickly introduced. In fact, within an hour or so after being with Natalee, Deepak sent an email to a buddy of his describing her "putting her hands down my pants." In every version of the hotel story, which they told the day she was reported missing, Deepak and Joran reported sexual contact with Natalee. They did the same thing even more graphically in their beach story, which they began telling about ten days later. And within twelve days of the crime Joran and Deepak spontaneously accused each other of rape. That fact leaps out from their police interviews. Early on, the suspects themselves gave every indication that Natalee suffered foul play directly related to sex.

## More News: Body Held Then Released

> *"i am one the the (sic) students they've **questioned and released** as they claimed in **the news** . [period]"*

It's as though Deepak continues:

Come back to my twin communication images which are designed to guide and alert you, *"students they've [police] questioned."* I'm also hinting that after Natalee died we 'released' her into the Caribbean Sea rather than hiding the body on the island. You bury bodies on land, but you release them into the ocean. Also, notice how I condensed this part of the story. I tell you why Natalee died and hinted at what we did with her body, all in one sentence. That's the way they do it on the news. My slip *"Hollaway"* was a one-word news flash. I hope you didn't miss these, Beth. I know you're not buying my cover-up story, but at the same time I don't know if the real story's getting through. Keep my news flash in mind and you'll see how I report the news in detail later on in my email.

If you're willing to dig deeper into my mind—and deeper into the sea—Natalee's body can be found. She can be set free. Wherever her body is now being held, it can be released. And don't worry—I'm not through. I'm also going to point you in the right direction so you'll know where to look.

## The News: Deepak's Enormous Guilt

> *"The missing girl natalee hollaway,**I spoke** to her , sunday she left **with me** , my brother and a friend from carlos n' charlies , it was **my car** like the news said she got in to, **I am one** of the persons of intrest , **i am one** the the students they've questioned and released as they claimed in the news."*

Step back, Beth, and see how guilty I am, how responsible I am, for Natalee's disappearance and death. I can't say it any stronger.

*"I spoke to her," "she left with **me**," "it was **my** car," "I am one of the persons of interest,"* and again *"I am one (they questioned)."* To make sure you hear me telling you who's responsible and who's guilty, I capitalized *"I"* twice. I, me, my. I did it with Joran and my brother. She's dead and we did it.

## Summary of New Information in Scene 2

- Powerful message marker *"The news."* Deepak makes it clear that he's unconsciously speaking for Natalee.

- Two other major communication images—*"students they've [police] questioned"*—suggest major clues and Deepak's guilt.

- Deepak is telling a logical story. After giving us a strong message in the first scene, telling us that Natalee died, Deepak now tells us what caused her death.

- The news: Deepak begins a string of sexual innuendos including *"I got into her," "I spoke . . . her/(poke her)," "I am one the the studs,"* pointing toward a sexual assault in which all three guys were involved.

- More news: He points strongly to Carlos'n Charlie's—a keyword used six times—suggesting someone there assisted the boys in entrapping Natalee, probably by pouring a drug into her drink.

- More news: One of Deepak favorite phrases is *"my car,"* suggesting the place of the assault.

- Deepak subtly suggests that Natalee died suddenly in the middle of a sexual assault involving a bondage scenario, which in some way caused her death, with distinct references to being held and released.

- More details: Deepak suggests that her body was eventually *"released"* into the sea. This matches his slip *"intrest"* suggesting "lying in rest" and *"Hollaway"* from first scene.

- Another key part of 'The News'—Deepak's enormous guilt. Image of "police" in *"they've questioned"* followed by confession in great detail suggests deep guilt. And Deepak can't say it enough, *"missing girl . . . I spoke to her . . . she left with **me** . . . it was **my** car . . . I am one of the persons of intrest , i am one.. they've questioned and released as they claimed in the news ."*

- Right off, Deepak's thoughtprints indicate that he is telling a plausible story, one which we can validate by decoding the balance of the email. He also demonstrates that his slips will contribute significantly to his continuing confession.

# 6
# Poker

## Scene 1: Deepak Promises to Tell All

> "*Let see where to start i don't even know where to begin these last days where so crazy for me i'm very tired haven't slept good in days : **The story** starts sunday night when a friend of mine was playing poker at a local casino (in the holiday inn) after he won the poker at the fourth place he decided to get up and play some blackjack so he went to the blackjack table and there was natalee (they were a lil drunk ) so my friend started playing blackjack and he was winning quite good , so then natalee approached him and introduced herself and said to him*" your a lucky guy , can you help me win some of my money back i lost $ 360 , "of my fathers money" so my friend said ok , why not ."*

Deepak's choice of the words "*The story*" reflects the most hopeful flashing-light message marker imaginable—unconscious confessions always tell a story, and because Deepak's email is so long we can expect it to reveal an especially detailed account of Natalee's disappearance. Adding the promise of "*the story*" to promises of "*the shocking truth*" and "*the news*," Deepak strongly insists that this forensic document contains his confession. He readily admits that he's tired and can't sleep, circumstances which invariably encourage a confession. His defenses are down and he's extremely vulnerable.

It's as though this now-infamous crime suspect is offering an exclusive email interview to the missing girl's mother:

> Beth, I promise to tell you *"The story"* of Natalee's last night. When you read that magic word *"story"* right after I've promised you *"shocking truth"* and *"the news,"* you have to know that, from beginning to end, this email will be my story of Natalee's disappearance. MY story. Stories can be fact or fiction. This is MY story. I'm the author of both the fiction and the facts behind it. In case you can't hear me, **I shout it out to you by capitalizing "The,"** which I then doubly emphasize with the colon.

87

Beth, you have to understand that on the surface I'm telling you a mostly fictional story. Sure, I've blended in some real events. I mean, we did meet Natalee in Oranjestad, and she went with us, but the rest of the story is mostly my little pack of lies.

By the time you read this you'll know that our initial story about dropping Natalee off at the Holiday Inn was a lie. Well, that's not the only lie. Lots of people know I'm lying when I tell you Natalee asked Joran to win some of her money back in the casino, and that Natalee was *"VERY drunk"* at Carlos'n Charlie's later that night. Even so, there's a message in my madness. I'm providing you and the authorities plenty of details about what really happened. Dig a little deeper and you'll find the truth.

Deepak's insistence that his L-2 mind is about to tell a hidden story clearly reflects what we now know about the deeper intelligence. It constantly tells stories, speaking indirectly and symbolically. The unconscious mind does the same thing when it speaks in dreams. While therapists now understand dreams in an entirely new way—as guided by a deeper intelligence—cutting-edge analysts have also learned to help patients access their L-2 minds by having them create fictional stories in therapy, which they then use to get to the truth. In a similar way, perpetrators driven by overwhelming L-2 guilt secretly tell the true story between the lines of forensic documents.

To say it most emphatically, forensic documents routinely contain hidden stories, which makes Deepak's promise of *"The story"* so striking.

## The Challenge: Break Key Parts of the Code

Just as any story is made up of major parts, Deepak's hidden story will have basically six major "mini-codes," or parts, which come together to make it cohesive. This means that specific mini-codes must be broken in order to read the whole story. This requires tracking matching sets of thoughtprints, with each set forming a key part of the story.

At times Deepak will present the key to a mini-code in one particular place, overtly defining the meaning of a repetitive keyword. For example, he will wait until a memorable moment in the email to provide the true meaning for the encoded word *"etc.,"* which he uses over and over. Break the code to that word, when he shows us what he really means by it, and you will understand a major part of the case.

Deepak has promised to tell us the entire story, and the unusual length of his email assures us that he'll provide plenty of thoughtprints, in code, to answer certain questions. Specifically these include:

- What happened to Natalee with the three guys? Is there a sexual-assault code, or instead a code about a third party taking her away?

- What happened that prevented her from returning? Is there a death code or a runaway code? We can expect Deepak to tell us quickly whether Natalee's dead or alive.

- How, specifically, did she die? Is there a cause-of-death code?

- Where did this happen? Is there a location-of-trauma code?

- What did they do with the body? Is there an intermediate-step code revealing where they took that body at first? If so, why? And who was involved?

- Where did they ultimately take the body? Is there a final-disposition or location-of-body code?

Already Deepak has started to answer these questions with the early development of several striking codes: a *death code*, a *sexual-assault code* and a *location-of-body* code. We will have every opportunity to see if he will continue these thoughtprint patterns.

## Natalee's death drives Deepak 'crazy'

*"Let see where to start i don't even know where to begin these last days where so crazy for me i'm very tired haven't slept good in days : The story starts sunday night"*

Through his denial, Deepak reveals keys to his symbolic story:

Notice that, before I announce the official beginning of *"The story,"* I tip you off with the phrase *"where to start."* It starts right here. Then I say, *"where to start i don't even know."* But that happens a lot. My real messages are disguised in blatant denials. Wherever you see a *"not,"* read the sentence without it. Read through the denial and you'll see that I'm telling you twice, 'I know exactly where to start—here!'

Now see how I write *"Where to start . . . where to begin . . . where so crazy . . . the story starts . . . "* and you can see my desperate, obsessive need to take you back to the beginning of the story. Pay attention to this sequence of **'where—where—where.'**

The story truly begins at this precise point, *"where so crazy,"* first translated 'where I—we—went so crazy.' I wrote *"where so crazy"* instead of 'were so crazy' to reveal not only that we did something very crazy and behaved very destructively but that things then got out of hand—*"where"* something *"crazy"* happened to Natalee, something really *"crazy."* That means you should be looking for some kind of clue about what disturbing event took place. Also, keep the specific word *"where"* in mind and you will soon understand more than you can imagine.

When you read the phrase, *" . . . know where to begin these **last days**,"* read it as 'know where to begin—the last day, specifically Natalee's last day.' That's where this story really started. *"Last"* is a major word that even by itself speaks volumes. Yeah, I'm already talking about her death, *"last days,"* and how it's linked to *"(last days) where so crazy."* I'm telling you that our crazy behavior resulted in her crazy death. Her 'last day' occupies my mind so thoroughly that I will soon speak for her in the first person two different times: *"Today is my last day,"* she says, followed by *"It's my last night."* Whenever I speak first person, particularly for Natalee, I'm doubly emphasizing the message.

You can also learn much more from *"where so crazy."* Her death happened at a specific place, but I'm also telling you *"where"* her body is now, where you'll find the evidence of our craziness. By repeating myself I'm shouting at you, 'Think where—where—where!' Isn't that the million-dollar question now summed up in the simple word *"where"*? Everyone's seeking the one answer that would set Natalee free in a new way. 'Where, oh, where is she?' Look again. *"Where to start . . . where to begin . . . where so crazy . . . the story starts"* begs for 'and where the story ends.' One place and one place alone. I'm telling you, 'Find the body.' I'm secretly promising you that information about her body's location is hidden in the pages of this email confession.

Now you can understand my reference to *"last days"* because the plural correctly reflects that the story started on Sunday and went on into early Monday morning. Beyond that it already shows you how that last day has stretched into *"days"* and *"days"* for me. And since you showed up, Beth, with your husband and all your friends, that has continued to drive me crazy. That's why you must—must!—find that special *"where."*

The unimaginably deep pain of causing Natalee's death has set in and is driving Deepak confession-crazy. That's exactly why he couldn't wait to tell Beth Twitty the truth. Throughout his long email, in which he mentions Natalee's name again an obsessive 24 times, he further indicates that he's consumed by thoughts of her brutal death. In a real way, Natalee's last day was also Deepak's last day, because his life will never again be the same—a fact he'll reiterate at the end of his email.

## Poker players—Sexual Innuendo Code from the Beginning

*"Let see where to <u>start</u> . . . where to begin . . . :[colon] The story <u>starts</u> sunday night when a friend of mine was **playing poker** at a local casino (in the holiday inn) after he won the **poker** at the fourth place [he decided to get up and **play** some blackjack]"*

With the crucial colon message marker, indicating that he's really getting down to business, Deepak now moves "officially" to the beginning of the confessional narrative. As promised, he immediately describes how the three boys behaved so crazily as to destroy Natalee Holloway.

Beth, you should have noticed that when *"The story starts"* I'm repeating *"starts"* or *"begin"* for the third time. That's because what I'm about to tell you is a central event in the story. First I linked the beginning of the story to our crazy behavior; now *"starts"* points to a specific event—*"playing poker at a local casino (in the holiday inn)."*

Before we get to the poker game, don't overlook my first reference to Holiday Inn, in special parentheses which highlight the message. Actually the story starts with the *"Holiday Inn"* and, as you'll see, it ends there too. Think of it this way: ***"Holiday Inn"* is code for the location of Natalee's body.** That's where we took the biggest gamble of our lives. That's where we bluffed our way through. That's where, as I will tell you, the key to the case remains for you to discover.

By now you know Joren's father told us 'no body' meant 'no case' but you find the body and you solve the case. So in the very first sentence, I'm slipping you a major clue about where we put the body—

the single-most important piece of evidence. That's the kind of mind you're dealing with here—unflinchingly honest and an expert in encoding messages. Read all of this as a spy letter, sending secret messages from behind enemy lines back to headquarters, disguised in a plain letter. And you're in charge at headquarters, Beth.

## The Player

Now back to where the story *"starts"*—playing poker. Yes, my tennis-playing friend, Joran van der Sloot, is 'a player.' And I'm not only talking about tennis or soccer. You know what a player is. He's always making plays for the girls. And he plays to win. But read it again: My friend Joran is playing *"poker"*—'poke-her.' It means he's having intercourse with her, but it's also the name of an object, a 'poker' used to stoke a fire, an obvious phallic symbol.

More important, notice where Joran is playing poker—and, Beth, this will be difficult for you but being brutally honest means being brutal. In the end, when you hear the entire story, you'll be better off because you'll cry out for justice. Joran is playing 'poke-her in the casino of the holiday inn'—the 'Holloway Inn' or 'Inn Holloway,' meaning inside Natalee Holloway. He—actually we—entered Natalee's private container, her vagina, during that time 'where we went so crazy.'

Isn't that the first question a DA would ask me on the witness stand? 'Specifically how and where, Mr. Kalpoe, did you assault Miss Holloway?' Well, I'm answering here and now, precisely and powerfully. Both *"hotel"* and *"casino"* are clear feminine-container images, as in 'where we stayed' and 'where we gambled.' We stayed and gambled inside Natalee's own personal 'Inn.' I 'got into her,' remember?

Notice also the sheer irony of how Holloway matches 'Holiday'—how perfect for a creative writer like my deeper mind! You can now see how easily 'Holloway Inn' also becomes 'Hollaway End.' Later, as I've told you, I will use 'Holiday Inn' in an entirely different way to tell you the location of Natalee's final destination, where her body ended up. Find the 'Hollaway Inn/End' and you find the body. The ocean, after all, is **the inn with Holloway in it.**

## Motives: A Game and a Lie

*"a friend of mine was playing poker at a local casino (in the holiday inn) after he won the poker at the fourth place"*

Deepak continues to speak:

It all started for us as a game—one big game, our own brand of *"poker."* What was our object? To win, of course. So, sure, he—we— *"won the poker"* and did what we wanted with Natalee. Winning means overpowering a little, blonde American schoolgirl—that was really the thrill of it all—that, and gambling that we could get away with it.

That's why I keep referring to gambling. We could play in Natalee's casino without any consequences—that's how crazy we were. Only this time the game unraveled. Man, it happened so fast it just spiraled out of control.

How appropriate that Deepak's story begins with an illegal act. Here we have the 17-year-old Joran van der Sloot, an underage minor, gambling in a casino. Deepak underscores that the story starts with a lie— an illegal act at the Holiday Inn where Joran was sitting in for his father, Paulus, in a Texas Hold 'em poker tournament that the father had entered. Deepak returns to this same theme elsewhere in his email, as he depicts Joran illegally gambling in several casinos over the next two days, with his father's permission. It's a confession—in its own way— right out of the box.

As Deepak's deeper intelligence reports:

The story starts Sunday night when a friend of mine was playing poker at the casino in the Holiday Inn—illegally, living a lie. But what was really illegal was the poker he played—we played—in Natalee's Inn. Yeah, we broke the law all right, but it had never seemed bad before. Nobody ever got really hurt. Until that night.

So, yes, it was all about having sex with these naïve tourist girls. I told you it was all a game that the three of us were playing—a crazy thing to do, I know now. I've got to admit that *"poker"* also suggests an aggressive assault, 'taking a poker to someone' the way an abusive husband or wife might beat their partner with a fireplace poker. And what we did was that vicious. She fought but we won. Three of us and one of her and that makes four. We won at the fourth place, get it? Then we moved on to the next game that we played when Joran continues to gamble for Natalee. Of course that will be another lie but a very revealing one. Just like I used one lie (Joran playing *"poker"* for Natalee) to tell you the truth about what we did to her, the second time he gambles for her will be just as revealing.

## Summary of New Information in Scene

- After promising to tell us *"the shocking truth"* and *"the news"* Deepak makes absolutely clear in a third message marker that his email is, between the lines, *"The story"* of the crime.

- With the key image *"crazy"* Deepak suggests that the boys' crazy behavior—the sexual assault—somehow led to Natalee's death, her *"last day."*

- Deepak puts much of the story in quotes here as he speaks for Natalee, in the first person, revealing that it's a crucial part of the story.

- He quickly moves to a powerful series of double entendres, increasingly crude, indicating a group sexual assault. First Joran was a *"player"* and his game was *"poker,"* suggesting that the boys played "poke-her" in the "Holloway Inn."

- Simultaneously Deepak suggests how easily *"Holiday Inn"* becomes "Holloway Inn/End" matching his earlier slip of "Hollaway." Deepak also uses *"Holiday Inn"* in an entirely different way to suggest where Natalee's body ended up. His use of *"Holiday Inn"* will be a key image, a key clue indicating the location of Natalee's body.

- By setting off *"Holiday Inn"* with parenthesis and linking it with gambling, Deepak points to the huge risk the boys took in disposing of the body there, whatever else he means by *"Holiday Inn."*

- As the story starts Sunday night at the Holiday Inn, he subtly leaves a major clue—repeating it three times—*"where"* the body can be discovered.

## Voyeurism and Gambling

Certainly gambling suggests voyeurism—an intense activity often watched by others. Voyeuristic images surfaced quickly in police interviews with all three suspects. Deepak first admitted *seeing* Joran's hands under Natalee's skirt while they were riding in the backseat of his car, then changed it to a classic denial in another interview, "I had not *seen* that Joran's hands were under the girl's skirt."

In turn, Satish initially admitted to seeing Joran finger Natalee in the backseat, then abruptly changed his story in a later police interview, again with classic denial. On another occasion Satish spontaneously volunteered, "At no moment had I *seen* the pants (underwear) of the girl. I only *saw* them French kissing." Such a spontaneous denial suggests precisely what Satish had seen, which certainly fits with his earlier report of watching Joran's finger penetrate Natalee.

In his email, Deepak draws attention to both his and his brother's voyeurism of Joran's sexual activity with Natalee. Under these circumstances the word "poker," repeatedly emphasized in Deepak's email, becomes an even more striking sexual innuendo.

And one last thing regarding voyeurism, in a police interview Deepak described how enamored he was *watching* Natalee's dancing in Carlos'n Charlie's on that fateful last night. He observed that Natalee danced "beautifully" and did not appear unsteady on her feet when she stepped off the stage—although earlier he had described her as greatly impaired.

## Police Interviews: 'Crazy' Behavior

To a man, all the suspects reveal themselves between the lines of their police interviews.

We start with Deepak's major thoughtprint, "crazy," and search the police interviews for similar references. (Several reliable sources including Dave Holloway told me personally that the police interviews now posted on the Internet are indeed accurate.) Exactly as in Deepak's email, the suspects quickly link "crazy" behavior to sex.

After Deepak and Joran concocted a second cover-up story in which Joran claims to have left Natalee alone on the beach, Deepak chastises Joran for doing so. "I even told him he was *sick* for doing that to the girl," Deepak told his interrogators. Barely into the subject, Deepak instantly labels his cohort "sick"—disturbed.

His brother, Satish, takes it far beyond that. Describing Joran's behavior in the backseat of Deepak's car with Natalee, he calls Joran "crazy" for indulging in a French kiss with a girl he had just met that day. He went on to say that, although it didn't bother him, Deepak thought it was "abnormal"—this from someone with Deepak's wild sexual history, someone who had DVD players in his car so he could show pornographic videos. Obviously Satish's "French kiss" story is phony, but what *does* fit with "crazy" and "abnormal" is an orgy—a group rape—which they forced upon Natalee, a girl they barely knew. Even the subtle reference to French kissing suggests both intercourse and oral sex—a body part of one person, a tongue, which extends and enters an orifice of the other. Remember, the L-2 mind specializes in specific symbolic communication reflecting details upon details—one image after another.

But we don't want to leave Deepak in the background. Taken in by his outwardly gentle demeanor, too many people who study this case have made that mistake. We will soon hear Deepak identify their actions as "perverted," clearly referring to the three guys' sexual behavior toward Natalee in the backseat of his Honda.

## Joran's Own Character Witness: His Book

As everyone knows, a good trial lawyer calls character witnesses to portray his client as a law-abiding, solid citizen. When suspects in major crimes write books, in effect they become their own character witnesses, making every effort to underscore their good names. Without question that was Joran van der Sloot's conscious intention in his book *The Natalee Holloway Case*. Stating a desire to set the record straight, Joran attempts to trade on his so-called newly learned honesty and maintain his innocence of any wrongdoing with Natalee Holloway. Without question, Joran has succeeded beyond his wildest dreams in letting us in on his character—warts and all. What unfolds, however, is the basic admission that he is simply one giant wart with only the slightest smattering of conscience left in his L-1 conscious mind.

From beginning to end, he tells one story after another of his continued deceitfulness, self-indulgence, and corruption—precisely as his incredibly honest deeper mind intended. Unconsciously, that was his purpose. As always we will read his narratives between the lines to determine the real story.

First he reveals his absolute obsession with being a "player," even adopting a motto of sorts: "Joran can get any girl." And indeed he brings to this game the same competitive spirit that he does to athletics and academics, in which he generally excels. As a player he is dominant. Joran tells us that to be a successful player you have to be really good. Players often have two or three cell phones, both to compete and to keep their women from discovering one another.

Frequently he is also sleeping with his "girlfriend" and multiple others behind her back. On one occasion his "on the side" girl tells his regular girlfriend about this, who then confronts him. He promptly denies the infidelity. Without blinking an eye, he immediately takes his regular girlfriend over to the bearer-of-bad-news girl, angrily asking her, "How dare you lie to my girlfriend?" Quickly the regular girlfriend sees right through him and breaks up with him—with Joran observing how she could always spot his lies. He then repeats the same pattern with two other girls, informing us in the process that he has learned nothing from his lying.

Joran writes about how much he loves gambling and how he derives a particular thrill from winning big pots, by bluffing at poker when he has no hand at all. He's clearly addicted to deceiving others. Deceit gives Joran a power rush. Joran brags about how he breaks his parents' rules at every turn, often in underhanded ways, such as stealing money from them or coming home at curfew only to sneak out minutes later with his friends. Eventually, his pattern of lying and stealing prompts his parents to take him to a psychiatrist, and Joran simply shifts his con to the doctor. After five sessions, not surprisingly, the psychiatrist tells his parents she thinks he's back on the right track. Five sessions, mind you! Joran then announces in his book—surprise, surprise—that he doesn't like psychiatrists.

We could go on and on but it's sufficient to note that Joran, ever the liar, has established beyond any reasonable doubt the exact nature of his character. Indeed he has proven himself a sterling character witness by attesting to his own lack of sterling character. Ironically, Joran has supporters who read his book and admire his honesty and candor. Many gullible observers have been taken in by Joran's superficial charm. Typical of players, Joran proudly utilizes that guile and charm to get what he wants. Like any good con man, he's an expert at the games he plays.

In this case, his first game was "Dominate Natalee." Now his game has shifted to "Bluff the Police." But it's still a game, and although his deeper intelligence sees through it, his cunning leads us to a serious question. Why should anyone believe Joran, who from the word go has established so thoroughly and convincingly that he is a natural liar? Now, with much higher stakes on the table, with his neck on the line and the death of a girl staring him in the face, how could we ever expect the truth from him?

When it comes to hidden confessions of bad character, brief stories are often worth many thousands of words. In his book Joran practically brags about being kicked out of his school's honor society—read "honest society." This brash admission is yet another revealing story from his L-2 mind. But most pertinent to this case, his book shines a clear light on his lying when it comes to girls and sex.

In his police interviews in June 2005, Joran portrayed Deepak as almost asexual, never involved with a girl, implying that Deepak would never assault a female. But in his book Joran describes Deepak stalking a girl from Cyberzone, the Internet café where he's employed. The girl had been having cybersex with her boyfriend online. Not only did Deepak secretly save her emails and read them later, he told Joran of stalking her and wanting to "f—k her." Clearly, according to Joran, Deepak admitted his potential for forcing himself upon a girl. In other words, while attempting to be Deepak's character witness Joran instead lets the cat out of the bag.

## Threesomes

But Joran, plenty bright but not very smart, has more cats to let out of the bag in his book. He tells us about one of his favorite activities as a player, renting a hotel room with his buddies for a few days of partying, including girls galore and absolutely no boundaries. On one such occasion he describes three guys, including Deepak, having sex with three different girls simultaneously in the same hotel room. Ostensibly reflecting his high moral standards, Joran declares that there were no threesomes. But we will also see later that, in a police interview he alluded to another story of a threesome with three guys and one girl in an automobile's backseat, actually introducing the idea in two separate stories.

Not to be outdone, in his police interviews Deepak also confirmed that on several occasions he had participated in orgies in hotel rooms with tourist girls. We now think back to Deepak's bragging about Natalee putting her hands down his pants on his genitals, an incident which he also sets in the backseat of his car. The story itself suggests a threesome, since Deepak now has Natalee touching or being touched sexually by more than one person. So much for Deepak's supposed sexual reticence.

## Chances of Sexual Assault

Given what we've learned so far from Deepak's email—and about the three guys' sexual appetites and Joran's insatiable desire to be a player—ask yourself what the odds are that Natalee was sexually assaulted by these three. Here we have a ringleader like Joran, who specializes in power "poker" and is also an admitted, pathological liar, leading two other desperately wannabe players into sexual battle. Natalee's disappearance was almost certainly triggered by a sexual assault. Given the circumstances of her fantasy island vacation, and the suspicious backgrounds of these three suspects, we can understand a sex act gone awry as a logical explanation. But if this is the case we can expect Deepak to tell us this even more forthrightly in his email, and we would expect confirmation in police interviews with all three suspects.

## Scene 2: Blackjack

## Things Get Physical: A New Game—'Blackjack'

> "after he won the poker at the fourth place he decided to get up and play some **blackjack** so he went to the **blackjack table** and there was natalee (they were a lil drunk ) so my friend started playing **blackjack**
>
> [and he was winning quite good , so then natalee approached him and introduced herself and said to him" **your a lucky guy** , can you help me win some of **my** money **back** i lost $ 360 , of my fathers money" so my friend said ok , why not . so he started playing]"

First, Deepak has opened his story with a powerful sexual innuendo depicting a rape and continuing it through "he [Joran] won the **poker** at the fourth place." But then the game changes. Joran decides to get up and play some blackjack, and there at the blackjack table was Natalee. Deepak adds in parenthesis, ("they were a lil drunk"). On the surface Deepak's scene involves just Joran and Natalee, with Deepak and his brother, Satish, still in the background. But here he provides another important message indicating that all three suspects were involved in the assault. As we will see, the clues are ripe for the picking.

In my cover story, the first thing Joran does after meeting a tipsy Natalee is to start playing a special game of poker—blackjack—and winning, again, like he always does. Playing and winning, with Natalee.

Beth, when I write *"so he went to the blackjack table and there was natalee (they were a lil drunk )"* you need to picture your daughter, Natalee, drunk at the blackjack table. Can you see my sexual innuendos getting stronger and stronger? I'm hinting at Natalee laying down now, on display, getting played and laid in the backseat of a car just as blackjack cards are laid on the table—a flat, felt surface.

Too coincidental, maybe? Ah, but such suggestive imagery when Joran has just met Natalee for the first time tells you this was our plan all along. And the sexual images will continue! So, when I write *"he decided to get up"* you know I'm really saying that Joran 'got it up'—an erection. He was gonna go first, just like we planned. The fun was just beginning. Later I tell you about all three of us having erections. One after another, inside my Honda, just like we planned it.

## Blackjack—Understanding the game

Deepak's L-2 sees the word *"blackjack"* complete with all its connotations. He further explains:

Here things get even more brutal, Beth, so prepare yourself. Early in our escapade the game suddenly changed for Natalee—from poker to blackjack. We were all players now. Blackjack is one mean word, Beth. 'Jack' is a slang term for 'penis,' so what's a 'black-jack'? Maybe some kind of 'evil penis'? A blackjack itself, a bludgeon, is shaped sort of like a penis.

What am I telling you? When someone uses a blackjack as a bludgeon, they sneak up on someone from behind. It's truly a violent 'betrayal.' Now look closely at what I wrote: *" . . . he decided to get up and play some **blackjack** so he went to the **blackjack** table and there was natalee (they were a lil drunk ) so my friend started playing **blackjack** and he was winning quite good . . . "*

Read it again. Joran 'gets up' from one poker game, changes positions, and is suddenly playing a very different, darker kind of poker game. In my story he meets Natalee for the first time when both are kind of impaired. So Joran becomes a player again, starting all over, a winning player no less—totally succeeding at another game and thoroughly enjoying himself.

## Three-way sexual assault

But pay attention to the important word *"blackjack."* I used it three times in rapid succession, SHOUTING at you that there were three of us who each became 'a black jack,' sneaking up behind her, gang raping her. You can see how well *"blackjack"* fits what we did to Natalee, and especially what my brother and I did.

As natives of Surinam, Satish and I are considered blacks. *"Blackjack"* also suggests sexual assaults by us, each with our own 'black jack.' The complete picture is that three of us, which includes two blacks—my brother and I—assaulted Natalee while she was lying on a flat, table-like surface, the backseat of my car. Remember, this happened 'as The Deepak News reported.' And now, the same news reveals that Joran never left the room where he was originally gambling, hinting that, for the most part, we never took Natalee out of the car. And we were all *"winning quite good"*—enjoying ourselves for sure. I write that *"my friend started playing"* telling you that Joran took Natalee first, followed by the two of us—the 'Kal-poke' brothers.

Deepak immediately harkens back to his story about black "ants" sneaking up on girls in his car and biting them—which fits perfectly with his idea here of "blackjacking" Natalee.

## A Chokehold and a Head Injury

Deepak's hidden confession reveals more details about the violent game the three boys were playing:

*"Blackjack"* suggests controlling someone from behind. We took turns manipulating a belt placed around Natalee's neck, but mainly Joran controlled her after he finished. The sound of the word 'poker' also suggests 'choker,' winning 'poker-choker' over Natalee by overpowering and controlling her. After he had his orgasm on top of Natalee, Joran got up and changed positions to play blackjack with Natalee— he got up and controlled her head and neck from behind. It was now a new game—blackjack. It was a group rape.

One more thing. Using a blackjack on somebody points to a head injury like what Natalee suffered while we were playing our sexual games. Keep in mind how well blackjack fits with poker—'taking a poker to someone.' Using a metal fireplace poker in an assault is not so uncommon in domestic disputes, sometimes resulting in a head injury. Beth, can you see that I'm telling you the exact sequence of what really happened?

As a profiler, I had seen striking revelations such as this in other hidden-story confessions in which a perpetrator's inordinate guilt caused him or her to lay out the crime's precise sequence of events. Again, Deepak's "sequence messaging" was eerily similar to that scene in the Ramsey ransom note in which the writer carefully described the chaotic chronology of events that had occurred so rapidly, resulting in JonBenét's death—a sexual assault gone bad, a sudden severe head injury leading to her unconsciousness and then a strangulation to hasten death—which resulted in a body needing burial.

## Police Interviews—Joran, the Rodeo Cowboy

Coincidentally, Joran told police he first met Natalee on Sunday, May 29, at the Holiday Inn's Excelsior Casino where he was playing "Texas Hold'em." Such suggestive details—volunteered completely spontaneously and naturally—are hallmarks of the confessing unconscious mind, a virtuoso with images. Joran could have easily offered any number of innocuous details, such as he was gambling or playing in a poker tournament, but he linked his initial encounter with Natalee to the rich image of "Texas Hold'em," suggesting a rodeo cowboy roping a young calf and wrestling it to the ground. In so doing he casually and unconsciously suggested using some type of rope or belt to control Natalee during the assault. In his email, Deepak indicates this very thing several times, and he specifically points to Joran as the bagman, the cowboy, the rope man.

For his part, Satish volunteered in police interviews that "Joran never had sex or got rough (savage) with Natalee" in the backseat on their ride alone with her. He invites us to read through both denials and understand that not only did Joran have sex with Natalee but he (and they) had to get rough with her in order for it to take place. This is not the last time we will see references to Natalee being choked.

## More Sexual Images—Joran a *'lucky guy'*

*"so then natalee approached him and introduced herself and said to him"*
*your a lucky guy , can you help me win some of my money back i lost $*
*360 , of my fathers money" so my friend said ok , why not . so he start-*
*ed playing and he won 100 $ for* **her back** *and he said hey thats the*
*best i can do".*

Deepak continues:

I've got plenty more to tell you about the sexual story. I can't leave
any doubt about what happened. That means one thing: more innuendos. So, when I quote Natalee saying to Joran *"your a lucky guy"*
it's pretty clear that he was about to get lucky—a familiar double
entendre referring to a guy 'getting lucky tonight' with a girl. See how
I write *"your a"*—that refers to Joran which is pronounced 'your-ahn.'
I'm speaking for Natalee as she meets Joran for the very first time,
calling him 'Joran lucky guy' and so naming him Joran Lucky Guy. In
my story his name is linked to Natalee from the very beginning, and
his name represents all our names, 'Deepak Lucky Guy' and 'Satish
Lucky Guy.' We all got lucky that night, at least for a while . . .

Now read " . . . *so then natalee approached him . . . and said to him*
*'Joran Lucky Guy . . . "* and you can see how much more personal
that makes my story. Look at the sequence now: *"Joran Lucky Guy*
*can you . . . Joran Lucky Guy can you win?"* It was all just a game to
us. And notice, also, that Joran/your-ahn also suggests 'Joran, you're
on.' Joran Lucky Guy was going to win with Natalee; he was going to
'score on her' as the ballplayers say—not for her but against her will.

I have to point out the obvious—if you switch one letter 'luck'
becomes 'f—.' That makes Joran a 'f—ky lucky guy.' Why didn't I
have Natalee say, 'This is your lucky day'? Because that wouldn't
quite say it right. Joran was one *"lucky guy"* who made his own luck
without any help from Natalee. I'm drawing attention again to his
being a male—to our being males.

Certainly the facts contradict Deepak's surface story. Natalee,
according to her classmates had no meaningful conversation with Joran
in the casino. In fact, Joran *did* play blackjack for one of the girls from
Mountain Brook, but never for Natalee, who was not wagering.

## Another Innuendo: 'On my back'

*"so then natalee approached him and introduced herself and said to him"* *your a lucky guy , can you help me win some of* **my** *money* **back** *<u>i lost</u>* *<u>$ 360 , of my fathers money</u>" so my friend said ok , why not . so he started playing and he won 100 $ for* **her back** *and he said hey thats the best i can do"*

Deepak continues his hidden confession:

So let me keep speaking for Natalee. You're never gonna hear her actual voice again, so you might as well hear her through me. Right after Natalee says Joran raped her—this guy who got lucky at *"black-jack"*— she asks him, *"can you help me win . . . my (money) back i lost $ 360 , of my fathers money."*

First get the big idea. Natalee has lost something valuable at poker, something she wants back, something connected to Joran's winning at poker. You can begin to see that I'm preoccupied with Natalee's back. When I write *"my (money) back I lost"* Natalee's really saying 'I lost my back' or 'I lost something while I was on my back'—something valuable of her father's. Remember, I've just pictured Natalee lying on her back, exposed on a table. What'd she lose while she was on her back, something which her father values so highly? Her personhood, her freedom, her right to choose for herself with whom she wanted to be involved. Without a doubt we robbed her of all her basic rights.

## Natalee's Virginity and Police Interviews

Deepak's idea that Natalee lost her father's valuables also suggests the loss of her virginity, as fathers value their daughter's chastity. There are other reasons to consider that Natalee lost her virginity as well as her life. Joran said that Natalee told him she was a virgin, and after he reported genital contact with her he stated in police interviews, "I don't think she was a virgin," which suggests that she probably was. In a police interview, one of her good friends also stated that Natalee was a virgin. I am aware from reliable sources (not including Beth Twitty) that two of Natalee's friends had discussed her virginity with her prior to her trip.

If Natalee was, indeed, a virgin, we would expect to find hints of that between the lines of police interviews, and impressively we do. First

Joran made a strange comment in describing sexual intercourse with a girl named Karen. First he  described a sexual encounter with Karen on the beach, but then he noted—out of the blue—that after having sex with her the second time on another occasion, "I do not know if she bled or not." This was most likely a disguised reference to Natalee, since it was so completely out of context with Karen obviously no virgin.

But in his own police interviews Deepak presented the most striking story in regard to Natalee's possible virginity. After police asked him about cleaning his car, specifically after Natalee had been in it, Deepak spontaneously described two incidents. First he told them of someone spilling a Cherry Coke on the seat of the passenger side where the hand-brake was located, with Satish also in the car.  The second time another car bumped him from behind while he was holding a whiskey Coke, and it fell between his legs, and also on the passenger seat along with the carpet on the passenger side.

Deepak strongly suggests sexual imagery—*someone else* spilled a "cherry coke" on the seat where a passenger was suggesting Joran (who went first as we will see) broke Natalee's hymen during the rape, which stained the backseat with Satish and Deepak looking on with no brake/self control being used. Then Deepak spilled something sticky between his legs and onto the "passenger" seat and carpet after someone jolted him from behind, strongly suggesting coitus interruptus with Natalee while Deepak was assaulting her, a likely event as we shall see.

Thus Deepak in two brief stories suggests two main events during the rape, additionally suggesting that his car was stained from Natalee's virgin blood and his own ejaculation—two very good reasons to clean his car so thoroughly. (Even though he was wearing a condom as will become clear later, a totally shocked Deepak easily could have stained his car with semen.) Deepak will also tell one other story, further suggesting that Natalee was a virgin, which we will review soon.

## Joran's Nickname

There's more to my story here. Now read my translation, and substitute my name for Joran:

" *So then Natalee  .  .  .   said to him Joran Lucky Guy can you win some of **my back** i lost $ 360 , of my fathers valuables" so my friend Joran Lucky Guy said ok , why not . So Joran Lucky Guy started playing and he won 100 $ for **her back** and he said hey thats the best  .  .  .*

Notice something else. *"So Joran Lucky Guy started playing and he won (100 $ for)* **her back** *and he said hey thats the best . . . "* I put that in quotes to emphasize it, because as Joran assaulted Natalee while she was on her back he told Satish and me, 'Hey guys, this is the best!'

But notice, *"he won* **100 $** *for her back."* What do you think that dollar sign is doing after the number? For one thing the '$' mark tells you 'we scored,' since '$' also suggests the G-clef in musical notation. But placing it after the number mainly tells you that, in playing such a juvenile game, we got the whole thing backwards. Our plan had backfired on us and—indeed—was backwards from the beginning.

With '1-0-0' I'm saying, Joran was the number 'one' who raped Natalee first, followed by two numbers who looked alike—Satish and me. Secretly I'm confessing we were just a couple of zeroes who longed for sexual power to make up for the fact that we had none. We saw ourselves as zeroes, as totally unimportant. Power was our most basic motive. Why do you think I keep highlighting that *"he won"*? We won! This is another reminder that this was all about dominance.

Power-hungry people looking for thrills want as many thrills as they can get, even if it means totally dominating a helpless female. We were crazy, sick for power, because otherwise we didn't have any power in our lives. People in Aruba, and even the tourists, look down on us Pakis. There's a two-class caste system here that nobody really discusses, but we all live it.

Now look back at Natalee speaking in *"my money back i lost $ 360,"* and how the number 360 implies 360 degrees. Now translate the message as 'It was a group assault; I lost all the way around.'

But there's another thing about 360 degrees—we lost all the way around too. When you travel that far, you're back where you started. Satish and I were still zeroes after all this was over, bigger zeroes even than before. We thought we were going somewhere and we weren't. Isn't that what you call 'crazy?'

The L-2 mind will often use a number code to communicate important messages (again eerily similar to elements of the Ramsey ransom note where the "kidnapper" demanded the unusual sum of $118,000). Here Deepak almost overpowers the reader with his increasingly vivid list of disturbing details. No matter how repulsive they are, however, we have to absorb these depressing details if we're ever going to understand Deepak's own verdict in this case. In the end Deepak will speak in the voice of the prosecuting attorney, making his closing argument and declaring what kind of punishment the three assailants deserve.

## Sodomy?

Taking one last look at "*can you win some of **my back** i lost $ 360*" it suggests both "can you win some of my back" and "some of my back I lost"—360 degrees. In short, Deepak points toward the possibility of sodomy in addition to vaginal rape, the idea of a 360-degree assault. Likewise "*and he won 100 $ for **her back**" suggests the identical possibility, particularly with the backwards "*100 $.*" Lastly, "blackjack" suggests "back jack" which conveys the same idea, possibly confirmed by the earlier idea "where so crazy," that it was a totally out-of-control sexual assault in every way. Whatever the case, Deepak has more than made it clear that it was one intense and brutal scenario.

## Deepak's Revealing Video Interview

In January, 2006, Deepak videotaped an interview with investigator Jamie Skeeters, a retired police commander from Oxnard, California who has since died. In the interview Deepak seemed to say that it was easy to get Natalee to go along with consensual group sex. Unfortunately, certain portions of the interview were not clearly audible. The tape's accuracy was questioned, and some viewers wondered whether it had been edited.

Later, Skeeters said that Deepak had told him about the "easy consensual sex" and denied editing the tape. While the original version of the tape has yet to be released, a reliable source told me that the unedited version supports Skeeters' claim. The tape was then played on Dr. Phil's television show, eventually resulting in a lawsuit by Deepak who was then denying such claims.

Despite his current denial of sexual contact with Natalee, Deepak went on in that same interview to strongly suggest that sexual activity had indeed occurred—as is so often the case when a guilty perpetrator evokes denial. Deepak could be clearly heard on the tape arrogantly berating Natalee for being "dressed like a slut" and insisting that only a slut would go off alone with three strange guys. At one point Deepak impulsively insisted, "Enough of this bulls—! She was a slut!"

In essence, Deepak betrays himself by confessing that indeed the three suspects treated her like a slut. Indirectly he also describes their plan to get Natalee to go off with *three strange guys* in a car"—making her think she was going off alone with Joran, who was not a stranger to her or her friends, with Deepak and Satish lurking in the background. With his thoughtprint and "strange guys" confession—*in the plural*—Deepak makes it plain that Natalee had not previously met the two brothers. Thus she wouldn't realize, until far too late, that a secret group attack was underway.

At the very moment he is lying, even taking it as far as suing Dr. Phil McGraw, Deepak reveals the truth. His verbal abuse of Natalee and his other thoughtprints suggest that a forcible sexual assault took place, not easy, casual sex. On the other hand, it was "easy sex"—that is, it was easy for three guys to overpower that petite girl.

## Interviews: F-Bombs and Calling Natalee Names

In various interviews the three suspects continually referred to Natalee in degrading ways. Certainly we recall Deepak's reference to Natalee as strictly a sexual object who had her hands on his privates. Deepak also reported that, on the day after the disappearance, as Joran and Deepak drove back to the van der Sloot compound to meet the Twittys, Joran exclaimed, "What the f—k is up with this bitch?"

*Vanity Fair* noted that, on that same night, Joran described Natalee to a confidant, Charles Croes: "She came onto me huge. Dancing suggestively. Like a slut." In a police interview Joran also claims that, after leaving Natalee alone at the beach, Deepak picked him up and immediately inquired, "Did you f—k her?"

After Joran changed his story to a second version, he reported that Satish picked him up and said, "F—k the bitch, somebody will find her tomorrow." Not to be outdone and ever the confessor, Joran told *Panorama* magazine that, after he left Natalee on the beach, he walked away in frustration saying, "F—k the bitch." Deepak also exemplifies this same hostile attitude toward girls in general, as we'll soon see when we take a close look at another scene from Carlos'n Charlie's.

Their consistently hostile attitude toward Natalee shows these three guys all caught up in their macho roles as "players" now spurred on by a feeding frenzy, with each inspiring the other. The scene was set for a testosterone-fueled sexual assault.

## Deceit: Natalee Alone with Three Guys

*he decided to get up and play some **blackjack** so he went to the **blackjack table** and there was natalee (they were a lil drunk ) so my friend started playing **blackjack***

As he continues to confess to Beth, Deepak appears anxious to explain his references to Natalee's drinking and the game of blackjack:

The obvious question is, how did we get Natalee to go off with us, alone with three guys? Remember, poker requires strategy. We had a definite strategy to get Natalee to go with us that night. You never show your hole cards when you're playing poker. There are the cards that are face up that everyone can see, and there are your hole cards, face down, and only you know what they are. Natalee would never know what hands we really held. She didn't know what kind of game Joran was playing until it was almost over. This was an important part of our strategy. Joran would deal to Natalee, betting that he could entice her into leaving—apparently alone—with him. But then the game suddenly changed: poker became blackjack.

There were two parts to our strategy. First, *"so he went to the blackjack table and there was natalee (they were a lil drunk )."* When I said that the very first time Joran met Natalee she bought him a drink there, it wasn't really true. What I'm actually doing is setting up what happened later in my story, when I describe Joran meeting her at Carlos'n Charlie's that night. The main thing to notice is how Natalee will progress from *"a lil drunk"* to *"VERY drunk."* At first *"lil drunk"* appears to be just an incidental fact, but notice how I emphasized it with parentheses, and for sure it will come into play in an even bigger way. The term *"lil drunk"* is a major hint that later in Carlos'n Charlie's, when Joran indeed buys Natalee a 'lil drink,' it was a drink with a 'little something in it.'

We knew that she'd be drinking at the nightclub and we wanted to give her a little booster. By spiking her drink we really blackjacked Natalee. We wanted to get Natalee a 'lil more drunk'—slip her some drugs to lower her inhibitions and mess up her judgment. Natalee got in way over her head, just as we planned it. We had this strategy down to a science; we thought. It was a game we knew how to play. We sure did.

Also, understand that drugs are everywhere in Aruba, cheap and easy to get. And we knew what we were doing. We knew what all those kids on senior trips and spring break were thinking. They wanted to cut loose. They were away from home and free to do whatever they pleased. Hey, Natalee was 'partying hearty,' and now she was alone with a smooth operator right after we slipped her some stuff that made her feel free and frisky.

In his videotaped interview with Jamie Skeeters, the investigator who was on Dr. Phil's television show in January 2006, Deepak said clearly that he had heard of Ecstasy being slipped into girls' drinks.

## Cab Ride Ruse

With blackjack's suggestion of deceit, I'm cluing you into another part of our strategy—to make Natalee think she was alone with Joran while the two of us hung in the background. Now how were we going to do that? She thought Satish and I were cabdrivers.

So, I played the part of the cabdriver and Satish sat in the front passenger seat. I swear, it was easy as pie for Joran. He just pretended that he'd ridden in our cab before and we could be completely trusted, reassuring Natalee who, by then, was already kind of messed up on drugs. Beth, I know you'd want to know Natalee didn't go willingly. Think back to how I described my first encounter with her:

*"The missing girl natalee hollaway,I spoke to her , sunday she left with me, my brother and a friend from carlos n' charlies , it was my car like* **the news** *said she got in to"*

What comes first and what happens after that? First, *"I spoke to her,"* then she left Carlos'n Charlie's 'like the news said in my car' with the three of us—the car *"she got into,"* just like you get into cabs. See the crucial news? We made her think my Honda was a taxicab. First you speak to the driver, you get into his car, and you leave.

The cabs in Aruba are normal, everyday cars, including lots of Hondas, and they're not at all distinguishable. Students on the trip with Natalee described the confusing and chaotic scene they encountered upon leaving Carlos'n Charlie's on that last night. Everyone—maybe 60 people in all—was searching for a taxi. Several had to walk a couple of blocks to where the cabs congregated. Clearly it would have been easy for the three suspects to take advantage of such circumstances, and for Joran to guide Natalee to a "cabdriver he knew."

Also, during their five-day stay in Aruba, Natalee's classmates later revealed that the 17-year-old Joran had been hanging around the hotel posing as a 19-year-old college student from Holland. Some students reported he claimed to be staying alone at the hotel. Never once was he seen with anyone else, including Deepak or Satish. In fact, Joran was already on the prowl, practicing his marksmanship, playing his game and setting up some poor girl to go off alone with him—or so she would think. He was also gaining Natalee's trust and lowering her suspicions. How could she imagine that anyone at the hotel who had clearly identified himself would be so brazen as to really bother her?

According to *Vanity Fair*, however, a hotel employee knew all about Joran. The employee's exact words to Beth Twitty—when she first arrived in Aruba to search for the missing Natalee—were, "He tends to prey upon young female tourists." Later, Joran would reveal in his book that he knew how to play the tourist game and would often wait until a girl's last night, when she would be at her most vulnerable, wanting to have one final fling before returning to the real world.

The facts are that around closing time, Natalee left Carlos'n Charlie's alone with Joran. No classmate of Natalee's known to me reported seeing Deepak or Satish in Carlos'n Charlie's. Natalee was overtly unimpaired, walking steadily toward the cabs which congregated close by. One eyewitness, a classmate of Natalee's, told me he walked out of the nightspot directly in front of Natalee and Joran, who was otherwise by himself. Joran was holding a souvenir cup from Carlos'n Charlie's and Natalee's classmate asked Joran for the cup if he was going to throw it away. Joran willingly handed it over.

In police interviews Joran described the identical scenario, with no mention of Satish, who was clearly in the background. A few minutes later another classmate passed Natalee and Joran, apparently walking by themselves toward the cabstand a few blocks away. All along, Beth Twitty has maintained that her daughter had been the victim of a cab-ride ruse. Deepak's thoughtprints resonate in living color, suggesting the same thing. It's likely that Joran, walking alone with Natalee, met up with Satish who guided him to a "cab."

Several of Natalee's classmates (and my own daughter), who once took a similar senior trip, have insisted to me that under no conditions would Natalee, no matter how impaired, have knowingly entered a car with three strangers. She had to have been duped. And, not only did the three guys likely fool her into thinking the Honda was a taxicab, they backed up that ruse with some chemical insurance: getting her *"a lil"* impaired by having her drink spiked at Carlos'n Charlie's. She wasn't drunk but she wasn't fully alert, either. Her guard was down, just as the three predators had planned.

Ironically, Deepak posted his email at age 21. Another name for the card game of blackjack is "21." Just as the crime involved three assailants, one white and two dark, the rules of blackjack call for each player to initially be dealt three cards, one exposed and two "in the hole." Ironically, it's as if Deepak is saying that, in their game of blackjack, they dealt Natalee three cards, one light-skinned and two dark-skinned, one standing right in front of her at Carlos'n Charlie's and two she couldn't see waiting outside in the dark. One guy first, two later.

Deepak also hinted at a cab-ride scenario in his police interviews when he said that he and Joran communicated in Papiamento, the local language, when they were leaving the nightclub with Natalee. That would have made it even more believable with Deepak, the supposed cabdriver at first apparently not fluent in English, allowing Joran to appear as the sophisticated, older Dutch student giving the cabbie instructions and directions. Joran and Deepak would then be able to discuss their true intentions without Natalee understanding a word they said. It would also allow Joran to turn and ask Natalee what she'd like to do. We can hear Joran telling Deepak, "Driver, why don't you drive around and let's listen to some music" as they casually drove to their pre-planned sex site.

In Joran's book, *The Natalee Holloway Case*, we find yet another clue about Deepak's car. Joran described Deepak's Honda as a "pimped up" car with a body kit, big rims, and two TV screens—one of the coolest cars on the island. Joran and his friends often had Deepak drive them to nightclubs. With these references, Joran clearly connects Deepak's car to pimping or picking up girls. Using Deepak as a driver strongly suggests they masqueraded as cabbie and customer in order to kidnap Natalee. More important, Joran's obsessive preoccupation with sex and pimping strongly supports my contention that Joran's book, like Deepak's email, is unconsciously intended as a confession.

We also find two overt references to cabs in relation to Natalee in Joran's book. First he tells of Deepak's driving them to his house. He intends to have sex with her there, and then to put her in a cab to her hotel. But Natalee refuses and instead wants to go to the beach. Later, when supposedly at the beach Joran becomes frustrated when Natalee doesn't want to go back to her hotel after he's ready to return home. He tries luring her back to the Holiday Inn by telling her he needs to order a cab there, but she will not budge. She supposedly refuses to go to the hotel.

## She 'lost' at Blackjack

*"i lost . . . "*

Deepak now moves to one last important matter in this scene:

Beth, here's one more image of the final play in our devastating game of blackjack, and again I'm speaking for Natalee: *"I lost."* She lost something far more valuable than her freedom—she lost her life. And speaking for her, she wants it back: *"can you help me win some of my money [valuables] back i lost."* Of course this is impossible, but what am I telling you?

I'm saying that, even from her grave, Natalee can have a victory of her own. That justice—a measure of having Natalee back—is possible. And you know there's only ONE way that would come about: if her body were discovered. That's the only evidence that will convict us. Then and only then will she have come full-circle, 360 degrees.

Consider Natalee's question again, the way I framed it: 'Can you help me recover my losses?' and you can hear her real question: 'Can you help me recover the body?' So don't miss my answer to her request for help, *"hey thats the best i can do."* I'm doing everything I can to direct you to the body. Like I've told you, my deeper intelligence is doing its absolute best to help you. And in a minute you will hear me promise you the same thing again. I can't say it enough. You're getting my best shot at helping you.

In the end, if you want to understand what happened to Natalee, Beth, you can sum up this entire story as poker and blackjack. And now that we're being pursued, now that we're the hunted, the game continues in an altogether different 'casino.' We're still playing mental poker. The question is whether we can bluff everyone else into folding.

## Police Interviews: Altercation with 'Tourist Natalee'

Again we examine police interviews for gambling references and stories in which the suspects make unconscious admissions about what happened with Natalee.

To this day, Deepak emphasizes poker—both in his email and interviews—as one of his grand metaphors for the entire scenario involving Natalee. He told one story to the police, which fits with his email confession in which he repeatedly revealed the three-way assault. Deepak described to interrogators a scene in a casino when he and another friend were watching Joran at the poker table: "At some point there was a verbal altercation between Joran and a tourist. The tourist was of the opinion we were helping Joran." The familiar idea of deceitful friends cheating to help Joran win a hand of poker identically mirrors what took place with Natalee. The three guys shared information, showed each other their cards—both activities against the rules of poker—and then they bluffed the little tourist girl out of her clothes and out of her life.

## Gambling and Losing

Certainly the three boys gambled that they could get away with the assault on Natalee, and at first they were raking in the chips. But then, their fortunes took a devastating turn and they lost almost all their winnings when they ended up taking Natalee's life. Then the stakes got higher and higher, and they were forced to stay in a far more serious game than they had ever intended to play.

Would they get away with the disposal of her body? It became the ultimate high-risk game of blackjack in which they didn't just sneak up on her and knock her out, but they killed her. Then they blackjacked her body and hid it. This leads us to the primary questions being asked by everyone who has examined this case: Will the boys suffer the ultimate loss they deserve, the loss of their freedom? Will the body ever be found?

## Summary of New Information in Scene

- Deepak continues with his striking double entendres as *"poker"* now becomes *"blackjack,"* suggesting a sudden sneak attack/rape on Natalee by the three guys with "jacks"—three boys who got *"lucky"* and won easily.

- He links this with further sexual images, suggesting Natalee *lying in a certain place* on a flat surface—such as the backseat of a car—and being "blackjacked"; that is, repeatedly raped.

- Deepak provides images of Joran changing positions with *"black-jack,"* now suggesting that he suddenly began controlling her neck from behind with some sort of choker collar.

- Deepak suggests Natalee's drink was spiked—a key part of their strategy to get her alone.

- Deepak underscores that Natalee was a *"lil drunk,"* a crucial idea that will later prove extremely important. He links her being assaulted while on her back shortly after she had been drinking.

- Deepak suggests that another key part of their strategy was a cab-ride ruse, a pretense carried out after making her think she was alone with Joran.

- He leaves no doubt that this eventually resulted in Natalee's death, even speaking for her in the first person, *"I lost."*

# 7
# The Moment of Death

## Coitus Interruptus: Moment of Death Suggested

> *"can you help me win some of my money back i lost $ 360 , of my fathers money"] so my friend said ok , **why not** . so he started playing and he won 100 $ for her back and he said hey thats the best i can do for you because i doubt it I can win more money for you so its better i quit so she said ok but at least let me buy you a drink so they went to the bar ( in the casino ). so they took a drink and started talking"*

Again, the action abruptly changes. First, Deepak describes a shift from one sexual assault, "poker," to a more ominous sexual assault, "blackjack." The guys are gambling that they can win and get away with it. Now he describes a third shift in the action—the card game suddenly ceases and the players stop playing.

At this point, since he has just provided details of the assault, we would now expect Deepak to deliver details about Natalee's death. We can also predict that he will not only continue to verify her death but will provide a more specific explanation as to why Natalee died so suddenly during their sexual assault.

> *"i doubt it I can win more money for you [so its better i quit so she said]"*

Beth, notice how in my story both Joran and Natalee quit gambling simultaneously. I'm telling you that at some point our game of blackjack—the sexual assault—abruptly ended. Both you and the authorities want to know why. I immediately answered your natural question, *"because i doubt it i can win more money for you [read: from you]"* and that's because, speaking for Natalee, *"i quit so she said."* We couldn't win any more valuables from Natalee because she had nothing left to give—she was no longer sexually available. We quit when she quit—when she died. Check out how well I've linked my messages—the gambling's over because there are no more valuables left to win because somebody quit.

117

See *"i quit"* speaks both for us and for her, but especially for her as I made plain in *"i quit so she said."* You have to find the second story in my sentences and read them a slightly different way, providing your own pauses and punctuation. Also, notice how well Natalee saying *"i quit"* matches her saying *"I lost."* I'm telling you in two different ways that Natalee died. And I'm pointing to the exact moment of her death as occurring in mid-sexual assault. Of course, now you want to know which one of us was having our way with her at the time—who was the specific sexual predator?

## Deepak Points to Himself

*"[so he started playing and he won 100 $ for her back and he said hey thats the best i can do for you] because i doubt it I can win more money for you so its better i quit"*

In the email, Deepak points toward Joran, but in the deeper story "Joran" simply represents "sexual assailant" so it could be any one of the three. Earlier, Deepak suggested that he himself was having intercourse with Natalee when she expired. There is no question that Deepak wants to tell us exactly which of the three it was. All we have to do is connect the thoughtprints.

Let's listen to how Deepak might explain it to the dead girl's mother:

Beth, I'll never forget that unbelievably shocking moment when Natalee quit responding. At that second, like I said in the same sentence, *"100 $ **for her back**,"* I was willing to give any amount of money to have her back, but we were totally helpless because, *"for her back . . . the best **i** can do for you– because **i** doubt it **I** can win more money for you."* We couldn't do enough for her—we couldn't bring her back.

Also, please look at that sentence again, where *"I"* is capitalized for only the second time in the email. By underscoring **the word "I" and using it quickly three times,** exactly when both Natalee and her sexual assailant quit, I'm strongly pointing to myself—'I, I, I.' Imagine you are at the peak of your sadistic, power-driven sexual excitement and your victim suddenly expires. Think you get over that easy? Not on your life. It was the most bizarre moment in my life—really the 'craziest moment,' having an orgasm while my 'partner' dies.

Deepak is describing the single most shocking event in his life. We can be sure he will tell us more. It would be impossible not to elaborate on such a moment.

## How Natalee Died—'Drink' and Death

["*so my friend said ok , why not . so he started playing and he won 100 $ for her back and he said hey thats the best i can do for you because i doubt it i can win more money for you so its better i quit]*

**so** *she said* <u>ok but</u> *at least let me buy you a* **drink** *so they went to the* **bar** *(in the* **casino***). so they took a* **drink** *and started talking"*

You want to know exactly how she died and what we did with her body? Notice how I take you there, right to the scene. I'll be brief.

Start with my short but important sentence within the long and winding unpunctuated sentence: *" . . . so its better i quit so she said ok but..."* I'm still speaking for Natalee, who has just told you she has died—she has quit. Quit what? You can finish that sentence. What do you quit when you die? You quit breathing. I'm drawing your attention to her mouth, and I'll keep doing it.

Now notice that she also adds, "[*so she said]* **ok but.***"* She's telling us that she wants to say one more thing from her grave right now, 'Yes, I just died—OK, but I have something to add to the picture.' Since this is the exact moment of death you can bet that what comes next will be extremely important.

## Natalee Picked Up Tab

So, what's the very first thing she tells you? *" . . . but at least let me buy you a drink . . . "* Of course I set it up first on the surface to look like a grateful Natalee was buying Joran a drink following his winning performance on the blackjack table, and at an intense game of poker. But the idea of 'treating Joran' tells you the real story. Once again I'm confessing that we all took a drink of Natalee later in my car, and confirmed it with the phrase *"**they** took a drink."* It was a group assault. In one way I'm using the word *"drink"* as code for 'Natalee'—a sexual vessel. Later, I'll describe how all three of us met Natalee at Carlos'n Charlie's, and connect her to a 'bar' and a 'drink,' suggesting again that she 'ended up buying us all drinks.' Of course the real truth is that Satish and I stayed in the background like good cabdrivers and never officially met Natalee until after leaving Carlos'n Charlie's.

## Police Interviews: Joran's Treat—'Caribbean Mother F—ker'

While the conscious mind carefully measures its words, checks itself, and often remains mum, the unconscious mind chatters on almost uncontrollably. In a police interview, Deepak provides us with another detail which he could have easily skipped but which his unconscious insisted on sharing. Immediately upon arriving at Carlos'n Charlie's on the night they met Natalee, Joran bought a house drink special known as a "Caribbean Mother F—ker." Later Satish reported Joran also bought them all a round of that particular drink.

It's not hard to read this thinly disguised story—Joran treated Deepak and Satish to that drink. As Deepak crudely confesses, they were three mean dudes, Caribbean Mother F—kers who did, in fact, "f—k her." But little did the three party boys know that, in the end, the Caribbean MF would prove to be a drink they couldn't begin to handle. Never lacking in creativity, Deepak's L-2 mind takes his own cocksure coarseness and rubs his nose in it, basically cursing himself. Throughout his email Deepak calls himself any number of vicious names but none more demeaning than Caribbean Mother F—ker. Nor as revealing.

## Natalee Resisted

*"she said **ok but** at **least** let me buy you a **drink**"*

Again, Beth, I want you to know that under no circumstances was Natalee a willing participant in this group-sex thing. I speak for her once again: 'OK, you may force me to be your drink, your momentary treat, but I'm going to be most unsatisfying drink you ever drank. You're going to get the least cooperation from me that I can give.'

But you want to know how she died and here's my story. Read between the lines ever so slightly and it will jump out at you.

## 'Drink' Points to Drowning—Aspiration

**Suggested reading of key sentence:** " . . . *it's better I quit," <u>so</u> she said. [Joran replies] OK, but at least let me buy you a **drink**. <u>so</u> they went to the bar (in the casino). <u>So</u> they took a **drink** and started talking"*

This sentence itself invites us to read it in a different way. The repeated "so" creates natural pauses in the action. And we should also read it differently because Natalee just suffered the maximum trauma and "quit," meaning "died." Then, it's as if Joran responds, *"OK, at least let me buy you a drink."* Deepak's first message tells us that something about buying Natalee a drink contributed to her death.

Then, Natalee herself—being the one who was given a drink—clarifies the situation. Even Joran has admitted to doing exactly that, sharing drinks with other tourist girls he scored with over the years.

Now we have to answer a simple question. How can taking a drink kill you? At the moment of her death, Natalee was drinking. Of course she wasn't still drinking alcohol because obviously the boys were too busy assaulting her. But drinking literally means to "take liquids orally," and if you suddenly die because you're swallowing some type of liquid that can only mean one thing—you drown. Deepak's words suggest some type of drowning, as in "too much liquid." He often repeats the word *"drink."*

So how could she have drowned? There's only one way. **Natalee drowned in her own vomit while being raped.** She breathed in her own puke after swallowing the drink that Joran bought her earlier that night at Carlos'n Charlie's, where he's friendly with the bartenders. In fact you can hear Joran's exact words to her, *"at least let me buy you a drink."* That's where it all started, see? As I told you before, Beth, the story really started in Carlos'n Charlie's because, if he hadn't bought her that drink, she wouldn't have thrown up. And he bought her one all right, bought and possessed her that very moment because she ended up buying his line. She bought our whole cockeyed plan. Believe it, too—we did our least for her.

## Another Matching Story from Joran's Book

As we examine these major issues surrounding Natalee's death, we could predict that, in his book, his own hidden confession, Joran would relate a story that matches Deepak's deeper revelations. Every time perpetrators speak, they present matching thoughtprints. From emails to police interviews to magazine articles to television appearances to books, thoughtprints can be tracked. So it's no surprise that in chapter 3 of *The Natalee Holloway Case* Joran recalls the three suspects all partying during carnival.

Deepak's Honda was their headquarters, parked in a perfect spot near the beach, rocking with music as they checked out the girls parading by in bikinis and skimpy halter-tops. A man approached the Honda and began harassing them. Satish told him to "piss off." In response, the man made a throat-slitting gesture and told Satish, "I'm going to kill you." When the man started to hit Satish, Joran picked him up and threw him off a nearby bridge. As the stranger splashed into the water, Joran suddenly realized the man might not be able to swim and could drown. Acting quickly, the three guys pulled their would-be assailant from the water.

Right after that, Joran reports that a cop walked by and told Joran he had done the right thing; the police ended up taking the soaked troublemaker into custody.

What do we have here? Well, here are the basic elements: (1) the three compadres are together and hot for girls, checking them out; (2) Deepak's car is in the center of things; (3) and then suddenly they're confronted with a crisis, with a person's life in danger from a throat injury. The next thing you know (4) another person, key to the story, is thrown in the water by Joran, who then fears that person will drown. In the end, (5) someone gets the punishment law enforcement says he deserves.

The parallels to Natalee's fate are clear. Joran was confessing, between the lines, what actually happened to Natalee. From beginning to end all the details are present, except for the vomiting although the throat injury hints at it. We would expect Joran to provide that detail later as well, and he won't disappoint. Like Deepak, he promised to tell us the story of what happened on May 29 and 30 and—sure enough—their hidden stories perfectly corroborate one another. Exactly as Deepak's story suggests, Joran was the main one who took Natalee's body out to sea, and Joran's unconscious mind thinks he deserves punishment by law enforcement.

## Natalee's Final Comment—'let me buy you'

*"she said **ok but** at **least** let me buy you a **drink**"*

Beth, you must hear one final comment Natalee makes from her grave, the message I'm personally delivering for her. It's true that we bought her a drink and forced her to be our drink. But now you can see why those words also fit Natalee. In return for our 'favor' you can hear her response, 'Now let me buy you a drink, boys. Better yet let me buy you, let me buy and sell you with the truth as payback for your false kindness to me that took away the rest of my life.'

If you hear her voice between the lines of my email, she can own us, all right! That's the kind of power she possesses from her grave—if you buy my messages, buy them enough to spend the money on the search. Because, one thing is for sure. In the end we will have owned her or she will have owned us. Are you going to help her?

## Overlooked Clue: Vomiting

An eyewitness, Charles Croes, an Aruban businessman who equipped the Twittys and friends with cell phones when they arrived on May 30, was with them early the next morning when they queried Joran at his house, twenty-four hours after Natalee's disappearance. Croes also spoke with Joran privately that night.

In a *Vanity Fair* magazine article published in January 2006, Croes said that after Joran drove an intoxicated Natalee to see the sharks, Joran reported that "Deepak was increasingly uncomfortable at the lighthouse, fearful that Natalee would 'make a mess' in the car, presumably by vomiting." On several other occasions Croes quoted Joran as saying that she had actually thrown up at Carlos'n Charlie's, which had turned Joran off. Later, Joran changed his story when he made his public-relations rounds on American television and made no mention of Natalee getting sick. By then, he was being careful to cover up anything to do with Natalee's vomiting. Joran even insisted that she wasn't drunk.

And yet, in this June 4 email, Deepak describes Natalee as absolutely intoxicated. Several eyewitness reports, made by his neighbors to police, indicate that Deepak went to great lengths to thoroughly clean his car—inside and out—on the morning of Natalee's disappearance. If Natalee got sick in his car, Deepak washed away the evidence.

Without question the issue of Natalee's vomiting that night was quickly swept under the rug by all three suspects, because such an occurrence would inevitably lead to questions about asphyxiation. But we have an eyewitness to Joran's comments right after Natalee's death, clearly recalling that Natalee's vomiting was a major concern for the three young guys that night. If asphyxiation due to aspiration of vomitus was the cause of death—which Deepak strongly suggests—we can anticipate that he will continue to find creative ways of telling us this in his email.

## 'Island Boy' Coughs It Up

We anticipated a major story about vomiting in Joran's book, and here he comes again at least fifty steps ahead of us. In his book *The Natalee Holloway Case* where appropriately the first chapter is entitled "Island Boy," Joran tells about the time he went out drinking at "a boat party," got inebriated, and threw up. Eventually he ends up mostly alone, ready for sleep but with no ride home. He has to call his mother to come get him, and she takes ten minutes to get there. A friend named Susana is with him, taking care of him.

Anita van der Sloot ends up giving Susana a ride home, and after dropping off the girl his mother lets Joran know how disappointed she is in him. She threatens to put him out of the car if he throws up. Again we find these thoughtprints: *excessive drinking with friends, someone vomiting, getting sleepy, left mostly alone, a boat, calling a parent, a journey taking 10 minutes, dropping a girl off in a vehicle, the fear someone might throw up in a car, and the possibility that the person could be kicked out of the vehicle precisely for vomiting.* These are all the same elements we hear again and again in the story of Natalee's last night.

But we're not through validating the thoughtprints. According to a police interview on June 12, 2005, with Joran's best friend, Freddy Zedan, Joran had told him that Natalee had fallen several times on the way to the beach that night when they were alone. Freddy also told the authorities that Joran had said that, at some point, "she no longer came around, no longer regained consciousness" and that he had left her on the beach. When asked about this in a June 2007 interview in *Panorama* magazine, Joran said, "I do not recall. I do not have an explanation for that."

Likewise Satish said in a police interview that he thought Natalee had drowned after Joran had left her on the beach, noting that she and Joran had been lying on the sand just three feet from the ocean. Joran expressed the same fear during his television appearances in the states in April 2006. All of these accounts corroborate Deepak's email, with numerous references to Natalee drowning.

## Natalee Quits Breathing and CPR Fails

*"so he started playing and he won 100 $ for her back and he said hey thats the best i can do for you because i doubt it i can win more money for you so its better i quit*

*[ so she said ok but at least let me buy you a drink"]*

Another way Natalee did the least possible was when she quit breathing and died. She could do no more. This suggests a command or a thought from her panicked assailants at the moment of her death, "At least you could breathe, Natalee!" Or, "At least you could stay alive, Natalee! Whatever you do, don't quit!"

Deepak's email reveals another action the boys would have taken immediately in such a crisis. Revelations such as this confirm in a fresh way that you're looking directly into the mind of a perpetrator in mid-confession. Here's one of those surprises, as Deepak continues his plea to Beth:

> You can imagine how panic-stricken we were when Natalee was gasping for air. Now look at my imagery: Natalee is on her back and Joran is now playing for her in another way—trying to bring her back, *"so he started playing . . . for her back."* Finally he reaches a point where he says, *"that's the best I can do for you . . . I quit."* In the story I tell, at the blackjack table Joran won back less than one-fourth of what she had lost—he couldn't get it all back; he couldn't get her all back. I'm telling you that Joran tried to resuscitate Natalee, tried CPR on her—even turned her over face-down in utter desperation and "played/worked on her back."
>
> In my slip—an unnecessary word *"it"* in *"hey that's the best I can do for you because **I doubt it** I can win . . . "*—you can even hear the question Satish and I asked of Joran during his desperate effort, 'Is she going to make it?' And you can hear his response, 'I doubt it.' We all watched an unresponsive Natalee. She stopped breathing completely.

## 'doubt it'—Confession of Staging and Failing Natalee

> *"hey that's the best I can do for you because **i doubt it** [I can win more money]."*

> But I can tell you more than one thing with one phrase. You can see again how clearly my slip *"I doubt it"* now naturally breaks the sentence into two parts: *"I doubt It—I can win more money."* It's another confession telling you that the entire scenario about winning money for Natalee is completely untrue. It's just part of the staging in the

email. In fact, the entire email is a cover-up story and you can sum up my staged version of the email in two words, "Doubt it!"

The image of Natalee lying dead before him haunts Deepak. He and his accomplices cannot undo what they've done, and there is much more to the story he has yet to tell us. He must elaborate on how a brutal sexual assault escalated to an even more disturbing level of trauma—an accidental murder. We would expect much more blatant thoughtprints of death, and more details as Deepak continues telling the secret story of that awful night. And at this point, in his completely voluntary, spontaneous communication, he still has much more to tell us.

Predictably, as we have just seen, Deepak has taken the next logical step in his hidden story and explained how Natalee died despite efforts to resuscitate her. And even though the thoughtprint story is subtle we have plenty of opportunities ahead to validate this early, very logical picture.

Next we should expect Deepak to describe their initial efforts to cover up their heinous crime. Deepak should reveal what they did with her body—which is precisely what he does. Having suggested that Natalee died by asphyxiation, he now points out that she was taken to another type of casino altogether. We must not miss the key sequence here: Natalee has died, the CPR rescue has failed, and now they buy her a drink, suggesting in a different light that whatever they did with the body has something to do with *"drink."*

## Moment of Death and 'So ... So ... So'—and the Hiding Place

> **Suggested reading of key sentence using keyword "so" as guide:**
> *"it's better I quit,"* **so** *she said. Ok, but at least let me buy you a <u>drink</u>. so they went to the <u>bar</u> (<u>in the casino</u>). [period]* **So** *they took a <u>drink</u> and started talking"*

Now, Beth, look at the sentence again where we find Natalee announcing the moment of her death, in *"it's better I quit, so she said."* This is followed by Joran's implied response: *"Ok, at least let me buy you a drink."* But keep reading, looking for key words.

You'll soon find the seemingly minor word, 'so,' but look again. It serves as a natural divider describing a series of actions. I again emphasize "drink." Then, **notice how I break the sentence into three separate actions with the word** *"so,"* describing a crucial three-part sequence.

(1) With the first *"so"* I've described the moment of Natalee's death (*"**I quit," so she said"**).* Joran then responds with an offer—a plan— *"let me buy you a drink."* See my confession? From this angle, Natalee has just died and Joran is buying her a drink. You don't have to be a genius to see that *"drink"* equals 'liquid' equals 'water' equals 'ocean.'

Keeping the question in mind at this point—'What did we do with the body?'—you can then see that *"let me buy you a drink"* reflects our immediate plan of dumping the body in the ocean. Earlier, when the question was 'How did she die?' I used *"drink"* to tell you she had drowned. Keep your eye on one question at a time and you can fol- low my confession. So we decided to put her in the ocean. And now the action picks up.

(2) Notice what comes next: *"**so** they went to the bar (in the casino)."* See the action? "They" moved; they traveled. All three of us were involved in the plan, and a group traveled somewhere with Natalee's body. And where did we take her? *"to the bar (in the casino)."*

Look closely when I clarify that the bar is *"(in the casino)"* inside parentheses. Of course you already know that, but I wanted to jar your thinking and make you think of another bar elsewhere, namely, a different kind of bar—a sandbar, which certainly follows in line with *"drink"* equals 'ocean.' I'm giving you a picture that we dumped Natalee's body in the ocean out past a sandbar. I put a period after *"bar"* to indicate something final is associated with a bar and with a drink. Later, in another crucial scene I will repeat *"bar"* two more times for emphasis.

Look even closer at the special parentheses to see which specific bar we took her to—*"the bar (in the casino)."* Read it as 'the bar in the Holiday Inn casino.' Very subtly but very clearly, I'm connecting Holiday Inn to a bar, suggesting 'sandbar,' and so the sandbar in the Holiday Inn/ocean means that *if a bar (in the Holiday Inn) is symboli- cally a sandbar, then the Holiday Inn is symbolically the ocean.* See? I'm validating the code, step-by-step: "*Holiday Inn*" means 'ocean.' Certainly the idea of a smaller place—the barroom—within the larger casino fits with the concept of a smaller sandbar within a larger ocean.

With *"casino"* I'm also telling you that we know we took a gamble that no one would find the body. That's the big wager on the table. Because right here I'm giving you a geographical location of the body—in the ocean and in a particular part of the ocean, located just as a bar is located in a particular part of a hotel or a casino.

I'm giving you a major key: use *"Holiday Inn"* as code for 'ocean' and pay attention whenever I use geographical references to the Holiday Inn, because at those moments I'm giving you more specific clues about the key to the case. If you're going to stay in this winner-take-all poker game, Beth, you've got to keep up with my mind, stay ahead of my corrupt self, and read my 'tells.' Like I said, my email is one big 'tell' but if you don't know how to read my eyes behind the sunglasses of my cover-up story, you don't stand a chance. Right now the authorities aren't even in the game. That's why I keep making all these gambling references—I'm inviting you to get in the game.

If you're following my hints, you should now think back to one of my most important slips—*"[Natalee] Hollaway."* We took Natalee's body away and put it in a 'holl' or a 'hole.' Like I said, her name 'Holloway' is so close to "Holiday" it's not funny! So decoding the particular clue **"Hollaway"** tells you that we took 'Holloway' away somewhere in the 'Holiday (Inn)/ocean' and put her body in some kind of hole or some kind of small space that would keep the body confined.

Like what? Try a container.

(3) Now look at my last *"so"*—**"so** *they took a* **drink** *and started talking."* I'm giving you a huge heads-up—just like the police say, '(he) started talking.' That shows I'm really spilling the beans here and emphasizing how, *"they took a* **drink**" explains Natalee's fate. Then I move on to another clear action, which suggests our response to Natalee's quitting (her death), 'At least let us buy you a different kind of drink.' Translated that means, 'Let us take you to the drink, to the ocean, where you can take one long, final drink.'

Pay real close attention to the word *"drink"* which also suggests 'water' and the picture of Natalee swallowing water—I'm confirming the location of her body.

Also, keep in mind the sequence, 'so drink,' 'so bar,' 'so drink.' My staccato chant *"drink"—"bar"—"drink"* gives you a key part of the story. I just gave you two final moments: one when she died, the second when—and where—we left her body once and for all.

We must not overlook the implied sarcasm and cold-hearted indifference to Natalee's death which comes shining through in this comment. Natalee has just died, and what's their response? "Oh, let us buy you a drink. Ho, ho, ho! Let us take you to the ocean and buy you one last nightcap—one for the road, one for the ocean. Ho, ho, ho."

This demonstrates that the three guys, in their desperate but devil-may-care ease, disposed of the body in the same cavalier way they assaulted Natalee, as Deepak next tells us. Properly heard, these three characters send a shiver up your spine. If we couldn't simultaneously hear Deepak's L-2 consciousness telling us how wrong and terrible their actions really were, we would be inclined to view them just as forensic experts often see such criminals—as complete sociopaths without consciences.

## *'why not'* Answered

> *"so my friend said ok ,* **why not** *. so he started playing and he won 100 $ for her back and he said hey thats the best i can do for you because i doubt it . . . better* **i quit** *so she said ok but at least let me buy you a drink so they went to the bar (in the casino)."*

Between the lines, Deepak is asking himself over and over, "Why did we ever do such a thing?" Look back at the final words in the previous sentence—the major question and message marker, *"why not."* Secretly Deepak has raised the question, "Why should we have not gotten involved with Natalee?" And in the next sentence he answers his own question for all to hear as he describes yet again the moment of Natalee's death: "I quit."

In retrospect Deepak now realizes that the three guys never should have targeted Natalee because their attack eventually blew up in their faces—she died during the assault and they couldn't save her life. As a statement, *"why not"* first reflects the off-hand bravado of all three perpetrators as Joran speaks for them, answering the call of the wild. Why not take this lovely blonde girl and have my way with her? Why not play blackjack with her, along with my two dark-skinned accomplices? Sure, why not?

And Deepak answers clearly: Because she died.

A crucial part of the Deepak Code has been broken—the location of the body. We might ask, however, whether "sandbar," in relation to the ocean, provides us with any significant clue.

Perhaps not coincidentally, Deputy Police Chief Gerold Dompig, the Aruban official in charge of the Holloway case, pointed out the same possibility in a January 2006 interview with *Vanity Fair* magazine. Dompig noted that it was widely known that a sandbar was located just 200 feet from shore on the northwestern side of the island, where Oranjestad and the Holiday Inn are situated. Just beyond this sandbar, strong sea currents would easily carry such evidence further out into the Caribbean Sea—causing Dompig to hypothesize that this was the easiest, fastest and most logical place for an ocean drop. If someone wanted to dump Natalee's body, they would have done it there, according to the chief Aruban investigator.

Dompig later urged Dave Holloway to search for the body in the ocean, specifically using the Holiday Inn as a reference point for a search pattern. While this was not mentioned in the *Vanity Fair* article, this implied that Dompig believed Natalee's body was dumped into the ocean in some type of heavy container where it could still be found. Thus the instincts of a key Aruban policeman match Deepak's revelation of the body being placed in a container that was then dropped into the ocean out beyond the sandbar.

## Summary of New Information in Scene

- Deepak continues to confirm that he is a reporter, unconsciously telling a logical, cohesive story.

- Even as we logically anticipated that he would describe in detail the cause of death, he does exactly that, with his description preceded by a detailed account of sexual assault in the previous scene.

- Deepak then describes a sudden change in the action—coitus interruptus—an abrupt end to the sexual assault linked to Natalee's death.

- Speaking in the first person for Natalee he links the moment of death, "I quit," to excessive drink.

- In similar fashion, Deepak links the crucial message marker *"started talking"* to Natalee drinking.

- Deepak suggests Natalee's accidental death by drowning—aspiration—while she was trying to throw up.

- He describes failed efforts at CPR.

- He suggests the body was dumped near a sandbar in the ocean, in the drink.

- Using the magic police words "started talking," Deepak instructs us to pay close attention to his confession, for continued revelations.

- We can expect Deepak to continue to make a strong case by providing more vivid images of an aspiration death, failed CPR, and Natalee's body in the ocean.

# 8
# The Witness Opens Up

## Conversation at Casino Bar: *'started talking'* and *'school'*

> *"so its better i quit so she said ok but at least let me buy you a drink so they went to the bar (in the casino ). so they took a drink and **started talking** etc. about **school**, the vacation etc.etc.afterwards my friend had to go and she said that "today is my last day i will be in carlos n' charlies will you be there" and my friend said well i have school tomorrow i don't think so . well she begged him and he still said yes i'll be there"*

> *"So they took a drink and started talking etc. about school."*

Again the scene shifts, subtly but powerfully. Natalee and Joran have started to converse, and immediately we find one of the most dramatic message markers in the entire email—the magic law enforcement term *"started talking"*—the words detectives use when a perpetrator is breaking, when the suspect is finally delivering crucial details about a crime. Without question, many more bombshell revelations will soon emerge.

*"Started talking"* points backward to what Deepak has just told us (the specifics of Natalee's death), even as it represents the strongest hint as to where her body lies. But *"started talking"* also points ahead. This message marker is accompanied by a powerful co-messenger—an equally striking marker—*"school."* In the science of thoughtprint decoding, such a potent combination says "High Alert Here—Key Message!"

With every new section, every paragraph, every sentence, and every word, Deepak's L-2 mind refuses to waste time. His unconscious L-2 mind has a plan, and with each new communication it adds important information.

## Prediction

Knowing that Deepak's thoughtprints have given us a strong case to go on so far, we might try to think ahead. Where is he going with his

133

story? As always, the answer is that he will tell us what we need to know to make a case against the three suspects.

Deepak has given us the first chapter of his story. Since he has given us a complete version of what happened, we would anticipate that he will now give us the second chapter. However, he must do several things at the same time. Mainly, he must go back and go over and over his confession until he is absolutely convincing. Thus we would expect him to emphasize key circumstances.

From beginning to end, his story will become more and more obvious as he gradually provides more obvious, less disguised thoughtprints, just as the unconscious mind performs in therapy. He'll deliver ever more blatant death images and will give us more images of the sexual assault.

Even so, to this point, the cover-up story has involved only Joran and Natalee. We can anticipate that Deepak will make it even plainer, between the lines, that all three suspects were involved. If drugs were involved, we should also expect that fact to become clearer. Then we would expect more distinct references to a drowning/aspiration incident, and more details about the location of the body.

We can even examine the beginning of each scene and predict where's he's going with it. Here Deepak will describe Joran and Natalee talking, allegedly for the first time. He should quickly reveal what took place between them. We would expect another version of the sexual assault scene, and how it ended up costing Natalee her life.

## 'etc.' Used Three Times

> "so they took a drink and _started talking_ **etc**. about _school_, the vacation _etc.etc._afterwards my friend"

Beth, again I'm giving you the magic words—"started talking"—and now see what follows. Don't miss the obvious. Notice the very next word, "etc." This little word is so important that I emphasize it by using it three times, one after the other. This triple usage, plus my surrounding it with those magic words—"started talking" on one side and "school" on the other, tells you that the importance of this single abbreviation cannot be overestimated. A complete understanding of the case hangs on this word—it's like a zoom lens bringing the picture up close and into clearer focus than almost anything else in the letter—and it's going to tell you what happened.

Etc." means to continue the same action, to continue doing the same thing you were doing. A period after it suggests a completed act—in this case, *three* completed acts. Remember, I'm speaking in code and at times I'll give you especially key words like *"etc."* It simply requires a certain amount of footwork to track down where else I use *"etc."* to see if I really emphasize the meaning. In this case it's as plain as the nose on your face. I'm practically shouting at you—"etc." is a **major key**!

Look ahead and you will find the most overtly intimate scene in my email.

## 'etc.' Means Sexual Assault—Three Altogether

*"so on my my to the lighthouse there was music playing and noone talking for a while when i looked in the backmirror my friend and natalee were kissing and touching (his hands **etc** was in her blouse but nothing nude or against natalees will )"*

I unmistakably connect *"etc."* with sexual activity—*"his hands **etc** was in her blouse."* And then I follow it with a classic denial—*"but nothing nude or against natalees will"*—telling you exactly what happened. By now you know that you have to read through my surface denials in order to clearly see the truth. So what am I telling you? Again, I have to be extremely graphic in my most vivid description of what we did to Natalee. First we stripped off all her clothes, leaving her nude. That was all part of the power trip designed to humiliate and frighten her. There's nothing new under the sun about that part of the assault. Like I've said, this was more about power than sex.

Then Joran's hands and his *"etc"* was in Natalee, penetrating her sexually, completely against her will. I used *"etc."* three times in rapid succession because Satish and I followed Joran, we each had our own "etc" in Natalee. Three assaults, three penetrations. *"Etc"* is code for 'sexual assault.' Yes, the three of us sexually assaulted her—back-to-back-to-back.

But there's more. I set the entire sentence off in its own parentheses, again to show how important it is. And notice that, in this sentence, when I define *"etc"* it has no period after it, suggesting ongoing sexual action. Previously, when I used the three *"etc"* in succession, each time I included periods, suggesting three completed sexual acts. To be plain, we all had orgasms. I know, shocking isn't it?

## Sexual Code Defined: New Insights

Now that you know the code, Beth, go back and substitute "sexual assault" for *"etc."* and you can see my confession even clearer.

(**Translation:** *"so they took a drink and started talking* **sexual assault**. *about school, the vacation* **sexual assault**.**sexual assault**.*afterwards my friend had to go and she said that "today is my last day I will be.."*)

The first "etc./sexual assault." occurs after Joran is drinking with Natalee—meaning enjoying some type of sexual gratification with Natalee associated with alcohol/drugs. In other words, Joran was the first to assault her. Notice the first *"etc."* by itself next to the word *"school"*—meaning 'go to school here and see how I describe the three assaults.' Next 'etc.etc./ sexual assault—sexual assault' tells you that there were definitely, without question—period, period 'that's it'—two more 'back-to-back' similar attacks by two people who looked virtually identical, Satish and me. Again, locating *"vacation"* between the assaults tells you once more that the three of us took a little vacation, had a little fun, at Natalee's expense.

## Police Interviews Reveal Natalee Stripped Nude

During the key police interview on June 11, 2005, when Deepak admitted to the beach story and his previous cover-up of the hotel story, he related another story specifically confirming how the suspects abused Natalee sexually. Riding along, with Natalee and Joran in the backseat, Deepak casually said that "Satish popped in a DVD that had nude scenes in it" with Natalee's immediate reaction, "Oh my God, what's that?" Deepak then responded to Joran, "The girl is going to think we're perverts." After a while, Joran reportedly said to Satish, "Switch off the DVD; she has had enough of it." Joran confirmed the identical story in his book, relating that one of the music videos was DJ Benny Benassi's version of "Satisfaction," featuring explicit images of scantily clad women wielding power tools.

Between the lines Deepak suggests both that they stripped Natalee and, with "Satish popped in a DVD . . . nude scene" that the boys "popped a cherry" when Natalee was nude. In other words, she was a virgin. Even the initials "DVD" ironically suggest "Deepak—van der Sloot—Deepak II/Satish." Notice too how both Deepak and Joran both admit that the three guys engaged in perverted sexual behavior in Deepak's car, behavior which not only shocked Natalee but killed her.

They also give us the strongest of hints that the moment Satish put that DVD in was the moment Natalee—suddenly shocked—realized she was in real trouble. For his part, Joran appears to be reliving the moment he gave the sudden command to stop the sexual activity after he realized that Natalee had had enough—that she was in distress. We will see this pattern over and over. In this story he tells Satish to stop, but other tales told by Joran will consistently recall him ordering Deepak to stop having intercourse with Natalee.

This fits with Deepak's earlier story about spilling the "Cherry Coke" in his car. The spilled soda suggests not only that Natalee was a virgin but that Joran's insistence that Deepak stop his assault was so urgent that Deepak partially ejaculated in his car. We find two specific reasons for Deepak and Satish obsessively cleaning the car—Deepak's seminal fluid and blood samples from Natalee's hymen.

## 'Island Boy' Confirms Natalee Exposed

In another story from his book, Joran discussed Natalee's short skirt. "Natalee did not want them seeing her underpants" he wrote, as he described her modestly holding her skirt down. But then he informs us that did no good because she couldn't cover herself up and he could clearly see her panties, which he described in remarkably specific detail—dark blue with flowers embroidered on them (her mother later confirmed she possessed such underwear).

Let's get real. In the dark, at night, with Natalee making a genuine effort to cover up, Joran would not be able to get that good of a look—sorry. Notice too his slip about "them" looking between her legs, making plain exactly how much Deepak and Satish were involved in the unfolding sexual scene. Both Deepak and Satish admitted they had each seen Joran's hands between Natalee's legs in the backseat before suddenly changing their story in classic denial.

For example, again Satish reports, "at no moment seen pants (underwear) of the girl." Unquestionably the message is clear—they *all* got a look at Natalee's panties and her private parts because they stripped her. No wonder Joran described giving Natalee a "sightseeing tour" in Deepak's car—she was the sight they all looked upon.

## 'etc.' Also Code for the Drug 'Ecstasy'

*"so they went to the bar (in the casino ). so they took a drink and started talking **etc.**"*

Now Beth look at *"etc."* again. Read the letters, 'e-t-c' and say them, 'E-tacy.' Then add the letter 'x' to 'etc' to make what I'm telling you a little plainer, and you have 'ex-t-c' or 'ecstasy.' Now you can see the same sexual code in yet another way, this time substituting 'ecstasy' for *"etc."*—*"so they took a drink and started talking **ecstasy**. about school, the vacation **ecstasy. ecstasy.**afterwards my friend had to go."*

But read the very beginning of this important sentence where it opens with *"So they took a drink"* as 'So they took the drug alcohol,' which further suggests other drugs. Remember, I've insisted in no uncertain terms that I'm really starting to talk here. Now I'm making our plan even clearer—to get Natalee intoxicated on alcohol and drugs to get her go along with the sex. I'm also strongly suggesting that the drug Ecstasy, or a similar drug, was involved in Natalee's assault and possibly in her death. Such drugs create an overexcited, hypersexual state. They also impair judgment and often cause dehydration or nausea.

In this context notice the similarities in *"started talking"* and 'started taking' (one letter apart), Beth. Now read the sentence through again as, *"so they took a drink and started taking Ecstasy."* You can see the strong hint that besides her drinking, Natalee had a little booster— and I'm even naming the drug. A second code word for *"etc"* is Ecstasy or 'X,' as it's more commonly known.

From its chemical name, MDMA, capsules of Ecstasy are also commonly called "mollies." Ecstasy is known to be popular in the Caribbean islands and is frequently used in liquid form to spike drinks. Deepak, as noted, was familiar with such practices and was well aware that Ecstasy was easily available in Aruba.

Reliable eyewitnesses described Natalee as appearing in control of her senses, and not overtly impaired by alcohol, when she left Carlos'n Charlie's with Joran. Such testimony would support a theory that Natalee was instead feeling the less-evident effects of a drug such as Ecstasy. The drug—true to its name—is known to greatly heighten a person's libido, even more so in combination with alcohol. Some users describe the combination as producing an almost irresistible drive for sexual activity.

When she was riding in the car right after leaving Carlos'n Charlie's, Natalee certainly behaved like someone on Ecstasy, reportedly opening a window to get some air, yelling euphorically to her friends and eventually getting nauseous.

In one of his police interviews, Joran specifically denied that Natalee used "narcotics"—an unusual description suggesting illicit, heavy drug use associated with a corrupt drug dealer. That's exactly the way Joran would have seen himself if he or an associate gave her a drug that eventually contributed to her death. At the same time another girl came forward later, telling a story of how Joran had seemingly spiked her drink on another occasion, causing her lips to tingle, although under pressure she recanted. Tingling lips, without any loss of consciousness whatsoever, would be most compatible with the use of Ecstasy, as opposed to a more specific date-rape drug.

Police also told Dave Holloway that whoever was using Paulus van der Sloot's computer the morning after Natalee went missing—likely Paulus himself—was using it to research alcohol and drugs on the Internet.

## Where Natalee Was Drugged

Deepak continues:

I will tell you more than once that Natalee was drugged but you want details: where was she drugged and who did it? Pay attention to my hints. Continue to substitute 'Ecstasy' for *"etc."* and keep reading.

**Translation:** *"so they took a drink and started taking Ecstasy. about school, the vacation Ecstasy.**Ecstasy**.afterwards my friend had to go and she said that 'today is **my last day I will be in Carlos n' Charlie's'"***

The phrase 'so they took a drink and started talking/ taking Ecstasy' suggests, in the strongest way, that Natalee's drink was spiked in a bar—the setting of my story. But which bar am I really talking about? And remember, she never had a drink with Joran at the Holiday Inn casino. That part of the story was total fiction.

So therefore, notice now which bar I connect it to—if you just read the two sentences together you can see the statement speaking for

Natalee, *"Ecstasy.Ecstasy. afterwards my friend had to go and she said today is the last day I will be in Carlos n' Charlie's."* Yeah, that bar played a major role in her demise. Remember? I previously pointed out Carlos'n Charlie's at the very beginning of my email, when I delivered the *"news"* (*" . . . Sunday she left with me , my brother and a friend from **carlos n' charlies**"*).

Also, don't forget how I pointed to another person of interest in the case, someone connected to Carlos'n Charlie's. Shortly, I'll describe Joran buying drinks in the same nightclub and Natalee being very drunk, implying that she was also drugged—the first time they really met. As mentioned, I'll use the word *"Carlos n' Charlie's"* six times, often at crucial points in my story. Enough said. If Natalee was drugged, you can see where I'm pointing.

The three guys, especially Joran, were regulars at Carlos'n Charlie's where they would have had ample opportunities to recruit staff members to participate in their predatory plans, perhaps repeatedly. Joran reportedly admitted to police that he had initiated brief affairs with at least twenty tourist girls over the preceding few years, and three of those girls reported him as a date-rapist to Aruban police, according to island authorities. In fact, Deepak implies that his friendship with Joran *"(a friend from carlos n' charlies)"* centers around the nightclub, depicting the bar as an important accessory-before-the-fact in their dangerous game. This stands as yet another suggestion that the three guys were experienced players in the game of "tourist poke-her," using their home-field advantage by playing at "Carlos'n Charlie's Park."

## *'afterwards'*—After Sex

Beth, notice now how smoothly and naturally I take you to the next part of my story. Read deeper into the sentence I previously described with *"etc"* meaning 'sexual assault' and we have . . .

**Translation:** *"so they took a drink and started talking **sexual assault**. about school, the vacation **sexual assault.sexual assault**.afterwards my friend had to go and she said that "today is my last day I will be."*

## Speaking for Natalee: *'today is my last day'*

Isn't that the most striking single sentence in my whole email? It really tells you what happened to Natalee—and when it happened to her as well—because I speak for her in the first person, putting it in quotes for emphasis.

I've just described an intense, brutal, non-stop sexual assault on Natalee and what happened as a result. Let her tell you, hear her voice speaking from her grave—"*today is my last day i will be . . . .'* Hear Natalee plainly, 'I have ceased to exist. This would be the last day I will be in Aruba or anywhere else. I am dead.'

## Going to School—Deepak Again Describes the Death

[See Explanation Below: *sexual assault.sexual assault.afterwards my friend had to go and she said that*]

"*today is my last day i will be in carlos n' charlies will you be there*" *and* **my friend said well i have <u>school</u> tomorrow i don't think so** . *well she begged him and he still said yes i'll be there.So that was in the casino i was not present* "

I mention the magic word "*school*" again, because I'm teaching you more about the moment we lost Natalee. I have to say it again in a different way to show you how much it haunts me. See my hidden phrase, " *. . . my friend said well I have school tomorrow I don't think so[.]*"—ending with a definite period.

You can hear Natalee's voice after her sudden, unexpected death plainly asking, 'Will I have school tomorrow?' Or better yet, 'Am I well? Will I have school tomorrow?' I use that magic word "*well*" to confess that Natalee's not well at all. Later I'll come back to it at the end of my email, just like I started with it in the first sentence. I'm under such great pressure to own up to what I've done, Beth, that I can't even slow down and take a normal breath, using normal punctuation. I just blurt out the answer to her question about school the next day: 'I don't think so, Natalee. School is out for you, Natalee. No school tomorrow because tomorrow will never come for you. You're dead—you no longer exist.'

The quick questions, the quick premature period, and the hint of urgency in "*my friend had to go*" all point toward that sudden death.

### 'afterwards' Again—Natalee Died During Third Assault

Beth, notice how I link Natalee's death to the three sexual assaults. Again I'm telling you the precise moment of Natalee's death—that she died during the third assault. Look again at the message substituting the code 'sexual assault' for *"etc."*

**Translation:** *"so they took a drink and started talking sexual assault. about school, the vacation sexual assault.sexual assault.afterwards my friend had to go and she said that "today is my last day I will be.."*)

Each of the three sexual assaults is followed by a period, indicating completion—orgasm. But, by running *"afterwards"* with the two sexual assaults *("etc.etc.afterwards"*) with no space, I'm telling you the third one of us who was with her wasn't completely finished. My turn with Natalee ended unexpectedly. *"Afterwards"*—her death—came very suddenly. I'm saying in another way that the third assailant was distracted as he neared orgasm and failed to notice Natalee's distress. I was that distracted assailant.

With *"etc.etc."* I'm also suggesting that two types of 'ecstasy' likely killed Natalee—sex and drugs. With the double periods I'm telling you 'This is the story of her end, that's it. Period. Period.'

Our conscious L-1 minds move past such details as spacing errors with nary a thought. But Deepak provides us with a treatise on how the L-2 mind of a perpetrator shifts into another gear and completely takes over a forensic document when the writer is confessing.

## Moment of Death: Were You There?

Deepak continues to tell Beth about the death of her daughter:

For more of my confession, look at the translation of the moment of death.

**Translation:** *"sexual assault.sexual assault.afterwards . . . she said that "today is my last day . . . will you be there" and my friend . . . said yes i'll be there. So that was in the casino i was not present ,"*

From the beginning I've promised you important revelations. At this most poignant of moments—Natalee's death—you can expect more major revelations. You can hear me speaking for Natalee immediately after she has died, and asking the question first of Joran: 'Will you be there—really, were you there, Joran—at my last day, my last moment?' Notice how close *"will you be there"* is to 'were you there.' To make sure no one can miss it I speak for Joran in the first person even as I quote him, *"Yes, I'll be there"* meaning 'Yes, Natalee, so that the world knows I, Joran van der Sloot, was there.'

And of course I'm speaking for all three of us. We were all there. I repeat the magic word *"there"* twice—the answer to the major cop question, 'Hey, Joran, Deepak, Satish—were you there when Natalee died? Were you there?'

I follow this with my typical cover-up denial, *"I was not present."* But secretly I'm telling you two things—confessing 'Yeah, man, I was there'—but also saying that I was out of it, the distracted third assailant who was in his own world, consumed by his own bizarre ecstasy when Natalee got in trouble.

## Deepak's Testimony: Natalee Begs Them to Stop

" *. . . sexual assault.sexual assault.afterwards . . . she said that "today is my last day . . . will you be there" . . . and my friend said i have <u>school</u> tomorrow i don't think so . well she begged him and he still said yes i'll be there.So . . . "*

I know this gets even harder for you, Beth, but I have to tell you again about Natalee's response, this time in more detail, using a different voice. Here my inner attorney shows up at the exact moment you would expect—when I'm recounting the moment Natalee departed this earth. You'll have to listen in a slightly different way. Maybe, strangely, it also will comfort you.

## Deepak As the Prosecuting Attorney

Let us now shift, for a moment, to see how Deepak's email confession might play out if its revelations were presented in court by a prosecutor who understood his thoughtprint messages. We'll specifically hear Deepak himself play the role of the prosecuting attorney. Deepak suggests that he unconsciously intended the email to be used in this way. In the end he'll make it plain that it is equivalent to a signed confession and will indirectly suggest that a prosecutor should use it in court. He will even go on to tell the court officials what his sentence should be.

We envision now that hypothetical courtroom scene at this crucial juncture in Deepak's confession. The courtroom scene would unfold after a search team had followed Deepak's email instructions and discovered the body, something Deepak has envisioned from the very beginning. Immediately after the most striking sentence in the email, declaring unequivocally that Natalee died, *"today is **my last day I will be**,"* it's as if Deepak takes on the voice of a prosecuting attorney, the DA who will one day interrogate him after Natalee's remains are discovered. We can hear the attorney, with Deepak's email in hand, continuing to question the suspect:

> "Following your admission that Natalee died, Mr. Kalpoe, your message marker *'school'* instructed us to really pay attention, since you've promised to give us exceedingly important information. In your classic denial *'I was not present,'* you've actually admitted unconsciously to being present at the sexual assault of Natalee Holloway that led to her sudden death. In a moment I will ask you to tell us what was going on with Natalee right before she died.
>
> "However, before you do that, Mr. Kalpoe, let's look at how you have already answered this natural question of what came next— *'she begged him.'* Within the context of a sexual assault against her will, *'she begged him'* can only mean one thing. Your blatant phrase *"she begged him [and he still said yes i'll be there]"* speaks volumes doesn't it? In that short sentence, with the definite period conclusion, you leave absolutely no doubt as to what happened. So I ask you now, what was your answer then and what is it now?

> Deepak replies to the DA, 'Sir, she begged us to stop.'

> "Now let's see what you told us next, Mr. Kalpoe, in the message, *'I have school tomorrow i don't think so . well she begged him and he still said yes I'll be there.'* At this point it's obvious that she was totally controlled by the three of you. She was completely helpless and was begging you to stop. Now you've given us a first-person response by Joran, even though you omitted the quotes, suggesting he speaks for all of you. And what do you have Joran saying to Natalee at her most desperate moment, after he seemingly refuses to meet Natalee later? You write that his response was, *'I have school tomorrow i don't think so.'*

In other words, in your alleged story Joran can't meet with Natalee because he has school tomorrow. But we know how you use key message markers such as 'school' to guide us to look deeper, to alert us that an important message is coming up. So now read what you reported that Joran said. Read it, Mr. Kalpoe.

On the witness stand Deepak looks at the blown-up copy [Exhibit A] of his email on the easel next to him and replies, "'he **still** said yes (I'll be there).'"

## Slip '*still*' Reveals Devious Plan

The attorney now continues:

"He still–still–still–said 'yes I'll be there.' '*Still*'—that one little word. '*Still*' is a huge slip of the tongue isn't it? It's another one in a long line of key slips you make, slips that reveal the real truth. It suggests that you three guys *still* continued assaulting Natalee, while she begged you to stop. This suggests to us that the cover-up story about meeting Natalee later was total fiction. In response to Natalee's pleading, 'begging you' in your own words, Joran spoke for all three of you, and I quote, '*Still* said yes (I'll be there).' Sounds like you completely ignored her pleas.

"You're suggesting that the three of you told her, 'You can beg us to stop, say 'No,' all you want, Natalee, but we're saying 'Yes,' count on it.' This was part of the power thrill all three of you sought. And you did make that slip, '*still*,' didn't you, Mr. Kalpoe?"

Deepak nods, quietly answering, "Yes."

"Your confession, then, that in the face of Natalee's protests you '*still* said yes' suggests that all along the three of you had a prior plan to assault Natalee or one of her friends later that night, and that Joran, masquerading as a traveling college student, had been sizing up this opportunity all week. Since you said '*still*,' that shines the light on your modus operandi—that you '*still*' continued your plan, that you smooth operators had your plan down to a science, and that this was a familiar game to you."

Deepak can only answer, "Yes, sir."

## No School for Natalee

"Now let's again look at the previous sentence. Read it, Mr. Kalpoe."

Following the attorney's instruction, Deepak responds, "'*I have school tomorrow i don't think so .*'" Not missing a beat, the prosecutor continues:

"Now, of course, on the surface you're referring to Joran, but in light of Natalee's death, who else didn't have school tomorrow? Let me help you, Mr. Kalpoe. Obviously Natalee didn't have school tomorrow, or the next day, or the day after that or ever again. That explains why you would put one of your rare periods here, suggesting finality. Allow me, then, to read the message according to your deeper story of sex and death. First, you're speaking for your deceased victim, Natalee, from the grave, as you are prone to do, saying '*I have school tomorrow i don't think so .*' In reality you are suggesting that she said 'I'll never ever have school again.'

"Isn't it true that, in just a few short months, Natalee was planning to go off to college on an academic scholarship, and was looking forward to some of the best years of her life? You knew that, so it would make perfect sense for you to speak those disappointing words of grief and loss for her.

"But we hear something else here, Mr. Kalpoe—we hear the sadism with which you boys carried out your attack. We can hear Natalee telling you, 'but I have school tomorrow, college ahead of me, I have to go home,' and we can hear your cold response, '*i don't think so.*' As you said, Natalee begged you, and we can hear more of her pleadings between the lines, something like, 'I came here to share a special trip, to create special memories with my high school friends before I went off to college, so don't ruin it. Please don't do this to me! This is my last day in Aruba, so please don't spoil it. Please, please stop!

"And once again came your suggested response: 'I don't think so, babe. Too bad—you know this is fun. You'll have a special memory. Just think how happy you made us.'

"Clearly linking Natalee to your references to 'school,' you suggest the obvious—that, in her pleas for mercy, Natalee mentioned her plan to attend college. You have admitted knowing about her college plans, isn't that correct, Mr. Kalpoe?"

Deepak says simply, "Yes."

## Natalee Begs for Air

*"she said that "today is my last day i will be . . .* **will you be air/there** *and my friend said well . . . i don't think so . well she begged him and he still said yes i'll be* **air/there.***"*

The prosecutor then continues:

"There seems to be one last important piece of information that we can gain from your description of Natalee, pleading with the three of you. 'Begging' also suggests being in great need physically. 'Begging for air' comes to mind since we have established that Miss Holloway drowned. Notice the repeated keyword *'there'* in your email. You did repeat that word, did you not?"

Again Deepak, "Yes, I repeated it." Picking back up, the DA then observes:

"And your word *'there'* even rhymes with 'air,' and in the context of her demise it invites the reading, *'today is my last day i will be . . . will you be my air and my friend said I don't think so. Well she begged him and he still said . . . I'll be your air.'*

"One way or the other the three of you were going to be Natalee's air, right Mr. Kalpoe? You're again suggesting that Natalee was being controlled by something around her neck—some type of rope or belt that could be tightened and then loosened by the three of you in your own game of sexual blackjack. And you were alternately choking her and letting her breathe, controlling her air, when everything suddenly fell apart and she was begging for air and couldn't get it because her lungs were filled with fluid. Isn't that what happened? Isn't that what you're actually telling us?"

Deepak's defense attorney interjects, "Objection your honor. He's asking the witness leading questions."

The DA responds:

"No, your honor, this witness's own ideas are leading him. I am just showing where his ideas are taking us. Your honor, the prosecution contends that this is a distinct, unconscious confession on the part of this witness, and that he wrote this thinly disguised email for the express purpose—*his* express purpose—of confessing as evidenced by how, in this very document, he has led the search team to find the victim's remains at a very specific place in the ocean. This is all in the context of the single most important sentence in his email, when he speaks for his victim, Natalee Holloway, and I repeat, says, '*Today is the last day I will be.*' The prosecution is simply following this witness, who was so overcome with guilt when he wrote '*Dear Betty*'—read 'Dear Beth,' the victim's mother—that these reflect his true sentiments. These are his ideas."

His honor replies, "Objection overruled. Please continue, counsel." And so the DA picks up again:

"Because we know you didn't intentionally strangle Natalee, the scenario of begging for air fits perfectly with somebody who is drowning doesn't it, Mr. Kalpoe? You can't deny that. It's common sense. You didn't intentionally strangle her, did you?"

"No," Deepak responds simply. Immediately the DA continues:

"So now, Mr. Kalpoe, Joran's words fit perfectly as you recounted them. In answering Natalee's implied question, 'Will you be my air,' he replied, 'I don't think so.' We can then hear Natalee's response to his refusal, 'So today will be my last day I will be.'

"Never were truer words spoken, correct? Because we all know by now—indeed –that it was Natalee's very last day alive.

"And, it certainly matches the moment Joran said to Natalee earlier in your email, 'better for you I quit playing poker'—suggesting 'better I stop assaulting her head, better I quit playing choker,' meaning that he was choking Natalee and had to stop abruptly. He had to stop because she couldn't breathe.

"You tell us something else that I find very fascinating, Mr. Kalpoe. You hint at a very personal encounter between Joran and Natalee as regards her being able to breathe. When you quote him as say- ing 'I'll be there,' suggesting 'I'll be your air, Natalee,' you're also suggesting that he was the one near her face, controlling her air by tightening and releasing the noose. He was the one she was plead- ing with most personally, face-to-face, when she died. The one choking her, the one who ignored her pleas, insisting, 'I'm staying put, so get used to it.'

"Just as you've already told us—and will tell us over and over in your email—*you* were the one who was raping Natalee when she choked. It fits doesn't it? And, as we read on, you will tell us that your own brother, Satish, was next to you doing his part control- ling Natalee. You will mention your own brother shortly in your email, will you not, Mr. Kalpoe?"

Deepak, looking down, quietly replies, "Yes."

"The story—your story—continues to hang together doesn't it, Mr. Kalpoe, just as you promised in the beginning when you said you would tell us *The Story, The News, The Truth?* In fact it comes together tightly—very tightly. We really must applaud your uncon- scious mind. It's as brilliant and honest as the day is long, as it continues to speak to us between the lines of this email."

## Email 'Body Language'

["*I have school tomorrow] i <u>don't think</u> so . well she begged him and he <u>still</u> said yes i'll be* **there***. So that was in the casino i **was not present**"

Standing beside the blow-up of the email with pointer in hand, the prosecutor now directs our attention to this brief sentence.

"I want everyone in this courtroom today to see how, in yet another familiar pattern, you used *two key periods* to give us a visual picture of that quick, final end which indeed shocked all three of you per- petrators. You follow Natalee's declaration, '*today is the last day I will be,*' with the confirming message—'*school tomorrow, I don't think so.*' Period, that's it, that's the final conclusion—Natalee has died.

"Immediately, you then repeat the message in the second-shortest sentence in the entire email—describing Natalee begging Joran for air, begging him to release his chokehold to let her breathe freely again. Then 'still' his response, you're quoting him as saying, in essence, 'No, I'm still going to be your air supply. I'm keeping the choker on your neck.' And then another period indicates 'the end—that was the end for Natalee'—because Joran continued to choke her. Finally, your brief sentence itself offers a nonverbal email 'body language' picture underscoring the brevity of life, both showing and telling us just how quickly things got out of hand and culminated in the end of Natalee's life, as in 'Period. It's over.'

"You know something else, Mr. Kalpoe? You never let up, never stop giving us detail after detail and never stop pointing to your own guilt. Look at your two words 'don't think,' suggesting how carelessly you three impulsive boys acted, giving nary a thought to potential consequences, remaining oblivious to Natalee's begging until it was too late. Again it's followed by the period, a punctuation picture translated as 'and that's a fact.'

"One thing is for sure—from the time you gave Natalee a ride in your car to the time you last saw her—you have to admit one thing, don't you? You boys didn't think. You didn't think about Natalee. You didn't think about consequences. You didn't even think about your own best interests. You didn't think you could ever end up in such a jam, did you, Deepak?"

Deepak remains silent as the prosecutor continues:

"When the night of May 29, 2005 began, you never thought you could end up here in this courtroom, on trial, facing murder charges, did you? Or that Natalee Holloway could end up dead at the bottom of the ocean, did you? In your worst nightmare you didn't think things could ever get this far out of hand, did you? You admitted in your email that when things got so crazy you were exhausted, you couldn't sleep. You were putting your family through so much that your mother was constantly crying and your father's blood pressure ran so high his hands were turning red.

"You also lost a lot of friends who, quote, 'thought you had something to do with this.' You and your brother each had to hire an attorney, and you were, quoting again, 'praying to God they find Natalee soon and find her well so that this nightmare—nightmare—ends.' You didn't think any of this could ever happen, did you?"

Deepak finally mumbles, "No . . . No, I didn't."

## Afterwards to Joran's House—and Then on Vacation

" . . . started talking etc. (sexual assault) about **school, the vacation** etc. etc. ( sexual assault.sexual assault) **afterwards my friend had to go** and she said that "today is my last day i will be in carlos n' charlies will you be there" and my friend said well **i have school tomorrow** i don't think so . well she begged him and he still said yes i'll be there."

After we have a feel from Deepak himself, as to how an attorney might use his own words to support a circumstantial evidence case, Deepak now picks up his own narrative again:

There are a couple of other things, Beth. Notice "*afterwards my friend had to go.*" After Natalee's death, where did Joran go? Where did we go? I'm implying Joran went home after he left the casino—also meaning we all went to his house after Natalee's traumatic death. And why? Because we now had to go to school. Once Natalee was dead we had to get down to business and come up with a plan to cover up our crime.

But pay attention—I've hinted again about what we did with the body. We sent Natalee away, sent her on vacation as the word "*school*" instructs you. It's one more hint that she is not on the island but in the ocean. When you go on vacation in or out of Aruba you have to go through or over the ocean. Over the sea and far away—or did we dump her far enough away? And did we really dump her in the ocean? Keep these questions in mind, Beth, and maybe you'll get answers.

We are still left with many questions at this point. With the phrase "*my friend had to go* (to his house)" Deepak subtly suggests a key part of their plan. With Natalee's body now in the car, they headed for Joran's house in Noord a few miles north of Oranjestad. Would they discuss the matter with Joran's drinking buddy, his legal-eagle father, Paulus van der Sloot immediately, or only later after disposing of the body? Remember, this is the same father who reportedly gave his underage son a line of credit at the Holiday Inn's Excelsior Casino and unquestionably encouraged his gambling.

## Joran's Crude Gesture Matches Email

Joran demonstrated his own urgent need to confess just as Deepak does in his email. In the presence of the men from Birmingham who showed up the next night at his house—after asking Natalee's stepfather, Jug Twitty, to leave the scene—Joran crudely described a sexual encounter with a "willing Natalee."

Holding up his hand and repeatedly gesturing, Joran said emphatically, "*I finger her, I finger her*," insisting she allowed it and that everything was completely consensual between them. Those words—and Joran's arrogant demeanor—still stick in the craw of one of those men whose daughter had been one of Natalee's roommates on the trip.

Don't overlook Joran's confession. Beneath his patina of politeness, Joran's raw comments spoke loud and clear, as though he were saying, "If you think I'm not the kind of guy who could have crudely and brutally assaulted Natalee and hidden her body after she accidentally died, think again." In a very real way, Joran was fingering himself and saying, "See how crude I am; see what I'm capable of; see how bad my judgment is; see how I'm pointing the finger at all of us; at me!" Given enough rope, perpetrators frequently hang themselves with hidden confessions in a thousand different ways.

Joran repeated the same scenario less crudely on his American talk-show tour in March 2006, this time casting Natalee as the more sexually aggressive of the two. Blaming the victim is an ancient game that sexual predators have played frequently throughout judicial history. But that first night, just twenty-four hours after Natalee's disappearance, Joran had already flashed his bloody shark's teeth.

## Summary: New Information from the Scene

What has Deepak now added to his story?

- Deepak fulfills two powerful back-to-back message markers— "*started talking*" and "*school*," one of the most unique sequences of markers in the email—to provide striking details of the crime.

- Unquestionably he has done *two primary things*—he has underscored that (1) a sexual assault (2) led to Natalee's death.

- As anticipated, Deepak has elaborated on the assault in this scene. He has underscored the rape in the most vivid terms as he directs us to fast-forward to the point in the email where he tells us that the three guys sexually assaulted a nude Natalee, after overpowering her. He describes a brutal assault as Natalee begs them to stop.

- Deepak uses *"etc."* as a code word for rape, pointing us to the clearest image of sex in the entire email and suggesting the details of stripping her naked and violating her repeatedly against her will. He describes three separate sexual attacks, two by men who appeared identical: Deepak himself, and Satish.

- Deepak hints that *"etc."* was also code for "ecstasy," suggesting that they spiked Natalee's drink to enhance her libido—and he points directly toward Carlos'n Charlie's as the place where the drugging occurred.

- Without question he is speaking for Natalee as he describes the exact moment of death in the single most powerful sentence in his email (*"today is the last day I will be"*)—and emphasizes that "we were all there." He then adds another death image for Natalee: "no school tomorrow."

- He re-confirms much of the previous story and says that Natalee died during the third assault, pointing to himself as the third assailant as he says again that she died from being unable to breathe and suggests that they immediately took her body to Joran's house before disposing of the body in the ocean.

- In another vivid message marker, Deepak sums up the entire escapade for the three careless predators—*"don't think"* meaning "we didn't think."

Deepak still has a long way to go, and we have a great opportunity to validate his story as we decode the rest of the email, but he has already made it clear that he's making one powerful L-2 confession.

# 9
# Planning the Cover-Up

*["she said that "today is my last day i will be in carlos n' charlies will you be there" and my friend said well i have school tomorrow i don't think so . well she begged him and he still]*

*said <u>yes i'll be there</u>.So that was in the casino i was not present , i was at work so my friend called me and said hey i met some girls in the casino and her friends and they want us to meet them in carlos tonight do you have to work tomorrow morning i said no , so he said pick me up later then i said ok.*

*so i got off my shift at 10 pm and went home took a bath had to fix something and then me and my younger brother went to pick up my friend was around 12.10 am so i came to his home and was talked for like 15 min"*

## Deepak: Multiple Sexual Innuendos Point to Rape—'Yes, I was there'

Deepak continues:

Beth, notice how I've focused on only one scene so far—the so-called meeting between Natalee and Joran in the casino—and this is just one-sixth of my story! Don't worry, though. I'm going to pick up the pace. My words will project a movie in your mind, and you'll watch the last evening of Natalee's life, scene by scene.

As each new scene unfolds, you may ask yourself, 'Why is Deepak telling me this?' But you already know the answer: I have to confess. I can't help myself. And I want to confess to YOU. As my little film flickers by, you'll see where I'm headed. You'll see the hidden story between the lines.

Here I quickly move to The Plan to "meet" a girl. (Prepare yourself for my sexual innuendos again. Also see how I repeat the keyword "meet" twice.) But really I'm describing two plans here—first the Sexual Plan, then The Cover-up Plan after our initial strategy of fun and games blew up in our faces. Now for our first plan: notice how, for the first time, I make it absolutely clear that our assault on some blonde girl was premeditated, and I was unquestionably involved.

Never lose sight of the deeper story line here as I continue telling my tale. Remember that, in the previous scene, Natalee has just died after being sexually assaulted, but Joran seems to be the only 'player' present. I begin the next scene with *"yes i'll be there.So that was in the casino i was not present, i was at work."* I seem to be claiming that in no way, shape or form was I involved in the previous scene, but you can read through my spontaneous denial—a dead tip-off—in *"I was not present"* to realize I'm telling you that I was in fact present. In a second way I cut through my denial with *"I was at work,"* declaring that I was not inactive but instead quite active.

To see the kind of work I was doing, simply look where *"I was not present"*—in the casino: in a gambling room, in a container. And what room would that be? To be blunt out of necessity—I was in Natalee's private container, her vagina, gambling that I could get away with being there. Like I've said, that was the huge gamble we all took, and I can tell you we never began to count how much we'd have to ante up

Between the lines I continue to describe my *"work"* in the sexual plan, describing the exact moment I was present. Merging two sentences without any space between them in, *"yes i'll be there.So . . . I was . . . present,"* tells you two things. First, at the very moment I deny being with Natalee I'm telling you once again that I was merged with her, having sex with her. The run-on sentences guide you to read the two sentences together as if there's no period. My deeper intelligence is The Guide for decoding this email, informing you here that I'm simply picking up in the sexual assault where Joran left off. I'm saying, 'So my turn came immediately after his. Yes, I was there doing exactly what he was doing. I was having my way with Natalee, playing poker/"poke her" and blackjack with her.'

## The Sexual Plan: Joran's First Phone Call

*"my friend called me and said hey i **met** <u>some girls</u> in the casino and <u>her</u> friends and they want us to **meet** them"*

Next we see how our plan unfolded. This is all after the fact. It's important that the plan started with a phone call—Joran supposedly calling me—and in a minute a phone call will take on far more significance in the second plan that night, the cover-up. I've already prepared you with some graphic sexual imagery, so by now you won't be surprised at more of the same. Our entire plan centered around meeting girls—get it?—'meat girls.' I mean, 'girls are meat,' right? Good-time party bars like Carlos'n Charlie's are known far and wide as 'meat markets,' places where guys can hook up for 'meating' or 'mating' with girls.

Notice the flow of the sexual assault. Joran says, *"Hey I met some girls."* That's part of *his* confession: 'Hey I meated some girls.' Notice the past tense *"met"*—clearly pointing to a done deed, a sexual encounter that had already taken place. I'm putting it crudely because crudeness reveals guilt like nothing else —Joran did 'meat' Natalee first .

## Revealing Slip: *'Her'* Friends—and Assault Order

Appreciate as always my slip in which Joran says, *"hey I met some **girls** and **her** friends."* I should have said, 'met a girl'—singular—'and her friends.' What I'm saying is that we turned Natalee into *"girls."* That's right, we all took turns. She became *"girls"*—plural—like she was more than one girl, one for each of us.

All along we planned just to meet only one girl, and at the time we weren't sure who it would be, just some girl. We didn't care who. Joran couldn't even remember the names of *"some girls"* he met from Mountain Brook, as he has testified several times. That tells you how much we cared about the girls we were hoping to 'meat.'

Where next Joran describes our plans the sequence of the assaults begins to emerge. I have him telling me *"some girls [really "girl"] . . . "they want **us** to meet/meat them tonight."* Specifically he has invited *"us"'* to join him in Natalee's casino, to 'meat them/her' after he did, and that's my way of confirming that Satish and I were in on it too.

We were like that huge fake shark painted over Carlos'n Charlie's front door. We were predators and she was our prey. Carlos'n Charlie's was a particular kind of market offering shark meat. Straight out, we were sharks **(later I will call us this very name!),** experienced predators who knew how to hunt and when to strike and who all got our fill of 'Natalee meat.' I say that because that's exactly how we treated her—crudely. And that's what we did to her—we sank our teeth into her. We ate her alive.

## The Sexual Assault Plan Continues

*"hey i met some girls in the casino and her friends and they want us to meet them in carlos tonight do you have to work tomorrow morning i said no , so he said pick me up later then i said ok. so i got off my shift at 10 pm and went home took a bath had to fix something . . ."*

Following Joran's invitation to *"us"* in "*they want us to meet/ 'meat' them in carlos tonight do you have work tomorrow,"*—translated 'do you want to meat Natalee too?'—I reply, 'No, we're not busy man! We're free to join you in meating this girl.' And we did.

When I say Joran "*said pick me up later,"* that's a distinct message that we can follow him in treating Natalee like a pickup, a prostitute we can treat any way our hearts desire. Leaving no doubt that I was involved, that I gave my full assent, *"then i said ok."*

Following Joran's instructions to *"pick me up later,"* I then took my turn after his. No doubt about it, "*i said ok,"*—fine with me, and it's one more way of saying, 'OK, I was really there.' Just to be perfectly clear, you're looking at that moment, "*then i said ok. so i got off my shift at 10 pm,"* and you can even see me getting off Natalee, off my shift, after I'm finished. At the end of my turn, "*i got off"* after 'I got on.' You get it. The truth is that Satish's shift came after Joran's and before mine. As you will see, the final shift was over at *"10 pm"* which you'll have to translate shortly to understand the actual time I'm referring to.

## More News: Satish Participated

*so i got off my shift . . . went home.. then **me and my younger brother** went to pick up my friend*

As much as I hate to say it, I stress something else here. When I say, *"me and my younger brother (Satish) went to pick up my friend (Joran). . . "* I'm admitting that both of us Kalpoes raped Natalee, treated her like a pickup. Yes, my little brother was involved, and as his older brother I feel terrible about getting him into this.

You can also see the order of the assaults here. We all did what we wanted with your daughter, and Joran had first shift, my brother picked up second and I worked the third shift, *"picked him up,"* stepped in where Satish left off.

## After Natalee's Death: The Second Plan, The Cover-up

## 'Not Present'—Out of It

*"yes i'll be there.So that was in the casino* **i was not present** *, i was* **at work so my friend called me** *and said hey i met some girls in the casino and her friends and they want us to meet them in carlos"*

Whenever I describe the sex I had with Natalee, even though I'm only describing it between the lines, notice how I continually refer to my being out of communication. That's another meaning of *"i was not present"*—**and notice that Joran called me.** Here I was, busy 'working away' in my own world, enjoying my turn with Natalee when all of a sudden Joran calls me to get my attention. This is another subtle picture that something was wrong with her, one reason I had to get *"off my shift"* with her. Over and over I'm telling you *"i was not present,"* another way of saying 'I was out of it.' That's my theme song, Beth. Can you hear the tune? There are more major clues here that something went wrong.

Now we shift to the second plan which we hatched after Natalee's death—the cover-up.

Surveillance videotapes and photos from the Holiday Inn Excelsior Casino, released long after Natalee's disappearance, show Natalee and Joran sitting not far from each other while he played blackjack on the evening of May 29. Joran had been hanging around the Holiday Inn and had carefully ingratiated himself with the Mountain Brook girls, putting them at ease by wagering somewhat successfully for one of Natalee's friends, Ruth McVey. He'd introduced himself as a student from Holland.

As we look at those photos, however, we can see Natalee resting comfortably, enjoying herself casually as she watches Joran and others gamble early Sunday evening. These photos speak volumes about a crucial part of Joran's strategy—to put a potential victim at ease. They make it clear that Natalee had spent enough time in his presence to let her guard down. We can see why Natalee might actually trust Joran to get her back to the hotel after Carlos'n Charlie's closed, never thinking he would be up to something devious. It's likely that Natalee found the tall, confident, outgoing Joran, the alleged college student with the Dutch accent, appealing and mysterious. For his part, Joran had plenty of prior experience at seducing tourist girls.

## Follow the Story Line—Fun Tonight, Work Tomorrow Morning

*"yes i'll be there.So that was in the casino i was not present , i was at* **work** *so my friend . . . i met some girls in the casino . . . they want us to meet them in carlos* **tonight** *do you have to* **work tomorrow morning** *i said no , so he said pick me up later then i said ok."*

As we continue with the second story about Natalee's death, I'll provide crucial information as to what took place. Pay attention to my keyword *"work"* and what time it occurs. First work *"tonight,"* second work *"tomorrow morning."*

First I've already described how I was at work 'meating girls/girl,' being with your daughter that **night,** which was really early the next morning on May 30. So the story starts that night with pleasure—fun and flirting games—but it turned into*". . . (do you have to)* **work tomorrow morning."**

Although I go on to deny that I had to work the next morning, read through my denial since I'm describing events after the murder. I'm telling you, 'Yes, I had more work to do later that morning.' Believe me, after the pleasure faded—and it faded fast—we had a lot of work to do that morning—*tons* of work. What might that work have been? Already I've hinted that Natalee died during the sex, specifically during my turn. So I could only be talking about one thing—getting rid of her body.

Now read the sentence without the denial, *"do you have to work tomorrow morning i said yes."* Then you can see what work I had to do by my very next actions, and by substituting 'she' for 'he' in what comes next since I'm speaking for Natalee—*"so **she** [vs 'he'] said pick me up **later** then i said ok."* I'm using the word *"later"* to show you I'm speaking for Natalee after she died, because in a minute I will quote her in almost identical sentences, using this exact word, about dropping her off **later** and giving her a lift **later**—picking her up later because she obviously couldn't pick herself up because she was dead. In both cases I'm referring to her body. And here, in a third way, I'm telling you that our work later that morning, after the assault, was to pick Natalee's body up—to lift it up and drop it off.

Notice another similarity. Later in my email when Natalee asks me if I will give her a lift home, I reply, *"then I said ok,"*—the same thing I say here when secretly referring to the same moment of dropping her body off. No question about it, I was in on the entire thing—the rape, the rape gone bad and getting rid of the evidence.

*"they want us to meet them in carlos tonight do you have to **work tomorrow morning** i said **no** , so he said pick me up later then i said ok."*

I tell you in even another way that Natalee has died, as I continually speak for her. See how similar *"work tomorrow morning . . . no"* is to the earlier idea, *"school tomorrow i don't think so,"* where I was also speaking for Natalee and, in both cases, talking about the same morning. School was out for Natalee and so was work. Never again on the face of this earth would she learn, work, or do all those things we do in life. No, she lost her life on this vacation island where people go crazy and lose control. They never think that there's any price to pay for going wild. Hell, we never thought we'd have to pay a price for helping ourselves to the fun. How crazy is that? Remember that word *"crazy"* in the very beginning of my story. Crazy sums up the whole freakin' thing.

## Deepak's Timeline Suggestions

*"so i got off my shift at **10 pm** and <u>went home</u> took a bath had to fix something and then me and my younger brother went to pick up my friend was around **12.10 am** so i <u>came to his home</u> and was talked for like **15 min** and then left to go to carlos (we all went out without or parents knew) so we <u>arrived</u> like **12.30 am** in carlos (carlos is closing **1 pm** ) and <u>headed straight</u> for the bar and bought **3 drinks** my friend paid for them"*

Suddenly Deepak is making numerous references to time as he reflects on the planning and preparations involved before heading out to Carlos'n Charlie's to meet some girls—specifically, one girl. Consciously he's recalling events prior to his meeting Natalee, but unconsciously he's drawing our attention to a hidden timeline regarding Natalee's death. This hidden timeline must be decoded in order for us to understand the central events: what happened, what was done with the body, and who was involved.

We must also closely examine Deepak's and Joran's supposedly "hard evidence" of computer and cell phone use in the early morning hours of May 30. As we scrutinize those emails, instant messages, text messages, and cell phone calls, we must remain on the lookout for suggestions of staging and establishing phony alibis. While we consider the possibilities, we'll see what Deepak tells us definitely and what he leaves open to speculation, to one degree or another.

## Assault Lasted 30 Minutes: Natalee Died at 2 am

Having extensively revealed that Natalee's death occurred during a brutal sexual assault we will now look ahead slightly, at one important timeline, which appears quite definite. Deepak reveals striking sexual imagery in the key sentence, *"so we arrived like 12.30 am in carlos (carlos is closing 1 pm )"* followed by *"and headed straight for the bar and bought 3 drinks my friend paid for them."* The imagery involves three guys, three heads, three straight heads proceeding directly to the bar, where Joran bought them three drinks.

Deepak's words suggest erections for all, and a group rape, during which the three guys all treat themselves to a drink of Natalee generously poured by Joran. Now we can put the timeline in perspective. They arrive *"in"* Carlos'n Charlie's, symbolic of Natalee via yet another container image. In a nutshell Deepak suggests three assaults, taking 30 minutes altogether—10 minutes per assailant—which Deepak further suggests when he tells us *"so i got off my shift at 10 pm"* (read after 10 minutes). Clearly the assaults ended because of *"closing"* time for Natalee, a distinct reference to her death.

Deepak indicates that the assaults started at about *"12:30 am,"* suggesting the embedded time of *"1:30 am."* That would fit perfectly with leaving the club with Natalee in tow between 1 and 1:15 am, a time which can be accurately determined in light of the bar's known closing time. It's further supported by the testimony of eyewitnesses who saw

Joran and Natalee leaving the club at that time. The bar's party atmosphere quickly gave way to another kind of party entirely, a sex party at which Natalee was an unwilling invitee. Once the guys got her in the car, her fate was sealed. In Deepak's story they head straight for the bar, and other such clues of a sudden, rapid assault will soon unfold, followed before long by images of an equally sudden, unexpected death.

All in all we find a striking suggestion that Natalee died about 2 am—precisely 30 minutes after the group rape started. In Deepak's embedded time frame, the closing time of 1 am becomes 2 am, **with all other times simply moved forward an hour.** If we then start with this time frame in mind it will help keep us oriented. We also notice Deepak's slip of "*1 pm*" instead of "1 am" (strikingly similar to "I am"), suggesting the condensed message and confession "I am responsible for Natalee being postmortem, post-murder," meaning "after I/we killed her." With "pm" we now have a second definitive suggestion that Natalee died at 2 am.

But look again at Deepak's declaration, "*i got off my shift at 10 pm*" and in "*10 pm*" we find another perfect embedded match. As cryptographers know well, to understand encoded numerology we must first pay primary attention to the numbers 1 to 9, ignoring all zeros, which makes "10 pm" the same as "1 pm" with Deepak's decoded message being "I got off Natalee at 2 am." Now we have yet a third definitive suggestion from Deepak's brilliant, unconscious mind that Natalee died at 2 am. (Previously Deepak has made it abundantly plain that he was sexually assaulting Natalee when she died.)

Once again Deepak appears to be speaking in Natalee's own voice as in "I am now postmortem, deceased. My life has suddenly fast-forwarded to its end." Mercifully for her sake, the rape was short-lived.

Now, as Deepak picks up his narrative, we turn to the important matter of phone calls relating to Natalee. Make no mistake about it—as in the rest of his email—all of his mentions of phone calls and timelines regarding Natalee contain deeper L-2 messages.

## Joran's Second Phone Call: Body Taken to Joran's House

"*i was at work so **my friend called me** and said hey i met some girls in the casino and her friends and they want us to meet them in carlos **tonight** do you have to **work** tomorrow morning i said no , so **he said pick me up later** then i said ok.so i got off my shift at 10 pm and went **home** took a bath had to fix something and then me and my younger*

*brother went to pick up my friend was around 12.10 am so i came to*
**his home"**

A lot went on at Joran's house that night. You want the truth, right, Beth? The deeper story? Just follow my deeper story line. Notice how quickly I bring his house into the story and how often. You can see how I immediately link the planning of the body drop to being at Joran's house. This is a major clue. Don't ignore it as just some minor detail. *Keep in mind that, unconsciously in my entire email, I'm always talking about what happened after Natalee's death.* That's when it was written. And in my deeper, non-cover-up story, Natalee has just died following our attack. I can't say it any more clearly than I just did, in Natalee's own voice: *"today is the last day I will be."*

Stay tuned to the subject matter, the flow of my ideas, and then you'll get the big picture. Here Joran makes a phone call to a friend to make plans about a girl he met, and arranges a meeting at his house to further discuss what everyone's going to do. See where I'm going? Sure, it just seems like I'm talking about picking up Joran earlier, but I'm also describing *"later"*—after Natalee's lying there dead in my car. That's why I used the word *"later"* so often.

Look again at what we did at Joran's house: in the deeper story we planned on checking out a girl he—or really we—*"met"* before. Since we've actually already *"met"* her by now and she's dead, what would you think we're planning next for Natalee? Of course: how to get rid of the body. And because all this planning happens after the fact at Joran's house, that tells you we had her body with us when we ended up at his place to figure out how to get rid of it. I'm telling you that a lot went on at Joran's house *after* Natalee died.

But notice something crucial: what brings us to Joran's house? A phone call, and somebody tells us to come over. In reality Natalee had just died in our arms, and Joran was dialing his cell. Who was he calling in the real story, to arrange this meeting at his house? Who am I suggesting was on the phone telling us to come to his house, even as I was by Joran's side? Obviously it could only be one person— Joran's father, Paulus van der Sloot. And just to make sure you get the picture, I confirm in vivid detail this same idea, later on in my email.

[Later in email] *"so i drove to whyndham and . . .* **my friends dad called him** *and said the police is at his home  . . .* **its about the girl** *you guys went out with yesterday , so my friend said wait there i be there, so* **we rushed _at_ my friends home"**

You can see the picture more clearly in a later scene in my surface story, when I describe the moment the police arrived at Joran's house the next night and Paulus called us to come home. Check out the flow of ideas: an emergency arises regarding Natalee, who is now missing; a phone call takes place between Paulus at home and Joran on his cell phone, with me at his side, with Joran being instructed to come home because we're in trouble with the police over Natalee.

Immediately we rushed to Joran's house—without Satish who was not with us—in such a panic I make a slip *"rushed at"* his house. Throughout my email I will often use one picture to describe two similar scenes. Without question, Joran called Paulus immediately when we were in trouble.

Of course we were panicked! What could be more important than to get rid of this dead tourist girl's body? That whole dark morning it seemed that I was constantly driving like a maniac over to Joran's house in Noord, all because of Natalee.

And my slip, *"we rushed **at** my friends home"* instead of the obvious 'rushed **to**' also tells you how rushed we were once we arrived at Joran's house in a panic, with Natalee's body. The meeting, as I'm about to tell you, lasted only 15 minutes. We had to move fast.

If you look closely you can also see that I earlier confirmed the idea of ending up at Joran's house by mentioning that detail three times altogether. Remember before, when I described Natalee's death, when I have her saying *"today is my last day"*? Yeah, that's the story I told the cops, too, about Joran and Natalee having a drink at a bar, and right after that I hinted that Joran left and returned to his house before going out that night—from where he called me. But go deeper. Follow my deeper line of thinking—all three times we end up at Joran's house after I've already made it clear that Natalee died. When I think of Natalee's death I think of going to Joran's house.

## News Clips: Assault, Death, to Joran's House

*"me and my younger brother went to pick up my friend was around 12.10 am so i came to his home"*

Now, Beth, re-arrange my sentence a bit and you'll see another way I describe the circumstances that turned our world upside down and brought us to Joran's house, scared out of our wits. Juts add in a few important pauses: " . . . *me and my younger brother went to [a] pick up–my friend was around–12:10 am–so I came–to his home . . . .*" Both Satish and I went to see a *"pick up"*—that is we had sex with Natalee, whom we treated like a prostitute just like Joran had—and Joran was right there *"around"* us, watching. Like I already told you, he was controlling Natalee while we did what we wanted.

You can also see again that I went last in having sex with her because I'm telling you the moment it was all over—the moment Natalee choked—and we had to take her to Joran's house: *". . . my friend was around–) so I came–to his home . . . ."* Just when *"I came,"* just when I was having a climax. I wasn't paying any attention to her because I was right in the middle of having an orgasm, and suddenly Natalee's dead, and before long we ended up at Joran's home. Think of TV news clips and you can see the news I strung together here— bang, bang, bang—using plain words packed with meaning.

And don't overlook my repeated suggestion in *"my friend was around–12:10 am–so I came"* that the time of Natalee's death was **about** 2:10 am, not far from the more precise time of 2 am. Clearly this fits with my other indications that the assault started at 1:30 am and she died at 2 am.

Certainly someone with such an obsessive time-consciousness as Deepak would know the exact time of death, especially a sudden death linked with his own sexual climax. As powerful an occurrence as an orgasm, linked inextricably to Natalee's death, would be frozen in his mind forever. Clearly, 2 to 2:10 am also fits well with the time of Natalee's death in yet another way, as we will see in a moment when we discuss the eyewitness who saw the three guys out in a car around 2:15 am.

# What Happened at Joran's Home—the Talk

*"to his home and **was talked for like 15 min** and then left to go to carlos (we all went out without **or parents knew**) so we arrived like 12.30 am in carlos (carlos is closing 1 pm ) . . . "*

So why did we go to Joran's house? Oops! Here's another slip! My slips are doors left open just a crack, doors for you to open wider, doors to the truth. Now you can see convincing clues that Joran called his father right after Natalee died.

My first slip was *"was talked (to)"* when I meant to say 'we talked'—and yes, I'm really talking, really confessing here. *"was talked to"* makes us look like passive sheep, like listeners being lectured by somebody. And who might that be? My next slip, the abbreviation *"min"* also implies 'men' or, to be specific, 'man.' I'm telling you we were talked to by a man for 15 minutes. He did most of the talking and he did it in Joran's home—and I was there. It's obvious I'm pointing to one man, Joran's father, Paulus. Like I said, that's why I keep mentioning Joran's home over and over again. Later I will describe exactly how Paulus *"talked to"* us, using those very words.

Are you still wondering when Paulus found out about Natalee's death, Beth? Well here's another big slip, *"we all went out without **or parents knew**."* Here I am trying to say that our parents didn't know we were out, but instead I tell you *"or parents knew."* And who knew the most? Paulus, because we brought Natalee's body home to him. And believe me, he wasn't happy about it.

Check it out. Here's what I'd be saying without the slip: *"we all went out—without our parents . . . "* That is, we all went out like we always do, we all thought about what we wanted to do, not what our parents would want us to do. We were our wild and crazy selves, and now Paulus was joining us, enabling us. Our mindset was that there's no parental supervision, nobody tells us what to do, and really, under the circumstances, that was Paulus' mindset too even though he'd have a hard time admitting it.

To remove all doubt that Paulus talked to us that night, there's one last slip when I say that *" . . . (was talked for like 15 min) and then left to go to **carlos** . . . so we arrived . . . in **carlos** (**carlos** is closing 1 pm ) . . . ."* Three times I turn Carlos'n Charlie's into the name of one man, Carlos, telling you that one specific man sent us on our way to dispose of the body—not 'Carlos' but Paulus. Just for good measure I put one man's signature all over the plan, 'carlos, carlos, carlos,' to clue you in to that the real Carlos, the man behind the plan, was Paulus. In fact, I put Paulus' name indirectly as *"parent"* right between the three *"carlos."* You must be able to see that, Beth. Since Joran was underage and his father, Paulus, always let him go to *"carlos,"* it's just natural to link their names, both of them six letters and each ending in 'los' or 'lus.'

But our fun was over and now we had to get to work. This work was so serious that we needed adult supervision. See, Paulus was OK with us being at Carlos'n Charlie's, our pickup spot, our meat market. Now he would help us hide our dirty deeds.

## More Suggestions of Paulus' Early Involvement

The above certainly fits with Dave Holloway's discussion with Paulus van der Sloot in June 2005, shortly after Natalee's disappearance. Dave talked to Paulus for 45 minutes after running into him at the jail in which Joran was incarcerated. Paulus told Dave that Joran wasn't raised to leave a young girl on the beach alone. Read between the lines of Paulus' response. Not only does he suggest that Joran indeed took Natalee's body to the beach—read "ocean"—he is linking himself, as Joran's parent, to Joran's actions.

In short, Paulus is suggesting that Joran didn't dump the body on his own but that Paulus helped him concoct the plan. Paulus also reportedly echoed his statements to Dave Holloway in a talk with the headmaster at Joran's school. Like Deepak Kalpoe, Paulus van der Sloot harbors a strong urge to confess.

In addition, several of Natalee's male classmates on the Aruba trip insisted to me that if they had found themselves in similar circumstances, with the untimely death of a girl on their hands—no matter what—they would first call their father. And Joran wouldn't even have had the normal teenager's hesitancy about involving his father, since the two of them were partying buddies. Paulus surely would have wanted to see the evidence himself, and he would have wanted some time to think the plan through from there. Deepak's email thoughtprints reveal that soon after Natalee's death Paulus was deeply involved in the cover-up.

## Next Step: The Plan to Dump the Body

*"so i came to his home and was talked for like 15 min and then left to go to carlos (we all went out without or parents knew) so we arrived like 12.30 am in carlos (carlos is closing 1 pm ) and headed straight for the bar and bought 3 drinks my friend paid for them"*

Deepak continues:

Paulus quickly helped us settle on a plan—like I said, we really rushed things at his house. When we got to Joran's house, his father didn't waste any time. We came up with a plan in *"like 15 min"* and we were on our way.

Remember how similar *"carlos"* is to 'Paulus'and you can see me telling you in more detail about our journey to Paulus' house and where we went after that. Again substituting 'Paulus' for *"carlos"* read the time sequence like this: *"left to go to Paulus (carlos)—Paulus (parent) knew—arrived in Paulus (carlos)—Paulus closing (soon-- we were not there long, 15 min as I just said)—and headed straight for bar."* Boom, boom, boom.

So where did we take the body? Paulus' plan was to head straight for the sandbar –to the ocean out beyond the sandbar--and to dump her body as fast as we could. It was closing time, all right, closing time for Natalee Holloway.

Something this important I will repeat, so later I'll describe Natalee on display next to a bar in Carlos'n Charlie's, her body standing out next to a bar. He wouldn't like this but they should name that sandbar 'Paulus.'

Already I told you in *"we arrived like 12.30 am in carlos . . . headed straight for the bar and **bought 3 drinks my friend paid for them**,"* about the sexual part of this story, but now I want you to think about yet another type of bar, the legal bar as in 'barrister' or 'lawyer.' Remember I'm still talking here about Paulus' plan. Before we headed out to carry out our plan, Paulus assured me that he'd help my brother and I get to that bar too. Look what else I'm suggesting—that Paulus promised he would help pay for legal expenses if my folks couldn't, and they didn't have a lot of money. I'll come back to that, so don't worry.

We've already heard about Paulus arranging for the Kalpoe brothers' attorney. It would make sense that Paulus, deeply concerned about Joran, would want to provide as much protection as possible for Joran's cohorts in crime, since they would be crucial to Joran's defense.

## The Fix: The Suspects' Staging and Natalee's Precise Time of Death

*"**work tomorrow morning** . . . so he [she] said pick me up later then i said ok. so i got off my shift at 10 pm and **went home took a bath had to fix something** . . . me and my younger brother"*

Now we return to the timeline the three guys attempted to establish. If someone was on Deepak's computer around 2:30 am, that means the boys had about 30 minutes after Natalee died to get their act together and decide what to do, particularly what to do with her body. How did they best shift into cover-up mode? After Natalee's sudden death and the failed resuscitation, the suspects' initial panic would have subsided. When they finally got a smattering of their wits about them, Joran called Paulus.

An eyewitness saw three guys in Deepak's Honda near the Fisherman's Huts at about 2:15 am, mere minutes after Natalee died. Knowing that they'd been spotted might've reignited their sense of panic, further prompting the call to Paulus—or perhaps they had just called him.

We can see another specific part of the timeline that leaps out at us in *"work tomorrow morning . . . so he [she] said pick me up later then i said ok. so i got off my shift at 10 pm and went home took a bath had to fix something . . . me and my younger brother."* Not long after Deepak, the last assailant, "got off his shift" and quit cruising with Natalee, he headed for home with his brother to take a bath and *"to fix something."* Right off, Deepak strongly suggests that he was personally involved in The Fix or staging, making things look one way when they're actually another.

The word "staging" typically describes murder scenes in which the perpetrator tried to disguise key features of the crime. In this case, the three guys resorted to staging to create false alibis and a false story about what happened to Natalee. Using "had" as in *"had to fix something"* further suggests that Deepak was acting in desperation.

In several different ways, Deepak suggests the fix was on soon after Natalee's death. First, immediately preceding *"fix"* he suggests the hidden sentence substituting "she" for "he": *"work tomorrow morning . . . so she [for he] said pick me up later then i said ok* ." This matches identically a later sentence in which Deepak quotes Natalee first-person, issuing the same command, suggesting strongly that Deepak's initial assignment was to set up an alibi before "later" disposing of Natalee's body.

This scenario also fits *"tomorrow morning,"* translated as some time later but still in the early morning. Also getting off his shift at the specific time of *"10 pm"* matches his slip *"1 pm"* (instead of 1 am), which we decoded as 2 am with pm suggesting postmortem. Not only does this fit perfectly with Deepak dismounting from his shift precisely at the moment of Natalee's death at 2 am, it is also further confirmation that Deepak was the assailant at the specific time of her death. Again with his unconscious mind now having suggested in *three distinctly different and precise ways*—powerful matching thoughtprints—*that Natalee died suddenly at 2 am*, we can now locate precisely the exact time of Natalee's death according to Deepak's email.

Now, with Deepak's immediate message *"went home took a bath had to fix something . . . me and my younger brother"* coming right on the heels of the specific time of death, *"i got off my shift at 10 pm"* (translated at 2 am) undeniably suggests one strong probability. Deepak and Satish quickly went to their house right after Natalee died, with plans to bury her body—literally to pick it up—later.

## Next: To Joran's House

*"and then me and my younger brother went to pick up my friend was around 12.10 am so i came to **his home** and was talked for like 15 min and then left to go to carlos (we all went out without or parents knew) so we arrived like 12.30 am in carlos (carlos is closing 1 pm ) and headed straight for the bar and bought 3 drinks my friend paid for them"*

The sequence is striking and so logical if, indeed, the fix was on. First swinging by Deepak's house in Hooiberg and "fixing something," the boys next headed for Joran's house to "pick him up" by helping him cover up.

Deepak suggests that what they fixed was to create the appearance that he was home on his computer. Given the 2:30 am computer-use timeline, it's likely that Satish logged onto Deepak's personal computer using Deepak's username and password. With that subterfuge in place, Deepak drove on to Joran's house with him, with Natalee's body in the trunk of Deepak's car. The idea of not having any work to do in the morning also suggests Satish was at home doing nothing, except pretending to be Deepak.

As they drove the six miles or so from Hooiberg to Noord, where they'd confer with Paulus, Deepak and Joran could have easily made it appear that they were communicating with each other from afar via their cell phones. We can almost hear them conspiring:

"We'll just say we dropped you and her off at the beach by the Marriott, Joran," Deepak might've said, dialing frantically. "People know she'd never go off alone with me and Satish."

"Yeah, man, and then you can call and check up on me. See if I got a ride home," Joran could have replied.

The so-called "hard evidence" timeline makes it look as though Joran was walking home, while all the time they were sitting side by side, first in Deepak's Honda and then in Joran's house. The reported time of the first cell phone call was about 2:50 am, in which Joran, reportedly out of breath, was supposedly walking 2.5 miles home but was not yet there. Decoding that message, we find the suggestion that the two boys were driving as fast as possible toward Joran's house to meet with Paulus, but they'd not yet arrived.

Along these lines Deepak, noted later in a police interview that when he was being questioned on the night following Natalee's disappearance, on May 31, 2005, he made a cell phone call to Satish on *his* cell phone while pretending to be calling home and speaking to his mother. In short, Deepak quickly confesses to establishing a pattern of phony communications by using cell phones.

Other factors suggesting Satish was at home include:

- Deepak wanted to protect his younger brother, so he left him at home to do some staging on the computer, but would not involve him with the body-dump.

- As Deepak described in his June 4 email, when the Twittys arrived later on May 30, he and Joran rushed to Noord without Satish to meet with Paulus and answer questions about Natalee being missing.

- On that next night, May 30, Deepak was at Joran's house without Satish, still working out their cover-up plans before the Twittys arrived.

Of course the idea of Deepak going home and taking a bath alludes to his attempt to cleanse himself of his guilt through a cover-up, and also how he and Satish thoroughly cleaned his car, which likely took place later in the morning. Staging such a computer cover-up again points to Paulus' early involvement and quick thinking. It's doubtful that three young men, inexperienced and in the jam of their lives, would have been able to come up with such strategy so quickly.

Deepak's cover-up also sheds light on a major disagreement between Joran and Deepak/Satish after they began blaming each other in different versions of the beach story. One major contention, though minor on the surface, was whether the boys had first taken Natalee by Joran's house before heading to the beach. While Joran insisted they had done so the Kalpoe brothers adamantly insisted that they had not—likely because they wanted to distance themselves from the possibility of having been at Joran's house after Natalee disappeared, and thus involved in disposing of her body.

> *"and then me and my younger brother went to pick up my friend was around 12.10 am so i came to **his home** and was talked for like 15 min and then left to go to carlos (we all went out without or parents knew) so we arrived like 12.30 am in carlos (carlos is closing 1 pm ) and headed straight for the bar and bought 3 drinks my friend paid for them"*

Continuing to follow Deepak's sequential messaging, he locates the arrival at Joran's house at *"like 12:10 am."* The main suggestion apparent here, given the known time frame, points to "12:10 am" as containing the embedded time "3:10 am" (12 am = 1 + 2 = 3 am, thus 3:10 am). If the boys got to Deepak's house around 2:30 am or slightly later, then 3:10 am wouldn't be out of the question.

But shortly, Deepak will make another suggestion about what they did. He continues to elaborate on time with a quick 15-minute lecture from Paulus. Perhaps with the words "no body, no case" ringing in their ears, Deepak and Joran then headed out for the ocean, out beyond the sandbar. But Deepak's message *"(we all went out without or parents knew),"* set off by the special parentheses marker, suggests that whoever provided the boat did indeed slip out without their parents' knowledge. In that short parenthetical phrase, Deepak unmistakably implies more than one set of parents.

So, now we have a possible explanation for the 40-minute time gap between dropping Satish home at 2:30 am and arriving at Joran's house at 3:10 am. It's possible that Joran and Deepak had taken time to pick up another teenager—the boat driver—who sneaked out of his home without his parents realizing it. Deepak could have easily swung by the driver's house and quietly picked him up, without awakening his parents, after initially making cell phone contact with him.

Deepak suggests that, after a harried 15-minute meeting, the boys headed straight for the ocean sandbar. In that case, they would have launched the boat around "12:30 am" which, as we've seen, can be decoded as 3:30 am. Also the idea of Joran buying three drinks suggests three boys were involved in taking Natalee's body to the ocean, treating her to a drink: Joran, Deepak, and one other. Thus we see how one story, about going to Carlos'n Charlie's, can be used in two different ways to describe both the rape and the cover-up.

Meanwhile, several times in his email, Deepak hints that he was there when they disposed of Natalee's body. He will hear Natalee say goodbye, and he will insist that he was present when they dropped her off into the ocean and helped lift her body into the water. The hotel story also supports the idea that Deepak was involved all the way to the end with Natalee's body.

A number of other possibilities certainly exist, particularly if no one was actually on Deepak's computer at 2:30 am. It's possible Deepak could have fixed things at his house by simply manipulating the computer time. Or Deepak and Satish could have gone home by themselves and let Joran dispose of the body, with Paulus' help, which would clearly have given them access to another car. Paulus then could have dropped Joran off near the marina and arranged a body-dump.

Overall, the crucial message is that the "fix" was in, one way or the other. This brings us to another idea about "bath," a key message that Deepak delivers. Let's let him explain it.

## To the Ocean in a Container

*"went home took a **bath** had to fix something . . . me and my younger brother"*

Now think of *"bath"* and think of Natalee's body, one of the main subjects of this entire email. A bath involves water, so I'm painting you a picture of where Natalee's body lies, surrounded by water. In other words, we dumped Natalee's body in the water, gave her a bath, dropped her in the drink.

Also, you take a bath in a bathtub—a container, a solid container that doesn't move, within a larger space like a house—and 'fixing' an object means to secure it in place. Now you have another picture that includes Natalee's body in water, within a solid container, surrounded by a larger body of water, the ocean. This explains how we solved our last dilemma, by putting Natalee's body into a container before we dumped it in the ocean. We put it into something guaranteed to get to the ocean floor and stay there. Notice how clearly the order speaks: first we put her in a container, *"the bath,"* so that we could then *"fix"* it in place at the bottom of the ocean.

By now you also know that right around this time a large, heavy fishing cage big enough to hold a body went missing from the Fisherman's Huts area next to the Holiday Inn. Under no circumstances did we want her body floating to the top, like the body of Scott Peterson's wife, Lacy. That was fresh on all our minds because we all watch cable TV news down here. Peterson dumped Lacy in San Francisco Bay, but it came back to haunt him. In fact, that was a big part of the discussion that night. You can see what we decided. We knew there were big cages at Fisherman's Huts, and so we took one.

In a revealing comment from a police interview Deepak gave another reason (in addition to ants in it) for vacuuming and cleaning his car right after the crime—because Joran had got sand in it from being in the water. The decoded message: we had to clean the car because Joran had gotten water and sand in it from dumping Natalee's body in the ocean.

## Definite Timeline

The more we decode Deepak's unconscious messages we are again struck by the absolute genius of the deeper mind. As we consider Deepak's fix—staging of the crime—we now have some definite confessions in place regarding the timeline. We can see that Deepak's elaborations have a purpose here, with repeated time references.

Almost certainly Deepak has revealed the following:

- Natalee was brutally assaulted shortly after they all left Carlos'n Charlie's, beginning at 1:30, by the three suspects.

- She died 30 minutes later, at 2 am.

- At that point, Deepak and Satish quickly went by their own house—around 2:30 am if Deepak's computer timeline is accurate—to establish an alibi even while Natalee's body was still in Deepak's car.

- Not long after that, with Satish staying at his and Deepak's house, Joran and Deepak proceeded to Joran's house where Paulus told the boys what to do with the body.

- Deepak also suggests that, prior to that meeting, he and Joran picked up another friend who sneaked out to provide the boat, and who was at the meeting with Paulus. Then they immediately proceeded to the ocean, using a boat to transport her body out past the sandbar.

All in all, Deepak's thoughtprints point to a swift assault on Natalee, a sudden death, a quick trip to Joran's to come up with a cover-up plan, and a short trip with the body to dump it in the sea. Later police reports will also suggest a quick disposal of the body. The girl's corpse was a damning piece of evidence. It had to be dealt with promptly.

## A Unique Witness

A witness, a local gardener named Chumpa, reportedly drove past the three boys around 2:15 am while they were parked in Deepak's Honda, on a side road near the Racquet Club directly behind the Fisherman's Huts area, on the beach next to the Holiday Inn. Dave Holloway personally had this witness checked out by his investigator, who validated that he was reliable. Aruban police, on the other hand, discounted his testimony. As he drove by, Joran sat in the driver's seat with Deepak next to him and Satish in the backseat, attempting to duck down to avoid being seen. Judging from this timeline and the one Deepak suggests, this sighting took place immediately following Natalee's death.

We can speculate about some reasonable possibilities. Surely after Natalee suddenly died on them, the three guys would be totally fixated on hiding the body. As an initial move, just to get it out of sight, they probably placed it in the trunk. They'd want to get their wits about them, to go someplace and think for a minute, to cool off and figure out how to come out clean. But for some reason Joran was driving even though he was underage and unlicensed.

Considering the plan they were formulating, however, it makes sense that Joran would drive. For one thing, Deepak was probably in a complete panic. With his father's connections, Joran would be the natural one to take over, putting aside any worries about driving without a license. Parking behind the Fisherman's Huts (from where the cage would soon go missing) implies that they had already eyeballed that area. On an island as small as Aruba their options were truly limited, as Deepak will soon remind us.

The fact that Satish tried to hide in the backseat suggests that the gardener caught them off guard as they were just beginning to plan their cover-up. They clearly had something to hide, and they were most likely already discussing plans to separate and cover up the otherwise incriminating fact that Natalee had last been seen with the three of them.

Obviously they did not want to be seen together. This suggests the three guys had already called Joran's father, far and away their most logical move.

## Deepak Makes Case for Paulus' Early Involvement

As we think back over the trip to Joran's house we can envision Deepak himself making the case for Paulus' early involvement. Surely Paulus called on everything within himself—his forceful, fatherly personality as well as his legal background—to try to calm the boys down.

> Now step back and look at this plan, Beth. Do you think we came up with it on our own, when all three of us were in a state of panic? Do you think we would have thought of things like quickly splitting up to establish alibis, getting on our computers and cell phones, putting the body in a container, and disposing of it in the ocean? Doesn't this plan have the ring of Paulus' famous words—"no body, no case"— written all over it? We considered other things, like burying the body on the island, but being in such a tremendous predicament, not sure about what to do, we needed a cooler, wiser head, like that of a good lawyer.

> Is there any wonder why, later in my email, I describe our talking with Paulus as, "*also his dad is pretty cool he calmes us down and **talks to us** also not to worry.*" My words –"*talks to*"—are now clearly connected to Paulus, talking to us, both confirming the earlier idea that indeed we were talked to by him shortly after Natalee died and that he tried to keep us from worrying.

## Police Interview Suggests Paulus' Early Involvement

It's well known that the chief of the Aruban Police Corps when Natalee disappeared was Jan van der Straten, a close friend of Paulus. In various interviews, Joran's parents repeatedly recalled calling 'Jan' frequently about various concerns they had early in the case. Van der Straten's official interview of Joran on June 13, 2005, as a major suspect in the case, was unimaginably lacking as an interrogation and equally as brief. In an early interview with Paulus around the same time, however, van der Straten actually accused his friend of concealing information: "I confront Paul with the proposition that he knows exactly what happened that night," the chief said.

Interestingly, in the same interview, van der Straten also commented, "I ask Paul if he thinks it is respectful to leave a girl of 18 years old alone on the beach after his son was satisfied," suggesting that unconsciously the police chief was picking up even more about Paulus' early involvement. Paulus responded, "No, for sure not. We as parents cannot agree with that." Reading through Paulus' denial—a key decoding tactic at select moments—we find Paulus suggesting himself that he was in on the cover-up from the beginning and specifically 'agreed' that Natalee's body should be dumped into the ocean.

## Joran's Buddies: Koen and Sander Gottenbos

To dump the body in the ocean the boys needed a boat. How easily could Joran have accessed a boat, and how quickly? As it happened, the father of one of Joran's best friends had a boat nearby. Koen Gottenbos was one of a tight circle of five young guys, which included Joran. According to statements Joran made to police, Koen's father had a "speedboat." It was moored nearby at the dock between the Holiday Inn and the Marriott, the northernmost hotel between two miles of barren beach and the lighthouse.

On the other (north) side of the Marriott, just a stone's throw away, was the Fisherman's Huts area—a beachfront dotted with small huts containing fishing gear. Many local fishermen routinely came and went from the huts. Dave Holloway saw a sandbar 15 feet in front of the secluded Fisherman's Huts area, a place where a boat could easily dock, allowing a body to be quickly loaded into the boat under the cover of darkness. "Coincidentally" the extra-large crab cage, big enough to hold a human body, went missing from the area around that time, again as has been commonly reported and confirmed to me by Dave Holloway through investigators.

Even more convincing is the police interview with Koen's younger brother. Aruban police spoke with Sander Gottenbos on June 16, 2005, approximately two weeks after Natalee's disappearance. Though doubts exist about whether the police actually interviewed Koen, they certainly did speak with his younger brother, Sander, and he revealed to them that he had invited Joran to ride on his father's *"speedboat"* around 11 am on Sunday, May 29, the same day on which Joran later met Natalee. Sander said that Joran declined, complaining that boat rides made him sick. Emphatically Sander insisted, *"Joran had never been on our boat!"* Even so, as we will explore below, Sander suggests that Joran had indeed been on his boat later that very day.

Then Sander made a far more telling comment during the interrogation: *"I say that I would put my hands in the fire for Joran. He would never do something like that. I would do also for Satish and Deepak, although I haven't known them as long."*

Sander's striking image, "Put my hands in the fire," suggests high-risk, potentially self-damaging behavior, meaning very dangerous involvement. "Hands in fire" further suggests something hot to the touch, a "hot potato." And "fire" indirectly calls for water to put out the fire, or to put "hands in water."

Clearly, Sander is putting his hands in something hot. Also, notice Sander's unique slip—it's not "a fire" but *"The Fire"* as in one particular fire, one particularly dangerous and difficult matter involving all three suspects. Subtly but strongly, Sander suggests here that he was involved in handling the hot potato—Natalee's body—probably touching it with his own hands, and that he helped take it to her ocean grave, maybe even putting his hands in the water as he lowered the cage which contained her body from his father's "speedboat." Though her body would have been cold by now, Sander suggests that Natalee's body in another way was hot as fire, and the water into which he helped dump her was boiling and bubbling with danger.

How well this fits with a red-hot case, with the authorities apparently in hot pursuit! The Natalee Holloway case was and is a hot story, with millions of people focusing on its details via the media and the Internet. Within the year the search for Natalee's body itself became a red-hot topic, as several teams of searchers scoured the island and made a series of deep-sea dives. As a possible accessory to a murder, as someone who helped hide the victim's body, Sander certainly placed himself in hot water. By disposing of that key evidence he unquestionably took a huge personal risk, especially if he had nothing to do with the crime itself. But don't forget why Sander was willing to risk everything. He said it himself: he did it for Joran.

As if his connection to Joran wasn't enough in itself, Sander volunteers that he'd do the same thing for Deepak and Satish, hinting that's exactly what he did, even though, in fact, he barely knew them. In saying he would put his "hands in the fire" for these three guys, Sander uses a vivid, hellish metaphor to say, "I took a huge risk, a foolish risk, as big a risk as you can take." Disposing of the body surely qualifies as such a gargantuan risk, potentially self-destructive to the extreme. Since it was his own metaphor, Sander surely felt a figurative pain in his hands, suggesting the image of an eternal pain inflicted on the guilty by the flames of hell.

Reviewing Sander's thoughtprints, we see that he suggests the following:

- He gave Joran a ride in his father's speedboat early on the morning of May 30, a ride that thoroughly upset Joran (and Sander himself)—made him sick—because he had to dispose of Natalee's body.

- In his reference to seasickness, Sander suggests also that Joran told him what had happened to Natalee—how she had got sick and stopped the ride they had all been enjoying in Deepak's car. We can easily imagine Joran recounting the most memorable events of that dark night.

- Sander's denial that Joran "had never been in our boat" suggests that clearly he had, and that "our" boat possibly meant that someone else went with them on the ride—if so, it would almost certainly have been his older brother, Koen, who was Joran's better friend. However, Deepak's email suggests that Koen probably did not go—just three people, total.

- By describing his family's fishing boat as a "speedboat," Sander suggests that when they disposed of the body the vessel did indeed become a fast boat, speeding out to its destination. In actuality his boat is reportedly not a true speedboat at all, but more of a fishing boat with a large open space in its center.

Sander then goes on to provide other details. His memory is shaky as to whether he had Internet or other contact with Joran on May 29 or

30. He told the authorities, *"I may have,"* suggesting that he did. Obviously he remembers dates well, and even specific times, such as inviting Joran at 11 am to ride in his father's boat. Yet Sander seems to suffer memory lapses when asked questions whose honest answers might implicate him or the others.

Coincidentally, he said he lost his cell phone at school on May 30, the day that Natalee died and was buried at sea. Is it possible that such a cell phone, one not belonging to Joran and not easily traceable, would have been used in working out the logistics for rapidly disposing of Natalee's body?

In his interview with police, Sander describes significant contact between Paulus and the Gottenbos parents regarding the situation. In the end, seemingly in response to all the pressure brought to bear by the investigative focus on his own sons, their father sold his business and moved the entire family to the United States. By relocating to North America, where they could find relative anonymity, Mr. Gottenbos suggests that he is protecting his two sons from falling under the growing cloud of suspicion in tiny Aruba. Koen reportedly now attends school in Holland.

Of course the police strongly suspected that Natalee's body was in the ocean, and that the Gottenbos brothers were involved. Additional clues could lay hidden in Koen's police interviews, if they were actually done and if they were thorough.

## Joran's Interviews and the Suspects' Behavior

In a police interview, Joran reported that late in the afternoon of May 30, some 18 hours after leaving Natalee on the beach, he walked from the Racquet Club to the casinos in the beach hotels, passing near to where he had left Natalee on the beach—but that he didn't stop to check to see if she was still lying there. Obviously we can see straight through Joran's ridiculous attempt at a cover-up story—the possibility that 18 hours later Natalee would still be lying on the beach.

But look at what else he suggests: that Natalee indeed is still lying near the beach, meaning in the ocean, permanently. He further suggests that he was checking to verify that her body remained lying in the ocean—just as he and Deepak apparently checked the beach to see if her body had washed up.

## Police Theory: Body Dumped Next Night

Dave Holloway said police believe that Natalee's body remained on the island for some 19 to 22 hours after she died, and that Joran, with assistance, dumped her in the Caribbean on the evening of May 30. Detectives surmised that the three suspects hid the body in the thick brush near the Fisherman's Huts right after Natalee died. At the same time, police believe that's when they spotted the large fishing cage supposedly unprotected outside the locked huts containing fishing gear—which they later stole. Then, sometime shortly after sunset of that same day, they stuffed Natalee's body into that cage and drove it out to sea.

Police have adopted this scenario because of significant gaps apparently arising in Joran's and Koen's time frames for the events of the afternoon of May 30. Their alibis for that day also remain unsubstantiated. Joran did not actually show up at the casinos early that evening as he reported, leaving a significant period of time unaccounted for. Joran also failed to attend school that day, which in itself suggests Paulus' early involvement. Interestingly, when he was interviewed by police Paulus could not remember for sure if Joran went to school that day.

## Police Theory: Paulus Involved Later

Police also believe Paulus became involved only *after* the disposal of the body had been completed. To some extent, Beth Twitty and Dave Holloway share this view of Paulus' involvement, believing that he may not have found out about his son's trouble until the early hours of May 31, when confronted by Beth and her entourage.

However, given the evidence at hand—and especially Deepak's hidden confession—it's apparent that the body was dumped before dawn. There are also major problems with the police's hidden-body scenario. The very idea of the three boys waiting to dispose of the body late on May 30, some 19 hours or so after Natalee's death, contradicts common sense. For one thing they'd be taking a huge risk of the body being discovered. Also, by late that afternoon rigor mortis would have set into Natalee's body making it difficult if not impossible to manipulate it into a cage. Putting her into the cage beforehand and then hiding the cage would have been even riskier than hiding the body by itself. Suppose the fisherman goes looking for his cage?

It's much more likely that, the minute they knew that Natalee was dead, Joran, Deepak and Satish would have realized they were operating in an entirely new world. They would have understood the need to leave no clues. They knew they had to get rid of that girl's body, and fast. They certainly would have wanted an on-the-spot consultation from an expert to make sure they weren't overlooking any obvious clues. Who better to call under those circumstances than Joran's father, Paulus?

Not only would Joran's party pal understand how a little "fun" from Carlos'n Charlie's could have turned into a nightmare, but with his legal background and his courtroom connections he could help them out of this jam. Because it had happened in Deepak's car, and because he and Satish came from a lower class, the Kalpoe brothers would have gladly welcomed the advice and assistance of their friend's father. Paulus would surely have reiterated the boys' own priority, the dire need to get rid of the body without delay. It was Paulus, remember, who reportedly uttered those infamous words, "no body, no case."

Did they have enough time during the darkness of those early-morning hours to get rid of the body? The pressure of the dawn deadline certainly explains Deepak's thoughtprint suggesting that they headed straight for the ocean with the body. Later he will emphasize heading forthwith to their final destination with Natalee—the Holiday Inn—when they decided to take her home.

Maybe they didn't want to chance an early-morning escapade during which they might have encountered fishermen, but it appears the boys still had time. Certainly, after observing that the area was deserted and enlisting the aid of one or two trusted friends with a boat, they could have made their move. Clearly they had time to steal the cage. Perhaps they even found the cage before going to Joran's house. After all, the gardener did see them in the Fisherman's Huts area around that time. The Racquet Club, where he basically ran into them again stands straight across the road from the huts.

Logic points toward the body being buried at sea during the early morning hours of May 30. And this logic stands completely apart from the overwhelming thoughtprint patterns that also point toward the same earlier drop, and toward Paulus' involvement from the beginning.

## Where Assault Took Place: Deepak's Car or Joran's House?

There is a question of where the assault occurred. Essentially it comes down to two probabilities—in the backseat of Deepak's Honda or in Joran's apartment, which is in a small, separate building next to his parents' house. *The thoughtprints universally point to Deepak's car—as we will continue to see throughout the email.*

Other convincing evidence also supports this theory:

- The Kalpoe brothers' obsessive cleaning of Deepak's car, in an extensive and secretive fashion

- The testimony of the eyewitness who saw the three boys at 2:15 am in Deepak's car, near the Racquet Club and Fisherman's Huts, trying to conceal the number in their group

- Joran's story about three boys having sex with a girl in the backseat of a car, specifically a Honda, suggests a perfect parallel with Natalee's situation and is a typical way in which perpetrators unconsciously confess.

## Summary of New Information

- Through classic denial—"*I was not present*"—and revealing thoughtprints, Deepak makes it clear that he was present at Natalee's rape and at her death.

- Deepak describes a brutal group sexual assault in a blatant sentence filled with sexual innuendos, "*some girls . . . they want us— to meet/ meat them tonight.*"

- Deepak describes Natalee dying at the moment he was having an orgasm while raping her, suggesting again that he was distracted.

- Largely Deepak describes the plan to dispose of Natalee's body in this scene—following their night of fun they suddenly and unexpectedly had work to do during the early morning.

- Deepak suggests that Joran's house was the central headquarters for developing the plan, and that Joran immediately called his father after Natalee died, prompting them to take her body there.

- Deepak suggests through key slips that he "*was talked to*" at Joran's house (*we all went out without **or parents knew**)*, that Paulus was involved in the plan to dispose of the body, and that he took charge and told them what to do.

- The plan involved a clear "fix" or "staging," with Deepak taking Satish home to establish an alibi by appearing to be Deepak on the computer. Meanwhile, Joran and Deepak likely arranged for a friend with a boat to help them dump Natalee's body in the ocean.

- Police interviews strongly point to one or both Gottenbos broth-ers—Sander and Koen—and suggest that they used their father's boat to help Joran bury the body at sea.

- With his obsessive preoccupation with time, Deepak offers a detailed time frame for key events including Natalee's death at 2 am following a 30 minute assault by the three suspects. Quickly, it seems that the suspects, with Paulus' counsel, established a cover-up and at about 3 am held a 15-minute meeting at Joran's house, with Paulus, before heading unimpeded to the ocean.

## Timeline Summary

**1:15 am**    Three suspects leave Carlos'n Charlie's with Natalee in Deepak's car.

**1:30 am**    Three suspects begin brutal rape on shocked Natalee.

**2:00 am**    Exactly thirty minutes later, Natalee dies suddenly and unexpectedly.

**2:10 am**    (approximately) Joran calls father, Paulus, who helps plan cover-up that includes plan to bring body to Joran's house.

**2:15 am**    (approximately) A gardener sees three suspects stopped near Racquet Club. One boy (Satish) tried to duck down out of sight. Obviously, suspects were already planning a cover-up, attempting to appear as if there were only two boys, and not three, together.

**2:30 am**    The three guys quickly drive to Deepak's house to establish an alibi, with Satish getting on computer and chatting, thus appearing to be Deepak.

**2:35 to 3:10 am** Deepak and Joran drive to Joran's house, staging phony cell phone calls/text messages to each other and thus appear to be apart, with Joran heading toward his house alone. Most likely they swung by friend/boat driver's house, where he snuck out to join Deepak and Joran. Meanwhile, Satish continues to chat intermittently on computer as Deepak.

| 3:10 am | Joran, Deepak, and boat driver arrive at Joran's house to confer with Paulus. |
|---|---|
| 3:13 am | Joran makes another phony cell phone call to Deepak: "Hey, swa (pal), I'm home." |
| 3:13 to 3:33 am | Paulus talks to three boys for fifteen minutes about plan to dump Natalee's body in ocean. Boys then immediately head for ocean/sandbar. |
| 3:25 am | Deepak (really Satish) sends two email messages to Joran, with no immediate response. |
| 3:33 to 3:56 am | Paulus on computer, appearing to be Joran, responds twice to Deepak (actually Satish), checks soccer scores, and watches porn. |
| 4:30 am | Joran is likely back home after disposing of body in ocean; visits Hotmail. Shortly thereafter, after dropping Joran off, Deepak arrives home where Satish waits. |
| 6:30 am | Paulus is on his own computer, researching the effects of drugs and alcohol together. |

# 10
# The Bar, the Drive, and the Scream

## Scene 1: Meeting Natalee at Carlos'n Charlie's

Deepak will soon return to "The Plan" that was developed after Natalee's death, but now he recalls the scene in which the three predators first met Natalee at Carlos'n Charlie's. This description of that meeting will be jam-packed with meaning. With the last scene specifically describing the plan to dispose of the body, we anticipate what details Deepak might add to clarify his story. At some point we would expect him to become more specific about the cause of death—and he'll certainly continue to tell us where the body is.

## Straight to the Bar: The 'Natalee' Drink

*"so we arrived like 12.30 am in carlos (carlos is closing 1 pm ) and headed straight for the bar and bought 3 drinks my friend paid for them, so besides the bar there is a stage and people were dancing and there was natalee dancing too (thats the first time i saw her )and she was calling my friend to get on the stage and dance with her my friend laughed and refused so after the song was finished she came up to my friend and asked why he won't dance with her , i only heared that part because i was talking to someone else so i don't know what he responded(by then natalee was VERY drunk)so as i said i was talking to someone when i turned i had lost my brother , natalee and my friend. [period] well **they were announced** that they were <u>closing soon </u>so i thought"*

Deepak continues:

Pay attention to when we walked into Carlos'n Charlie's. We *"headed straight"* for the bar right next to the stage where Natalee was dancing. Three guys all with straight heads. Get it? We all had erections and we were "headed" to exactly where Natalee was.

187

So my friend, Joran, paid for the 3 drinks. He stepped up to the bar and said, "I'll have 3 'Natalee's' for me and my friends, thank you.' He set it up and we each took a drink of her—3 drinks—and pleasured ourselves. Natalee was the special drink at the bar for at least that one night.

Already we can see that Deepak, with his own guilt surely suffocating him, is beginning to blame the whole thing on Joran. It was Joran who called Deepak and Satish. It was Joran who concocted the plan. It was Joran who bought them the "Natalee Drink." It's no wonder, then, that when their cover story began to fall apart early in the investigation, Deepak quickly spoke up for himself and his brother, throwing Joran under the bus.

In his own mind Deepak was surely thinking, "None of this would have happened if it hadn't been for Joran!" Yet he repeatedly berates himself far more severely for participating. Deepak can't shift the guilt so easily. It eats at him from the inside out.

## Voyeurism: 'Dancing'—'Get On'

*"(that's the first time i saw her )and she was calling my friend to get on"*

In my story, after heading for the bar, I tell you about seeing Natalee for the first time, although I was intentionally watching her from a distance while appearing disconnected from Joran. She was practically on display—on a bar—dancing, *'besides the bar is a stage.'* And we were all looking at her—*"there was Natalee dancing . . . (the first time I saw her) . . . "*—watching her body move seductively. That was a rush, and we knew there were more to come.

The story continues and I make it clear what happened. As soon as she sees Joran, Natalee wants him to *"dance with her."* She wants him to *"get on"* the dance floor with her—to 'get it on with her' or "get on her," to put it more crudely. Remember, this is the cover-up story—we were the ones who got on her. A common euphemism for sex is *"dance"*—"Are you going to 'dance' with me baby?" And I said it twice to make it clear that "dance" is definitely code for sex: Joran *dancing* with Natalee.

Look at the picture again—*"there was Natalee dancing . . . (the first time I saw her) . . . she was calling my friend to **get on** . . . and dance with her."*

**Translation:** The first time I 'really saw' Natalee she was on display, dancing, with Joran inviting himself to get on her—I was watching her have sex. He got the first dance, but in the end it was a dance of death for all of us.

Just for the record, in my story I'm talking about dancing—sex—and somebody refusing to dance with somebody else. Who do you think resisted whom? Of course: Natalee resisted all of us. I wrote, "she begged him" to stop, remember? All my shocking sexual innuendos about the quick hook-up between Joran and Natalee, as soon as we walked in the bar, tell you again that we didn't waste any time assaulting her once we got her alone.

Also, whenever I mention the time, pay close attention. Here I describe *"the first time I saw her"* with parentheses for emphasis, and I'm watching Natalee dance, watching her have sex with Joran. *I'm telling you that, in truth, the first time I met Natalee wasn't until we got her off in my car and shortly before we began assaulting her.*

And the first night I met her was the last night I would meet her—the last night of her life. "First" and "last" are important words. I use them over and over, and in my mind they're linked because, as you know, Beth, I met her for the first and only time that night. One person, one night that forever changed my life—and hers.

Once again, no one among Natalee's friends saw either Deepak or Satish in Carlos'n Charlie's that night. Earlier in his story Deepak claims *"I was not present"* when Joran first met Natalee, allegedly at the Holiday Inn's Excelsior Casino. In actuality, he suggests again a key part of their plan—for Deepak and Satish to stay in the background at Carlos'n Charlie's so that Joran could seduce Natalee on his own. Deepak has also shifted his story here, making it even clearer that all three guys were personally involved in the brutal sexual attack.

## 'VERY drunk'

*"i was talking to someone else so i don't know what he responded(by then natalee was VERY drunk)so as i said i was talking"*

This is exactly where I mention that Natalee was *"VERY drunk."* She progressed from being *"a lil drunk"* when I had her buying Joran a drink in the casino (which really she didn't) to *"VERY drunk."* But in Carlos'n Charlie's, Joran is buying others a drink, and yeah, he bought Natalee a drink there as well. Put the two pieces of the drinking puzzle together. I'm saying Joran bought Natalee a *"lil drink"*— once more a drink with a little something in it from the bartender that produced a big change. This is how Natalee was primed to go— fueled with alcohol, primed with pills, and ready for a good time. But pay attention here, because by writing *"VERY drunk"* I'm telling you that is a HUGE part of the story. This is one of just three times in the whole email where I practically shout the story at you.

## The Announcement: Natalee's Obituary

*"so we arrived like 12.30 am in carlos (carlos is <u>closing</u> 1 pm ) . . . and headed straight for the bar and bought 3 drinks my friend paid for them, so besides the bar there is a stage and people were <u>dancing</u> and there was natalee <u>dancing</u> too (thats the first time i saw her )and she was calling my friend to get on the stage and <u>dance</u> with her my friend laughed and refused so <u>after the song was finished</u> she came up to my friend and asked why he <u>won't dance</u> with her , i only heared that part because i was talking to someone else so i don't know what he responded (by then natalee was VERY drunk)so as i said i was talking to someone when i turned <u>i had lost</u> my brother , <u>natalee</u> and my friend. well they were **announced** that they were <u>closing soon</u>"*

In the Carlos'n Charlie's scene where we met Natalee, I make no bones about the fact that she's dead: the music stopped—*"the song was finished," "closing time,"* the dancing is over and I use the phrase *"I lost . . . Natalee."* That says it all. But I've already told you in many other ways that Natalee has died—so think like an investigator. What else could I be telling you when I'm shouting at you, *"VERY drunk"*? Figure that out and you'll figure out exactly how she died and when—**because I'm clearly linking *"VERY drunk"* to *"I lost Natalee"*— to her death.**

And remember, between the lines of my story we're all now in the middle of "dancing" with Natalee. So what happened to her? Listen closely to my *"song"* here because I'm singing for all I'm worth—and I keep hearing that same song over and over. I'm telling you again that at that moment I was distracted. I've got to say it twice, *"I was talking to someone else."* When I suddenly came to my senses—Natalee had died, I had lost her. That was the moment when the music died for all of us.

Now for what specifically happened. My words are important but so are my punctuation marks. "*i don't know what he responded***(by then natalee was VERY drunk)***so as i said . . . [I had lost Natalee].*" See the deeper story: We're on Natalee "dancing" with her and the music suddenly stops—because she is very drunk. By emphasizing *"VERY drunk"* I'm telling you that Natalee consumed huge amounts of liquid. But 'VERY great amount of liquid' is linked with Natalee's death, because in reality she wasn't that drunk at all. It means only one thing—she vomited and choked, and that's when she took in a lot of liquids and was suddenly completely out of it, unconscious.

See how it came on me in a flash? Notice there are *no spaces* between my being out of touch and suddenly, *"by then"* she has taken in vast amounts of liquids. She died before I could turn around, and I'll never get over that shock. She tried to throw up and she couldn't. She drowned from too much drink.

Now look again at my sentence and see first my question speaking for Natalee after she died, *"asked why . . . won't dance . . . her"* meaning she asked why she 'won't or can't dance.' Now substitute "she" for *"he"* right after this in the  sentence as the flow suggests, *"i only heared that part because i was talking to someone else so i don't know what **she**[he] responded(by then natalee was VERY drunk)"* and you can see me telling you Natalee couldn't respond and couldn't dance. Suddenly she couldn't speak because she was too busy taking in fluids, silenced by her own vomitus. I also draw your attention to her silence in another way—*"I only heared"* what was said right before she was so drunk, implying that she was drowning and couldn't speak. The parenthesis without spaces also suggests fullness.

This is when she died. And to highlight it I surround the moment *"VERY drunk"* with five images that say **"The End."** On one side the music (1) *"was finished"* along with (2) *"won't dance with her"* imply-ing "can't dance" –and on the other side (3) *"I lost . . . Natalee"* immediately followed by a definite period meaning (4) "the end," and then (5) *"they were **announced** that they were **closing soon**."* I've used the word *"announced"* here for the only time in my email, which fits perfectly with the shout, *"VERY drunk."* I've chosen this moment above all others—speaking for all three of us, *"they"*— to make the announcement of Natalee's death and why it occurred. This is both her obituary in The Deepak News and the front-page story.

## Speaking for Natalee Again: Deepak's Climax

Now looking back you can see me speaking for Natalee, protesting what happened to her. Here she is looking at the moment she died—the music has stopped and notice what Natalee said, *"so after the song was finished she came up to my friend and asked why he won't dance with her , i only . . . ."* She came up to *"friend,"* one of the three of us, and asked *"why he won't dance with her,"* which is translated as "Why did you want to dance with me? Look what happened: I died." And which of her three friends do I have her talking to at the time, *"I only"*—only me. See, once more I was the one who was right in the middle of dancing with Natalee when it happened. As you can see from the lack of spacing both before and after my highlighting parenthesis marker in, *"he responded(by then natalee was VERY drunk)so as I,"* at that moment I was merged with her.

Notice another crucial message and read the sentence this way: *"so after the song was finished (she)–came–up–(to) my friend"* and you can see me describing the moment of my climax, the moment I finished with her—*"came"*—my erection, my friend, still *"up,"* being friendly. That was simultaneously the moment the music stopped for Natalee. Ironic, isn't it? Two climaxes—mine sexual and hers the end of her life. Sex and death. Quite a price for a little selfish fun.

## Deepak's News: Perfect Timing

We would expect that the central trauma that caused Natalee's death would definitely be hidden in Deepak's email in several places. He had no other real reason to write such a treatise to "Betty." And we certainly would expect it at precisely this point, when he describes meeting Natalee for the first time, because he would inextricably link the "first" and "last" time with Natalee in his mind. He has already implied such. Deepak's pattern is always to quickly get down to business, so we should expect a powerful, coherent message here that continues to tell the real story.

Remember, our task from the beginning was to break key parts of the Deepak Code. When we find a plausible part of the code exactly where we would expect to find it, that's a powerful validation that we're on the right track toward understanding the embedded story. We could also expect to find a crucial signal, such as "song/singing" at just such a point. It announces not only that he's confessing, but that he's confessing to the central part of the story that everybody wants to know: What happened? That adds yet another level of confirmation.

All these underlying factors point to one thing. Like the newspaper reporter he promised to be, Deepak has unmistakably pulled together the key ideas to make the compelling announcement that the crucial issue in Natalee's death was "VERY drunk." As we have seen, he has pointed toward aspiration of her vomitus during the attack because she was prevented from throwing up, in part because Deepak was on top of her. We would expect more details in the email about how they controlled a stubbornly resistant Natalee—a chokehold of some type would be the most logical. But we must let Deepak tell us in his own way.

In fact, the most common cause of death among rape victims is strangulation.

## Where Is the Body Located?

Deepak continues:

When thoughts such as 'look how she died and you caused it' stay on your mind hour after hour, you know what else you want to shout out? You can't stop your mind from shouting it from the rooftops like I do with these all-caps messages: 'I feel so awful I have to tell you where the body is.' Now you can see the other major clue in my shout, "*VERY drunk.*" I'm telling you where her body is—in the ocean, **in the "VERY drink"** where she "swallowed" a tremendous amount of liquid. We all ended up buying her a very big drink called the ocean.

Another clue for you here, another part of my story here that matches: I'm "*talking to someone else*" when Natalee died. Remember, I've told you right *after* she died, we talked to someone else: Paulus van der Sloot.

## Police Interviews: Joran Validates Vomiting Episode

As we consider the most central issue in this chapter—the cause of death—we need to leave Deepak's confession for a moment to *review Joran's police interviews*. Joran repeatedly made numerous suggestions pointing toward a vomiting/aspiration scenario in several different stories. Not surprisingly, in Joran's first (publicly released) police interview on June 9, 2005—some five days after Deepak's historic email treatise arrived in Betty's computer—we find some astounding matches and elaboration, leaving no question about what happened to Natalee Holloway.

## Jelly Shot

The unconscious mind speaks best through detailed stories, and right off Joran obliges us. First Joran noted that the *first time* he met Natalee, *"I saw that Natalee wasn't holding a drink"*—far too coincidental a comment. Then he described the first part of the meeting in Carlos'n Charlie's where he *"had to drink a jelly shot"* off of Natalee's belly button as she lay on the bar. He suggests a liquid on her body, shooting out like jelly, something she had to do as she lay flat on her back. He added, *"Natalee asked for a jelly shot"* suggesting a request for a shot not only into her mouth but out of her mouth. A "shot" itself suggests something quick and impulsive associated with drink. We can translate his comment: *"Natalee asked to make a jelly shot—she asked if she could throw up."*

## The Smell

Most strikingly of all, Joran recalls vividly, *"(When Natalee got onto the bar) I thought she was drunk. I could <u>smell</u> this from the <u>smell</u> that came out of Natalee's mouth"*—obsessed with the keyword "smell" he uses twice. His comment is at once beyond belief, yet on a deeper level it is a blatant confession. Here Joran was drinking alcohol himself, had been drinking earlier, was surrounded by numerous others drinking, with alcohol being served all around him, and yet he distinctly recalls the smell of alcohol coming out of Natalee's mouth. That's a very unusual description to say the least.

But more important, *beyond this is the basic fact that people who are drinking simply can't smell alcohol on another drinker's breath.* However, indeed there was an unforgettable smell emanating from Natalee's mouth—but it was the smell of her vomitus. Joran would have been intimately familiar with that smell, particularly if he tried some type of CPR on her. Clearly, Joran is describing Natalee's vomiting and death.

Later Joran changed his story on his Fox television interview in March of 2006, when he completely denied that Natalee was drunk. Obviously Joran wanted to distance himself from any recollection of Natalee's being drunk. There are more implications from Joran's stories: excessive drink itself also suggests a drowning. "Shot" as in "jelly shot" also suggests a violent act. And in linking a "jelly shot" to Natalee, Joran suggests that Natalee took another type of jelly shot from him when she couldn't expel her drink, aspirated, and died.

She turned to jelly, every bit as though he himself had shot and killed her. His thoughtprints continue to give him away.

## The Chaser

In another incident at Carlos'n Charlie's, Joran describes buying Natalee a shot of Bacardi 151 rum—*"Natalee asked me if she should drink the Bacardi in one go."* He told of Natalee drinking the shot in two gulps, suggesting the idea of Natalee not being able to hold a drink down and being in some distress. Drinking associated with "two goes" suggests two separate aspects to drinking—now and later—pointing to two distinct periods of swallowing liquids. Not only does this imply first drinking liquids and then later regurgitating them, it also suggests that one effort at swallowing is followed by another.

All of this implies that Natalee vomited at least twice. And even more strongly in this vignette, Joran noted that she needed a chaser—a drink of his whiskey coke—to get the shot down, again suggesting a picture of Natalee being unable to keep a drink down. A "chaser" also implies another liquid linked with alcohol. Indeed, Natalee had a reverse chaser with her drinking, when it unexpectedly wanted to come back up and the three boys inadvertently prevented the chaser from being expelled.

Joran repeatedly paints a picture of vomiting, with Natalee having a distinct smell on her breath, repeatedly having difficulty with drinking—keeping a liquid down—and he does so in his initial interviews. Such details strongly indicate how badly he really needs to confess, just as Deepak does. We find striking images—repeat thoughtprints—from Joran that confirm that Natalee indeed vomited. These thoughtprints are precisely the kind of vivid, relevant, right-brain pictures—symbolic pictures—we would expect to find in such a vital part of the story.

## The Final Chaser—Natalee's Body

Giving the phenomenal right brain its due, there is one final meaning in the end of Joran's story of Natalee taking a "chaser" to hold down her drink. Since a "chaser" is a second maneuver involving liquids designed to hold something down—to prevent it from surfacing—we find a subtle suggestion of a second maneuver, something specific holding Natalee's body down. In short, Joran points to another type of "chaser"—the container *chasing* or *going with* her body into the ocean to make sure it *stays down.*

Ironically, Joran tried to tell the police all about the chaser they should be chasing, but as yet they don't have a clue as to his message. The would-be chasers—the authorities—are missing out on the chase. Unquestionably Joran has demonstrated how much police can glean from a suspect between the lines of his cover-up story—and how much the Aruban authorities overlooked.

Leave it to a perpetrator to reveal that we are in an entirely new day and age for interrogating suspects, thus inadvertently advancing the cause of forensic science!

## Summary of New Information in Scene

- Deepak first repeats the sexual-assault story with distinctive sexual innuendos drawn from the three suspects' first official meeting with Natalee, including the suggestion of the three suspects having erections in "headed straight" to the bar where Natalee was, and Natalee supposedly calling out for Joran to "get on" her and to "dance" with her. Above all, this scene most clearly defines the moment of death and its exact cause.

- With repeated images Deepak again declares that Natalee has died: *"the music stopped," "closing time," "won't dance"* implying "can't dance anymore," and, most strikingly, Deepak describes the moment *"I lost Natalee."*

- In a key all-caps message further highlighted by his characteristic *parenthesis marker*, Deepak points to the cause of death. Natalee was *"VERY drunk"* suggesting not only aspiration of vomitus but that her body is in the ocean where she continues *"VERY drunk."*

- Again Deepak confesses how he was the one raping Natalee at the moment of death, and how he was distracted, repeating twice (*"so as i said)– i was talking to someone"* and then *"when i turned i had lost . . . natalee."*

- Deepak vividly connects the specific moment of his climax—when he "finished"—with the moment of Natalee's death in "the song was finished."

- Deepak's image of Natalee being "VERY drunk" takes us back to when she was *"a lil drunk"* while having a drink with Joran, suggesting again that she was drugged, which contributed to her vomiting.

- Deepak uses striking messages markers, *"song"* as in singing/confessing, shouting at us in all-caps *"VERY drunk,"* and *"announced"* to make it plain that this is Natalee's obituary in *The Deepak News.*

- Joran's striking police interview suggests the identical vomiting/aspiration scenario, with images such as the first time he met her *"she wasn't holding a drink,"* "jelly shooting on Natalee's body," Natalee turning to "jelly, having to use a "chaser" to hold a drink down, and the striking "smell" coming from Natalee's mouth.

- Joran also suggests that Natalee's body is now "the chaser" after her three assailants, and if it isn't held down she indeed will capture them.

## Scene 2: Cruising

*"when i turned i had lost my brother , natalee and my friend. well they were announced that they were closing soon so i thought well maybe they' re waiting for me by the car its better i go there so i went to my car and nobody was there so i started playing music and was waiting on **my brother and my friend.i waited** for like 10 min and then i saw my brother stepping in the car and my friend who was **with natalee. so i** was surprised but anyways i started the engine and my brother was besides me and my friend and natalee were in the backseat so i started cruising in the area and asked my friend whats going on so natalee responded to me ''hey its no prob let us just drive around and have fun its my last night"*

Deepak shifts the story into high gear again. Having lost contact with Joran, Satish, and Natalee, Deepak has gone outside the bar to his car, to wait for them alone. Soon he is joined by the other three, and he immediately drives away. Thus we have strong suggestions that Deepak was waiting for Joran and Natalee in the car, masquerading as a cabdriver assisted by his brother, Satish.

In describing their experience of driving around with Natalee in his car—*the first time she was alone with the three of them*—we can expect to see suggestions as to how the young islanders arranged their three-on-one outing with Natalee Holloway, and how it so brutally unfolded. With Natalee riding off into the night with three strangers in the backseat of Deepak's car, here above all other places in his email we would expect him to tell us precisely what happened.

First we would anticipate his sexual innuendos to become much more blatant, since this was what led to the problem. Then we would expect thoughtprints clearly referring to Natalee's death. Given Deepak's tendencies we can rest assured he'll get quickly to the point. However, as always we can also expect surprises.

## The Cabdriver

Deepak continues his story.

I'm always going back and forth between two stories: what we did to her and then Natalee's death. As I begin to tell you about Natalee's joy ride with us, don't forget that this is being *"announced,"* alerting you to pay keen attention for even more information. First, here we come to the assault.

*"well they were **announced** that they were closing soon so i thought well maybe they' re waiting for me by the car its better i go there so i went to my car and nobody was there so i started playing music and was waiting"*

Once again you can see our plans to get Natalee into the car alone with us, to close the deal. Listen and you'll hear me speaking for Natalee again, "*well they were announced that they were closing soon so i thought well maybe they' re waiting for me.*" Yeah, we were waiting on her, getting ready to close in. *"They' re waiting for me . . . nobody was there"* sums it all up. See, we were waiting on her, but nobody was there for her at all—none of her friends or her teachers. Nobody—certainly not the three of us. We were there only for ourselves. But that's what my email is all about—I'm being there for Natalee now. As best I can.

So there I was waiting by the car, waiting for my passengers to get in, which again suggests what? Yes, a cabdriver. And don't buy all this garbage about my getting separated from everyone else inside Carlos'n Charlie's. Decode the message. The truth is that I intentionally stayed in the background, separating myself from Joran both inside and outside Carlos'n Charlie's. Then you can also understand our plan—why it was *"better i go there,"* to my car alone, so Natalee wouldn't get suspicious.

So, Joran left Carlos'n Charlie's alone with Natalee. He met up with Satish between my car and the bar. It would have been very easy for him to say he had arranged a cab to pick him up right after Carlos'n Charlie's closed, and that Satish had come to find him. If Natalee thought she was getting into a taxicab when she got into my Honda, fine. One way or another we had to get her in the car. And we did.

One last thing, in *"announced . . . they were closing soon,"* I'm announcing—making it official— that Natalee died not long after the assaults started—like I said before, within 30 minutes. Now I'm about to tell you again how long we each took with her.

## The Three Assaults

*"was waiting on* **my brother and my friend.i waited** *for like <u>10 min</u> and then i saw my brother <u>stepping in the car</u> and my friend who was* **with natalee.so** *i was surprised but anyways i started the engine and my brother was besides me and my friend and natalee were in the back-seet so i started cruising in the area"*

As soon as Natalee gets in the car I immediately tell you what really happened. For instance, *"so i started playing music and was waiting on my brother and my* **friend.i** *waited for like 10 min."* I'm describing how I waited on my brother and my friend, Joran, to make music with Natalee, to dance with her—to rape her —before I got my 10 minutes with her. Notice how I subtly create pictures of the first two assaults, but when my turn comes my thoughtprints will leap off the page at you.

First, *"then i saw my brother stepping in the car"*—I was watching my brother put his foot in my car. The "car" represents Natalee. I'm watching—watching like a voyeur—my brother put his extremity, his penis, in Natalee's car/container. Next I'm watching *"my friend who was with natalee,"* meaning 'be **with** Natalee, or having sex with her.' All along I'm watching, ever the voyeur. With a definite period here, I picture how they both finished their turns with Natalee and how I went third. And I'm also leaving no doubt that Satish participated. My deeper mind tells the truth on everybody.

And for the record, usually you 'step into' cabs and you 'get into' cars—another clue to our cab-ride charade. Also keep in mind the idea of two people helping Natalee into a container.

But continuing with the assault, once more you can also see me speaking for Natalee here: "*i waited for . . . 10 min,*" telling us that her assault was 'like waiting on 10 men to gang rape me.' Another abbreviation, "*min,*" suggesting "men," speaks volumes, linking it to the word "*waiting,*" telling you that Natalee had to wait while each one of us finished. At the same time you can see a picture of just how anxious I was for my turn, because I left no space between their completion and my waiting, "*on my brother and my **friend.i waited** for like 10 min.*"

Like I said, we each assaulted Natalee about 10 minutes. I waited until this specific scene to really emphasize the time factor. So I waited 10 minutes while Joran and Deepak were with her, and that number takes you back to my earlier comment, I "*got off my shift at 10*" meaning my shift with Natalee lasted about 10 minutes too. You might think I'm preoccupied with the number 10. My brother and I picked up Joran at 12:10 am—which itself tells you, "1, 2, and I'm 3. I am. I am. And we each had a 10-minute ride, each one of us dancing to the music in our self-absorbed minds."

## Joran's Book and Another Clue: 'Leg Hanging Out'

In Joran's book we find another highly suggestive sexual image, precisely matching Deepak's email story. Deepak reported to the police that immediately after leaving Carlos'n Charlie's, before anyone else arrived, he was waiting in his car with "my leg hanging out." In a nutshell he summarizes the boys' entire mission. They all had their legs hanging out just like they headed straight to the bar when they arrived at Carlos'n Charlie's. Deepak implies that not only were their legs hanging out, they were all straight. How easily Deepak could have left out this little description, yet how rich the confession. With "leg" as slang for "penis," decoding Deepak's message is not difficult, nor is it the last time the suspects will use the common vernacular "leg."

## The Backseat

*["waiting on my brother and my friend.i waited for like 10 min and then i saw my brother stepping in the car and my friend who was with natalee. so]*

*i was surprised but anyways i started the engine and my brother was besides me and my friend and natalee were in the backseet so i started cruising in the area and asked my friend whats going on so natalee responded to me "hey its no prob let us just drive around and have fun its my last night , she said you can drop me off later at holiday inn anyways right" i said sure why not so"*

Right after the three of them get in the car, I write (and read it this way): *"anyways I started the engine—and my brother was beside me and my friend and natalee were in the backseet so I started cruising in the area."* See how I'm describing me now being in the backseat with Natalee? And, as I continue you can see how I leave no doubt that's the case here. *"Anyways"* suggests "in a ways" and then *"I started the engine,"* I started moving—*"cruising"* 'in' and 'out.' Everybody knows what *"cruising"* really means—looking for sex, having sex. One sexual image after another. I was taking my turn sexually — *"cruising"*—with Natalee just like my two compadres did, and now they surrounded me, watching, while I had sex with your daughter.

First I told you the order of the assaults, then I went into detail about what I did with Natalee, and what I was doing when she died.

Again I speak for Natalee at a truly crucial moment. My friend asks, *"what's going on"*—the critical question, 'What happened, Natalee? What happened in the backseat?' Notice how I set up the answer, depicting a guy and a girl in the backseat at night, in the dark, driving around on a getaway island right after partying hearty. Already you can see where I'm headed with this, but just to triple-underscore the scene I answer through Natalee, *"Hey it's no **prob** (sic) let us just drive around and have fun it's my last night."*

Never overlook an abbreviation slip—like *"prob."* That's my second abbreviation, almost back-to-back, with sexual connotations. What's a *"prob"*? It's a blatant phallic symbol—a 'probe'—not very well-disguised at all. Remember the 'poke-her' game?

You can hear Natalee's protest too, 'Hey no probe, no penis, no more assault!' Almost immediately after Natalee got in my car I began cruising. That tells you, again, that we started in on her very quickly after she got in. After all, Joran had school the next day. I know, Beth, another crude, crude image—but that was us. You've got to know and I've got to tell you.

And hear a final first-person comment from Natalee, *"Hey it's no prob (sic) let us just drive around and have fun **it's my last night**."* Her last night—and you can hear her admit, 'Yeah, it's a problem, a big problem! You wanted to know what's going on. I died, that's what! This assault has cost me my life. This was the last night of my life.'

Her words—both in first-person, no less—exactly match that earlier statement, *"Today is my last day I will be."* That should eliminate any doubts that your daughter is dead, any doubts that we had  sex with her against her will, and any doubts that I am confessing to the crime. The last day, the last night of her life and she spent it with us being prodded and poked. Some way to go out, huh? It's a problem all right—the biggest problem we've had in our lives.

The words *"last night"* also point out that Natalee died that night—and quickly. She died when we were driving around, not at Joran's house. She died in the backseat. And once that happened, I'm lost. I'm out of touch and again asking, 'What's going on in the backseat?' That's where my slip *"prob"* has another meaning about the problem that developed during my turn with Natalee. When all of a sudden she's dead, that interrupted me and shut down my enjoyment. But far more important than that, it left us with a huge 'problem' on our hands—a *"prob"* by the name of Natalee who turned the tables on us.

## Slip: *"Backseet"*

Our problem came on us so suddenly our heads were spinning. Look at my slip, *"backseet."* Then read my sentence another way, *" . . . – anyways—i started the engine—and my brother was besides me— and my friend—and natalee were [was] in the **backseet** so i started cruising in the area—and asked my friend whats going on—so natalee responded to me "hey its no prob – . . . just drive around* *and have fun its my last night."* Hear my voice say *"backseet?"* I'm so beside myself, I'm running the two words together. 'Backseat with Natalee, oh seet, oh shet, oh s—t!' I was in the backseat cruising with Natalee, having started my engine, taking my turn, when suddenly Natalee went into total shock!

'back seet' suggesting also implies we used a sheet or a blanket over my backseat. It even suggests Natalee's 'back seat'—sodomy, and more. Conjures up a lot of ideas, doesn't it? Go with them, Beth. I'm leading you outside the box to the answers. I must confess how brutal we were.

## 'Back sheet' Matches 'Blackjack'

Deepak makes another powerful suggestion with his slip *"backseet"* suggesting "back sheet." First, tying a "sheet" in knots is a familiar image in stories often used when people want to escape from an entrapment—a jail or a burning apartment, for example. And it's a striking image of someone being in a life-or-death situation, as they depend on the sheet's holding its knot. Combining the idea of tying a sheet with the image of somebody's back, we indeed have another type of "back sheet"—controlling someone from behind by tying some type of noose around their neck. How powerfully then "back sheet" matches "blackjack," but at the same time providing yet another detail in Deepak's email saga.

## The Body Again—'Later'

*"she said you can drop me off later at holiday inn anyways right"*

There's something else. Remember the question I asked your daughter, "Hey Natalee, what's going on in the backseat?" Beth, I've got to keep shouting it. After *"hey no prob . . . have fun its my last night"* listen good, *"she said 'you can drop me off later at holiday inn anyways (sic) right."* It's a logical sequence of events. I've just told you Natalee died, and how, and now I'm telling you what we did with her body. I'm giving you every kind of clue with *"later"*—what comes after death, *"later"*? Getting rid of the body. I've told you before we disposed of the body, but I get more specific here.

So what happened to her body? We dropped it off later at the Holiday Inn, which is once more code for ocean and for "inn/in/end." Think of

'Holiday Inn on the Ocean,' or actually 'in' the ocean. Hey, it's not just me saying it. It's Natalee herself who answers the question, 'Where did they drop your body off?' She replies, 'Look in the ocean, no question about it.'

See, there are three issues that I've got to have Natalee address personally—*what we did to her, how she died and where we hid the body. In my entire email, nowhere else do I speak so plainly for her, combining those three major events into one sentence.* Before long I'm going to narrow the search down for you, letting Natalee speak again in her own voice. If you still have doubts what the Holiday Inn really means, I promise to make it even clearer. One thing for sure—Holiday Inn is a major part of the code. So, understand what it means and you'll know where we dropped the body.

Pay close attention: "*she said you can **drop me** off later at holiday inn.*" We dropped her. You bury bodies on land, but you either release them (as I mentioned before) or you drop them into the ocean. The Drop. Her body is in the ocean. Find the drop and you'll find us. That's one last meaning of *"prob"*— probe the case like a detective should; search for the body. I'm shouting at you again: probe the waters and you will find The Drop.

## Location of Body: 'Anyways Right'

Now back to one last thing here. I told you that Natalee's own voice would help you narrow the ocean search. Listen again, "*. . . its my last night , she said you can drop me off later <u>at holiday inn</u> **anyways right"** i said <u>sure why not so.</u>*"

With *"anyways right"* I'm confessing that we treated her any way we wanted, treated her carelessly. But I'm also telling you something much more important about dropping her off at the end of her time with us. Pay close attention to the geographical references that come after I talk about us dropping the body off. Take it word by word.

First, I've told you *"Holiday Inn"* and located her body in the ocean for you. But I don't stop there. Next, it's *"anyways,"* suggesting 'in ways' or 'in a ways.' So in a ways from what? *"At Holiday Inn anyways/ in a ways"* I'm using *"Holiday Inn"* in two ways—literally as a reference point with the key geographical marker *"at"* and then pointing you 'in a ways' from there, which could only be toward the ocean and the obvious translation: 'Holiday Inn/ocean in a ways' suggests a short distance into the ocean.

But I still have one more geographical clue for you here—one simple word, *"right."* So put the two geographical clues together: going out from the Holiday Inn the body was dropped "a ways" into the ocean after we turned right. This locates the body in the ocean toward the northwest end of the island, where only a few lights barely illuminate the shore. And also notice a typical thing I do—I confirm the message, as in: *"i said sure why not so."*

Again, think like an investigator, Beth. In my email, when I focus specifically on leaving Natalee—dropping her off later on her last night—those are the most important sections, because that's what will finally bring resolution. The one thing I *can* do to begin to make up for what we've done is to tell you where Natalee's remains are located.

If we examine the vertical messages here we find the suggestions: "cruise the area—probe, drive around—the holiday inn/ the ocean." **Translation:** Search the ocean. Remember, at key moments the deeper intelligence communicates in vertical messages, as though it's writing out the answers to a crossword puzzle. The specific area in the ocean suggested by Deepak fits well with the known facts surrounding the case. Around this particular issue, Deepak's thoughtprints coalesce swiftly and surely.

## Alone

> *"VERY drunk . . . when i turned i had lost my brother , natalee and my friend. well **they were announced** that they were <u>closing soon</u> so i thought well maybe they' re waiting for me by the car its better i go there so i went to my car and nobody was there so i started playing music and was waiting"*

Now come back to one other thing. When I was talking about being 'alone in the car' unexpectedly, I'm also describing how Joran, Satish, and I were unexpectedly alone at the moment Natalee died. I repeat myself by writing, *"so i went to my car and nobody was there"* because—suddenly—Natalee was no longer there. She was dead.

But that's not all; I'm painting a distinct picture of somebody all alone, way off by themselves in a car/container. That's Natalee, lying underwater in the cage. That's where my slip, *"they were announced,"* comes in. Read *"they were announced"* as 'the perpetrators made an announcement that Natalee was lost, off by herself in a container in the ocean, in the drink.' That's what *"the news"* does, makes announcements about people, and from the beginning I've told you that this was *The Deepak News*. The biggest news is 'Natalee has died,' followed by 'Suspects confess.'

You can then see the next bit of news in my slip, *"[i had lost– my brother . . . –and my friend.] well **they were announced** that they were closing soon so i thought well maybe they' re waiting for me."* The news here is that the authorities were waiting on us, were closing us down. Along those lines, *"they were announced"* is quite similar to 'they were pronounced'—guilty. You can hear the final verdict now if you listen, 'We, the jury, pronounce these three suspects guilty of murder/manslaughter in the . . . degree.'

All along we tried to tell ourselves that hiding the body would solve our problems, would close the case for good. But deep down you can see I really doubted that solution. Deep down I knew the truth, as shown in *"well they were announced that they were closing soon **so i thought**"*– meaning so I thought at the time. But I knew better. Our solution was just a temporary fix and I knew unconsciously I had given the authorities a clear confession, including a map to Natalee's grave. Find her grave and you find ours.

## Summary of New Information in Scene

- Deepak provides crucial information in his story by describing the first time the three boys were alone with Natalee.

- He again suggests the boys used a cab ride ruse to entice Natalee as he waited alone in his car before she and Joran "stepped into" it.

- As expected, he immediately describes a vivid sexual scene in which, after waiting his turn after Joran and Satish, he "starts his engine," *"cruising"* in Natalee like the other two, who are now beside him, controlling Natalee.

- In the single most revealing sentence in the email, *"so natalee responded to me "hey its no **prob** let us just drive around and have fun* *its my last night* , *she said you can* **drop me off later** *at* **holiday inn** *anyways right"* Deepak tells us about the group rape, how it led to her death, and what they did with the body.

- In his major slip, Natalee has a *"prob"* in the backseat, meaning she is being probed and raped. This results in her *"last night"* alive, where afterwards Deepak notes that they *dropped* her body off in the ocean.

- Once again Deepak confirms the message and the code: *"Holiday Inn"* (where they allegedly dropped her off) means *"ocean."*

- Deepak then makes it plain that he is unconsciously guiding the search for the body, instructing the authorities by providing important details about where to search in the ocean—straight out from the Holiday Inn and slightly to the right.

- Deepak also clearly establishes that the repeated rape occurred in his car's backseat, probably covered by a sheet or a blanket.

- All in all, here we find one of the two most revealing scenes in his entire email, packed with important information as Deepak approaches the end of his story.

## Scene 3

### Injury and Screams

The action changes once more. Now cruising down the road with Natalee, the three guys suddenly come across Natalee's friends, who urge her to get out of the strangers' car. Using vivid message markers, Deepak suggests that another crucial communication is coming up. He doesn't disappoint. We must pay close attention—this is one of the most action-packed scenes, which tells us that something crucial happened here.

### Prediction

In the previous scene, while Natalee was alone with the three guys for the first time as they rode in Deepak's car, we anticipated that he would describe the strategy used to isolate Natalee, the sexual assault, and other key details. Now in the current scene, since Deepak is clearly unfolding a logical story and continuing to build the case against himself, we might expect him to elaborate on key components, such as how she died and where the assault took place. And all along we will contin-ue to expect tips about the body's location—emphasizing location, means of dumping, and in what kind of container they placed the body.

Deepak resumes his commentary:

> Beth, take a quick read of this next part and you'll see I use the word "*scream*" twice. I'm screaming something really important at you here about this case. Notice, too, I mention her friends three times. They come into play here more than anywhere else. Believe it or not, I'm also referring to the part of **me** that is Natalee's friend, that speaks the truth for her. Let's take the screams one by one.

*["have fun its my last night , she said you can drop me off later at holi-day inn anyways right" i said sure why not]*

*so as i was drove out of the carlos road and got on the mainroad there were natalees friends and she , pushed het head out of the window and* **screamed** *something i can't recall.so i was driving very slow to make a left to get in the next road and then one of natalees friend* **screamed** *for her to get out of the car , and she refused so then i stopped my car and i said natalee if your friends want you to go with them its better you go listen to them and go with them , she said no i will stay with you guys i will get a lift from you anways later, so she said bye to her friends and i drove away, so then we were just talking etc, in the car"*

## Where We Assaulted Her

> We'll start with the second scream, with her friends screaming at Natalee, because this is where I stopped my car. Don't forget, *in my deeper, hidden story I'm always looking back, telling two stories, one about the assault and one about Natalee's death.* What I'm really referring to here is when we three guys, her new "friends," screamed at her when we suddenly stopped the car on a secluded side road after we finally got her alone, not long after leaving Carlos'n Charlie's and seeing her friends on the way. We had not planned on running into Natalee's friends, or having her spontaneously yell out to them, but we had to act as if it didn't bother us when she spotted them.

> We drove around a little while to let Joran get her warmed up in the backseat. But it wasn't long before we got to our planned destination and I suddenly stopped my car. There were two screams: Natalee

screams at her friends but can't be understood with her head partially out of the car. Her friends scream back at her to get out of the car, but Natalee refuses. Notice the set-up: "*so i was driving very slow to make a left to get in the next road and then one of natalees friend screamed for her to get out of the car,*" just driving along very casually; then a sudden change in the action with someone now screaming at Natalee. That's us: we suddenly stopped the car and opened the doors. Joran—"*one of natalees friend*"— went out the door ahead of her.

At first he gradually began pushing Natalee's head down toward one side of the backseat, partially out the door, encouraging her to lay down so we could have our way with her. He was also preparing to control her head. It was a slick maneuver. And notice the sequence, "*and she refused so then i stopped . . . and i said natalee if your friends want you to go with them its better you go listen to them and go with them.*"

At this point, we were 'gentlemen' still trying to sweet-talk Natalee into going along with us voluntarily. See my key word "*go*" used three times, meaning 'go along' (with us). We tried to tell her, 'Look, sit back and enjoy it, this is going to happen so go along with us.' But Natalee "*she said no*"—in fact she shouted at us, screamed at us "*No,*" and then we had to scream at her. We had to overpower her.

You can imagine the sheer terror on her face. This was the power trip we lived for. Like I told you earlier when she had a problem with my probe, with our probes, we asked, 'W*hy not baby?'* She fought us the whole way. With Natalee resisting our offer then we had to control her quickly—to take her clothes off, to get her to go along, and to keep her from screaming. And this, of course, is where the chokehold came into play.

## The Sexual Assault Again: Repeated Innuendos

"*as i was drove out of the carlos road and got on the mainroad there were natalees [friends] and she , pushed [het head out of the window] and screamed [something i can't recall].so i was driving very slow to make a left to get in the next road*"

"*she said no i will stay with you guys i will get a lift from you anways later (so she said bye to her friends . . . )*"

Of course then the rapes started. Natalee is being violated repeatedly as I tell you that again here—pretty explicitly. Remember how, in my story, I'm on my shift following Joran and Deepak? Here I'm telling you again the order: follow *"as i was drove out of the carlos road and got on the mainroad there were natalees [friends]"* and read it: "As I drove out of the carlos road there was Natalee (the mainroad) surrounded by her friends, Joran and Satish, who had just been with her on the 'carlos road'—referring back to Carlos'n Charlie's in my story where she was with them. Now I *"got on the mainroad,"* you know, *"got on"* the Natalee road, the main road I'd been looking for, the road called 'my turn.' Now I'm driving and notice my slip, *"so i was driving very slow to make a left to get **in** the next road."* See I'm not getting 'on' the next road but *'in'* it, meaning **to get *"in"* Natalee**—and suggesting I'm continually driving 'into' her. And what was Natalee doing in the beginning: *"she , pushed . . . and **screamed"**—*resisting the chokehold.

Now look at: *"she said no i will stay with **you guys i will get a lift from you anways.**"* We gave her repeated lifts all right—*"anways"* suggesting 'in ways'—on the way into her. Just like I told you earlier, we blackjacked her, we repeatedly jacked her up. And *"later"* came very quickly for Natalee, as soon as we were alone with her, but I'm also telling you something else about *"later"* after it was all over. Stay tuned.

## Notes and Police Interviews

Having previously observed how Deepak's slip *"backseet"* suggests "back sheet," and the use of a sheet or blanket over the backseat, it's likely the three boys commanded Natalee to get out of the car at some point, to strip her and prepare the backseat by covering it with a sheet. This is also when they would have used their "back sheet" noose like a blackjack to control her. Almost certainly the rapes took place there in Deepak's grey Honda, where Natalee died in mid-assault.

In police interviews, Joran described how Deepak and Satish adjusted the front seats of the Honda that night to give him "leg room" in the backseat with Natalee. **Translation:** the three boys moved the front seats forward to give themselves enough room to be able to operate freely. Again, with "leg" being slang for "penis," Joran is confessing that in the backseat he found a room for his penis in Natalee.

## Rape Scene in Email Matches Police Interviews

*"as i was drove out of the carlos road and got on the mainroad there were natalees friends and she , **pushed het head** out of the window and **screamed something** i can't **recall.so** i was driving very slow to make a left to get in the next road"*

In Deepak's email, the scene in which he stops the car is exactly where he tells us what happened when they really did stop the car, and not surprisingly, it's here that Deepak tells us between the lines all about the sexual assault. Not coincidentally he provides us the email's most vivid picture of Natalee being injured with his slip "het head," suggesting "hit head." We will see that there were two types of head injuries, the first of which was sexual. Deepak will shortly tell us, first-person, about the second head injury, which was fatal. First we must examine the sexual injury.

Before getting to the email version let's first look back at two sexually charged stories that emerged during police interviews—one from Deepak and the other from Joran. Both fit hand-in-glove with the sexual assault on the side of the road.

Importantly, Deepak's story began when he stopped his car on the *side of the road* at Arashi beach with Joran and Natalee in the backseat. He describes getting out of the car—in which everyone was awake—to relieve himself before driving on to the lighthouse.

Since Deepak's unconscious mind confesses through specific images in stories, let's decode the image. Deepak stops his car (a phallic image all its own), unzips his pants, pulls his penis out, exposed on the side of the road outside the boundaries of a normal restroom, which he could have used at the nightclub, and relieves himself. With a girl in the backseat, this action suggests crudity and disrespect, along with desperation and an inability to control himself. It's also a story of his phallus exposed to Natalee—the same phallus he insisted Natalee touched in his reported cover-up email to John Croes immediately after Natalee's death. In short, the imagery fits exactly a desperate rape on the side of the road whereby Deepak relieves himself at Natalee's expense, without any regard for her whatsoever.

Notice again that Deepak stops his car on a side road, again suggesting the assault took place in a pre-planned spot on a secluded road familiar to the three suspects. He seemingly confirmed the same idea in another police interview, when Deepak volunteered that "We drove until we got to roundabout." Consciously he was referring to a road known as the roundabout, but unconsciously he described exactly what happened: they boys drove Natalee around until they stopped for the violent "roundabout" on their special side road. It was a wild and dizzying merry-go-round that Deepak continues to ride.

## Joran's Matching Honda Story Points to Rape

Now we turn to another story Joran told in a police interview. In the end, this points to a paper-thin version of what happened with Natalee. Joran described an earlier occasion when his friend, Freddy, had sex with a girl in the backseat of their mutual friend Jamie Carrasquilla's "famous" four-door Honda, a car renowned for such escapades. As Freddy became intimate with the girl, Joran and Jamie stood at the trunk of Jamie's car and drank alcohol. Before the sex act, Joran handed Freddy a condom.

Here we have the thinly disguised picture of three boys indulging themselves, having sex with a girl—treating themselves to a drink of her—in a now-famous four-door Honda, using condoms, with one boy standing down at the foot and the other near the head, or upper torso. Now we have another striking detail, as Joran suggests that the three boys used condoms when they raped Natalee.

To validate this detail, Joran introduced the idea himself in various interviews, and in his book he reported that he didn't have sex with Natalee because he didn't have a condom with him that night. Of course we read through his denial, which suggests that having planned the attack all along, all of them had condoms with them, with Joran possibly supplying them. On one occasion Joran referred to not having a condom when he was with Natalee as "the end of the party," a striking reference to what was the end result of the assault. Once again in a brief phrase, "end of the party," one of the three suspects succinctly sums up the entire matter.

With these clear sexual stories in mind, now we can understand "het head" as in "there were natalees friends— and she , pushed—het (by) head out— of the window." The imagery suggests Natalee was injured by the boys pushing their heads in and out of her, in a real way hitting or damaging her. The idea of sticking a head out a window suggests the "in and out" of sexual intercourse, back and forth through an opening. Clearly this fits with Deepak relieving himself with his head out, and with sex in the backseat of a well-known Honda with three guys using condoms. And it fits with vaginal bleeding from a "head injury." Once again the unconscious mind is an expert with descriptive images, becoming as crude as the event that it describes.

## Forced Oral Sex?

But there's even more sexual brutality to the story. In *"she , pushed het head out of the window and screamed something i can't recall.so i was driving very slow"* Deepak also suggests forcing Natalee to perform oral sex, whereby she couldn't speak because a boy had "slowly" pushed his head into another of her orifices, thus preventing her from speaking.

Deepak had meant to say, "Pushed her head," which suggests forced her head or forced her to give them "head." Charles Croes, Joran's previously mentioned confidant the night of Beth Twitty's arrival, reported that Joran told him Natalee gave him a "blow job" in the backseat. Confirming the same idea, Satish reported that in the backseat Natalee had fallen asleep in Joran's lap.

Next, Joran adds his own confirming imagery, when he describes in both a police interview and in his book, how Natalee fell asleep on his leg as they drove past the Marriott. Just for good measure, along these identical lines, Joran reported in the same interview as his famous Honda story how "I had (a girl) to give me a blow-job . . . " while Joran's friend, Chato, "saw that (the girl) was giving me head in his four door pickup." Once again, here's Joran implying a girl "had to" perform oral sex on him in the back of a friend's four-door car while the friend watched.

Later the friend had Joran ask the girl if they could have group sex, but she refused. Again in his story, the girl resists. And Joran goes on to report he later took the girl to his apartment to spend the night and have sex again, with his mother being fully informed that the girl would be there. The suggestions are strong and consistent that the three boys forced Natalee to perform fellatio.

To continue describing this sordid picture, Joran told police that Natalee declined to have sex with Deepak or Satish. Already we know about Deepak putting a pornographic video in his car's DVD player and implying that Natalee was offended by the X-rated imagery. This further suggests that the three guys briefly encouraged Natalee to engage in group sex by playing a porn video. Deepak has told us in numerous ways in his email, as has Joran in various stories, that Natalee refused, and that they then proceeded to overpower her. Joran's mention of a porn video is a clear confession of participation in a group sexual assault,

214 — Into the Deep

complete with its voyeuristic thrills. Also, the reference to scantily clad women wielding power tools suggests that, for these three, the various sexual assaults allowed them to create their own "power tools" in their minds to compensate for their personal powerlessness.

Deepak had also suffered a major emotional trauma in May, 2005— as he told Betty in a previous email that month. He had been refused entrance to a college outside Aruba in part related to his difficulties getting a visa. So immediately prior to Natalee's assault Deepak would have been feeling significantly powerless and looking for a power trip. Stuck on the same road to nowhere life owed him something and he was going to take it.

Now we move from sex to death, just the way it transpired. For sure, Joran had it right—the party ended abruptly.

## Cause of Death: A Stifled Scream and 'Het Head'

Now Deepak brings us back to the first scream.

*"as i was drove out of the carlos road and got on the mainroad there were natalees friends and she , **pushed het head** out of the window and **screamed something** i can't **recall**.so i was driving very slow to make a left to get in the next road"*

So I'm giving Natalee a lift like Joran and Satish did. I'm the one who is now with her, surrounded by my two associates. And Natalee suddenly makes a move. In my story she pushes her head out the window and screams. In actuality she suddenly renewed her effort to push us off, to resist. She felt a desperate urge to scream. But notice my slip, "*het head*" suggesting 'hit head.' I'm saying that, while I was taking my turn, her head was injured somehow, leading to a stifled scream, a silent scream.

My not being able to hear Natalee's scream suggests the *exact moment of the fatal injury.* She can't speak at all; her voice is cut off. Look at the scene again—she's pushing her head out the window, meaning that her head is framed by a "window," or something around it. This is a picture of the noose we had around her neck. And when you try to scream with something tied around your neck, if it's tight enough you can't.

How was she injured? She *"screamed something i can't recall"* meaning that she couldn't scream because there was a noose around her neck—one reason for the noose in the first place. When Natalee panicked and tried to push away from me while I was on top of her, when she realized she was about to vomit, Joran momentarily pulled the chokehold even tighter and held her down even harder. All the while I'd gotten off in my own world and was completely oblivious to her distress.

And what happens when you start to throw up and can't? What happens when you're being held down with one guy on top of you and another with a chokehold around your neck, and you're a 5'4" girl weighing all of 110 pounds? I'll tell you what happens. You can't "scream" meaning you can't vomit, and when you're trying to vomit and can't, you die. You are then *"VERY drunk."* You drown in your own bodily fluids.

Later on I make the same slip again: *"het"* instead of 'her' in *"my friend offered to help **het** to her room,"* making it clear that Joran was the one holding the noose. The final period here makes it plain that this is where she was injured and died. "*Screamed something I can't recall [.] (period)*" means 'can't scream' means 'strangulation,' with the period declaring 'that was the end for Natalee, the final moment.' This is how I link her death to the stifled scream, when she was trying to vomit. Before we knew it she was unconscious and was gone. It was all over.

"Scream" is a common colloquialism for vomiting or throwing up, and is often associated with sticking one's head out the window to do so. Eerily, what happened to Natalee matched that exact image in Deepak's story. Also, "scream" translated as "vomiting/aspirating" fits perfectly with Deepak's major shout-out, "VERY *drunk,*" which further links Natalee's death to aspiration.

"Scream" and "VERY drunk" are two of the most vivid message markers in the entire email, and together verify exactly how Natalee aspirated to death at the hands of the three suspects. Again, it reminds us of Joran's private conversation with Charles Croes the night after Natalee disappeared. Croes reported that Joran denied having sex with Natalee because she had thrown up at Carlos'n Charlie's. Of course this is just one version of many lies Joran will tell—but in every lie there's often a piece of truth.

Importantly, this is only one of two scenes in which violence is overtly linked to Natalee—both times through slips where she is "het" or "hit."

## A Wrong Turn and The Second Scream—Joran

*"screamed something **i can't recall.so i was** driving very slow to make a **left** to get **in** the next road"*

Here I'm showing you yet again that when I failed to understand Natalee's scream, her need to throw up, I was merged with her. The lack of spacing after the period connects the two of us—*"**i can't recall.so i was** driving"* suggesting 'sex and merger.' Notice, too, that I'm making a wrong turn—a left one instead of a right one **to get *"in"* not "on" the next road.** Plus, I have to remind you again that at the time of her death the one who was out of contact—the one who can't recall what was said about Natalee—was me. Now I also want you to notice something else.

*"and then one of natalees friend **screamed** for her to get out of the car , and she refused **so then i stopped my car.**"*

Here I was oblivious to Natalee's distress, in my own world, which takes us to the *second scream*—when a friend of Natalee's screamed and what happened? First I'm telling you I came to my senses and stopped driving my car, stopped having sex with Natalee only when Joran—Natalee's friend at that moment of crisis—screamed at me to stop, for me to "get out of" her. Of course Natalee "refused" to get out of the car, refused to move because she was totally helpless and controlled. She couldn't get away from me.

Joran had suddenly recognized that Natalee had choked. With the noose around her neck and me on top of her, Joran then screamed at me to stop, which finally got my attention. And I saw her face change colors when she couldn't breathe.

## Failed Resuscitation and Regret

*"and i said natalee if your friends <u>want you to</u> **go** with them its <u>better</u> <u>you</u> **go** listen to them and **go** <u>with them</u> , she said no i will stay with you guys i will get a lift from you anways later, so she said bye to her friends and i drove away, so then we were just talking etc, in the car"*

But that wasn't all. Joran then lifted her out of the car onto the ground to try and resuscitate her. You can see that moment in the key word "*go,*" with us shouting, 'Listen to us! Go Natalee, go Natalee— breathe, breathe!' *'Go'* meaning life, energy. But we got only silence from Natalee's motionless body, which spoke volumes as it shouted back at us: " *she said no i will stay with you guys i will get a lift from you anways later.*"

In other words, 'I'm not coming back, I'm staying with you guys and you're going to have to deal with taking care of my body—have to give it a lift and put it somewhere later.' And, for sure, she wasn't coming back. We lost her when she drowned. She was staying with us now—forever.

At this moment of death, Deepak refers to lifting Natalee, an image he will return to when he describes her falling out of the car at the final drop-off. Clearly lifting Natalee's body also suggests resuscitation efforts. Joran will later describe lying alongside a sleeping Natalee on the beach suggesting both of them on the ground together at the moment of Natalee's death/sleep—another image confirming a desperate effort at CPR.

## Deepak's Scream of Guilt

At that moment I also wanted to scream—one more personal meaning of *"scream"* to me. As Natalee's *"friend,"* looking back I should have screamed at her to get out of the car because she should never have taken off with us. I'm screaming now, if you can hear me, that it would have been better for Natalee to have gone with her friends. I'm screaming at myself, at Joran, and even at my brother, Satish, for doing what we did. I'm looking back at Natalee and four different times I'm screaming: *"Get out of the car," "Go with them," "Better you go listen to them," "Go with them." "Go–go–go Natalee, why didn't you go?"* If only, if only, if only . . .

## Deepak Says Goodbye for Natalee

" *she said no i will stay with you guys i will get a lift from you anways later, **so she said bye to her friends** and i drove away, so then we were just talking etc, in the car*"

But I'm not through speaking for her. Keep going with my flow here. Listen to Natalee's words, *"she screamed something i can't recall,"* something I don't want to recall. And what was that? How about "*she said bye to her friends (and i drove away).*" See how clearly the story hangs together. I'm describing her death again, in two ways, not only her inability to speak but saying goodbye to her friends and her family for the final time.

This is a sad moment for me, so awful I can't tell you. Imagine never being able to say goodbye to your friends, and most of all to your family: your mother, your father, your brother and two little sisters. I have too good of an idea of what that must feel like. So I said it for her, right here. Exactly like I tell you, "*she said bye to her friends*"— and family—she and I said "*bye.*"

Also, when I tell you that Natalee screamed, "*something i can't recall*"—well, that's not totally true. I remember all too well what really happened at the end of her life, and I'm telling you here. That's why I also said, "*(something i can't recall.) so i was driving very slow*"— I'm taking you through these events slowly, step-by-step, so you can see my confession.

## Lifting the Body—'In Ways'

"*she said no i will stay with you guys i will get **a lift from you anways later**, so she said bye to her friends*"

There's still one more thing I'm screaming, something else I want you to know about where we put her body. Notice that Natalee is unequiv-ocally pointing to her death saying, 'No, I will get a lift in ways [anways] from you later.' This translates to 'In ways I will get a type of lift from you later, a different kind of lift when I'm no longer alive and you dispose of my body.'

Once more in my story I describe a vehicle that's stopped, and Natalee (in the first person, no less) talks about us giving her a lift later, a lift "*anways,*" suggesting that, after we stopped the boat, we lifted her body and put it into the ocean. But read the slip "*anways*" again as 'in ways' or 'in a ways'– virtually identical to my previous slip and geographical marker, "*anyways*" with both slips connected to "*later.*"

I'm confirming that after Natalee died we lifted her body into the ocean after going 'in a ways.' I'm giving you the same distance.

Natalee's body is not too far out into the ocean—you only have to go 'in a ways.'

That magic word *"stay"* also contains another important clue. Wherever we lifted Natalee's body into the ocean, there she stays. She isn't moving. This is one more confession and clue: look for her body in a container that doesn't move. So you're to look in the ocean—go "in a ways" and search for a container. But you need to know more, such as what area of the ocean to search. You have to see one last clue.

## Location of Body—a Perfect Fit

*"she said you can drop me off later at holiday inn anyways right" i said sure why not so as i was drove out of the <u>carlos road</u> and got on the <u>mainroad</u> there were natalees friends and she , pushed het head out of the window and screamed something i can't recall.so i was driving <u>very slow to make a left</u> to get in the next road and then one of natalees friend screamed for her to get out of the car , and she refused so then <u>i stopped my car</u>"*

Let's look more closely at Natalee's goodbye. The image of saying goodbye to her friends as she pulls away in some sort of transport also conjures up the image of friends standing at the dock, waving goodbye as her ship pulls off. I'm pointing to a second goodbye later—when we got rid of her body, the exact moment of the final goodbye linked to a ride in a vehicle with somebody driving immediately away—a boat ride during which we dumped the body.

Pay attention to the *geographical* clues I drop along the way. The trip starts on the road coming out of the Carlos road, and quickly I'm on the main road, but before driving very far I stop the car just before turning left because we've now run into Natalee's friends. At that point someone urges Natalee to get out of the car—twice.

In other words, this is all about the moment we dumped her body, the moment she got out of the boat. *The route of the car suggests in some ways the route of the boat.* I've quickly merged from one road onto the main road, gone straight for only a short while, and finally stopped just before turning back to my left. Remember Paulus' instructions when we took the "Carlos/Paulus" road to the sandbar, which would fit with Fisherman's Huts. Assuming we picked her body up at the Fisherman's Huts, this fits exactly with going out not very far into the ocean, and then stopping to let Natalee out before circling back to my left to head back to the marina at the Holiday Inn.

Thus the main message is that she's generally straight out into the ocean from where we picked up the body.

With me using Natalee's voice to tell you *"she said no i will stay with you guys i will"* I am not only confessing that Natalee never actually left us that night but, instead, stayed with us until she died. I'm also telling you that she has stayed with us even after we got rid of her body. She lingers in our minds in a real way. She's dominant, the most unforgettable person in our lives. It's as though I'm trapped right there with Natalee in the ocean—held captive in the prison of my mind, as police detectives say. And no matter how hard they try to cover up, Joran and Satish feel exactly the same way.

The boat Joran probably used was docked at the marina between the Marriott Hotel and the Holiday Inn, a bit closer to the Holiday Inn. It would have been a short trip to the obscure Fisherman's Huts area just north of the Marriott, where the crab cage went missing the same night. That would have been the easiest place to load the body. On one hand Deepak describes going straight out into the ocean from the Holiday Inn—the suggested reference point—and taking a right before shortly dropping off the body. This seems to match his idea of heading straight out from the Fisherman's Huts area and taking a left. Using two reference points—going left from Fisherman's Huts and right from the Holiday Inn—their paths would come together.

## Avoiding Group Assault Image

Although the three suspects have found themselves at odds since June 2005, in their current propaganda campaign they have denied any idea of a group assault and any suggestion that they were in Natalee's presence at the end. While the van der Sloot and Kalpoe camps shift blame among themselves, and debate which of the three guys was with her last, such discussions are mere distractions.

She was with all of them at the moment she died, and then they disposed of her body. Unconsciously, Deepak continually attempts to establish that truth as if he's writing a lawyer's brief to refute the cover-up version. Here and elsewhere Deepak makes it plain that "it was them," all three of them, all the way.

## Summary of New Information in Scene

- In one of the most striking action scenes in his email, Deepak takes us back to the details of their sneak attack—how, after driving Natalee to a secluded place, they suddenly stopped the car.

- Deepak has described the exact scene of Natalee's crisis in the most vivid terms, as he tells a chronological story just as a reporter would do.

- After Natalee refused to go along with the rape, Deepak describes how they pushed her from the car, stripped her, and prepared the backseat in order to rape her.

- Again Deepak confirms that Natalee died in his car as a result of the rape's brutality.

- Using one of his most vivid message markers, "*scream,*" Deepak tells us how Natalee choked while trying to throw up/"*scream.*"

- Next Deepak reveals how Joran "*screamed*" at him to get his attention at the moment of crisis, while he was off in his own world of ecstasy with Natalee totally helpless and controlled.

- Two vivid message markers—"*scream*" and "*VERY drunk*"—match perfectly to reveal that Natalee died from aspiration.

- Here is only one of two places where Deepak overtly describes Natalee suffering violence—through the key slip "*het head.*"

- Deepak confirms again how the boys' panicked efforts to resuscitate Natalee failed.

- Deepak provides another memorable picture of Natalee's death: saying goodbye to her friends.

- He notes how they lifted the body into the ocean—and how it can be lifted out—with geographical clues about where to search.

- He suggests again that the body was placed in a container.

- Deepak sums up the case in a key sentence, "*she said no i will stay with you guys i will get **a lift from you anways later**, so she said bye to her friends.*"

- From beginning to end Deepak reveals how his conscience continues to "*scream*" at him for what he did—and how his email is one earsplitting "*scream*" for justice on Natalee's behalf.

# 11
# Dropping Off Natalee

## Scene 1: On the Way to the Lighthouse

## Key Message Markers: 'Talking'–'Lighthouse'–'Trafficlights'

*"so **she said bye** to her friends and i drove away, so then we were **just talking** etc, in the car and then she said she wanted to see sharks ,it was by the **lighthouse** she saw them before that can we go , my friend said ok ,deepak lets go. so on my my to the **lighthouse** there was music playing and noone talking for a while when i looked in the backmirror my friend and natalee were kissing and touching (his hands etc was in her blouse but nothing nude or against natalees will ) so my brother siad just leave them for a while untill we get to the **lighthouse**, when i arrived at the **lighthouse** i said well here is the **lighthouse** they did not pay attention to me , so my brother said lets return (i did not stop anywhere not for a min only **trafficlights**) so after like 10 min my friend is telling me that natalee **fell asleep"***

## Anticipation

Natalee is dead but her body remains in the car as the three suspects begin to fathom the depths of their difficulty. What will Deepak tell us next? Better yet, what do we need to know? Deepak's deeper intelligence is locked into a pattern of revelations that explain exactly what Natalee's family and investigating authorities most need to know.

Disposal of the body is certainly the ultimate item on the agenda. Deepak has two scenes left before he reaches the end of his story, detailing the three suspects' first-hand contact with Natalee. In the last scene he will describe dropping Natalee off at her hotel, and certainly there we would expect a vivid description of exactly where her body now lies. Because the location of the body is so important—the most vital piece of evidence in the whole case—we could predict that Deepak will also provide striking clues.

Since he has already repeatedly pointed us to the location of the body—in a container in the ocean—we can anticipate particularly vivid matching thoughtprints conveying the same message. Deepak will also highlight central issues in his story to make his case—just as an attorney would do in a closing argument—leaving no doubt about what happened to Natalee Holloway. We might even expect him to go over the sexual assault in detail once more, and in a less-disguised way to confirm exactly what led to Natalee's death.

Thus Deepak begins this scene with one of the most dazzling message markers in his entire email.

## First: Strongest Confession of Sex—and the Noose

> *"and i drove away, so then we were just <u>talking</u> etc, in the car and then she said she wanted to see* **sharks**

> *it was by the lighthouse she saw them— before that can we go . . . there was music playing and* **noone** <u>*talking*</u> *for a while when i looked in the backmirror my friend and natalee were kissing and touching (***his hands etc was in her*** blouse but* **nothing nude** *or* **against natalees will***)"*

First, let me tell you something really important. When I use a word like *"talking"* that tells you I'm going to reveal plenty. So pay special attention right here.

I've just finished describing the sex, how we gave Natalee a lift, how I was "driving away" non-stop. And now I link *"talking"* to *"etc"*—another code word for sex. This is the most crystal-clear description of sex in my email: I'm looking in the back mirror and describing a sexual scene, in which Joran has *"his hands **etc** in her."* I might deny it on the surface, but this activity with Joran was totally, completely against Natalee's will. She was nude, and Joran's "etc"—his penis—was in Natalee. He was touching her body, doing whatever he wanted. The music was playing. I merge 'no' and 'one' in ***"noone** talking for a while,"* again showing how we merged/raped her; how we ran completely over her *"no."*

Also, *"noone"* is one letter from **'noose'** and is connected to the idea of not talking, which would certainly explain why Natalee couldn't talk. Sex in the backseat with a nude Natalee, resisting while being controlled with a noose around her neck.

And why were we going to the lighthouse? So Natalee could see the sharks. Get it? We were the sharks. We were the predators—sexual predators. See how clearly they all come together—*"sharks"* and *"lighthouse"* and Natalee? And sharks are silent predators. You can't see them coming and they attack without warning. Natalee never saw us coming. We were too fast.

Deepak has surpassed expectations again, leaving no doubt as to the phenomenal mental ability and total truthfulness of his unconscious mind. First, via the word "talking" he told us, "Be prepared; major information coming here," and then he followed up with two key revelations. Immediately, we find a string of sexual images unlike anywhere else in the email, adding vivid new details despite his blatant denials, of Natalee stripped nude and assaulted against her will.

And he has saved his most vicious sexual image for last—*"sharks,"* ravenous predators which completely destroy their victims. Like a prosecuting attorney, Deepak has argued strongly that this victim was sexually assaulted and that the assault unquestionably caused Natalee's death. Secondly, with a telling slip, *"noone/noose,"* he reiterates the fact that the three perpetrators controlled Natalee with some type of noose—most likely Joran's belt. Deepak clearly links the ligature to Natalee's inability to speak. Interestingly, old photographs of Joran jokingly controlling a friend with a belt around the friend's neck surfaced on the Internet in July 2005, shortly after Natalee's disappearance—and were quickly removed.

## Police Interviews Suggest Natalee Controlled by Belt

Ever attuned to important details, especially one as important as a possible neck-hold, we would expect confirmation of that in police interviews and elsewhere. Deepak doesn't disappoint us as he provides a detail that matches his slip "noone"/noose. When describing to police how he drove around immediately after picking up Natalee, he said he avoided passing by Carlos'n Charlie's again and turned left toward another nearby bar called "Choose a Name," because he saw police officers standing at the corner and he was not wearing his seatbelt.

Truly it's amazing how many messages Deepak's unconscious mind can pack into one brief sentence. Here he intentionally avoids the police over a seatbelt/"belt" matter with Natalee in the backseat of his car, confessing obviously that indeed—in complete violation of the law—they used a belt to control Natalee in the backseat. At the same time his powerful image of lacking a seatbelt himself in this context represents another aspect to his confession: read "I/we were totally out of control in the backseat."

Even the detail "Choose a Name" reflects their strategy of entrapping the easiest victim. How well this matches Joran's declaration when initially confronted about Natalee's disappearance twenty-four hours later, when he denied even knowing her—and several times when he claimed he couldn't even remember her name. In a real sense the boys had no idea who Natalee was—they didn't know her and they didn't care to know her. Once again a brief symbol, this time "Choose a Name," sums up their strategy in spades.

## Lighthouse: A Phallic Symbol

Deepak continues:

Now think about how a lighthouse looks. It's a phallic symbol with a light on its head. To put it graphically, I'm shining the light on one giant penis; really, three of them. And lighthouses attract boats, supposedly to serve and protect them. But our lighthouse was different. It wasn't there to guide Natalee through the night. By repeating "lighthouse" I'm shouting at you that we each attacked Natalee with our own long, tall lighthouse. That's the second meaning of "lighthouse." See how I continue to shine the light of sexual imagery on what happened?

And notice what Joran says, speaking for all of us, when Natalee wants to see the sharks: "*OK, Deepak let's go, let's do it.*"

But just to show you how versatile one image can be, "*lighthouse*" has another sexual meaning, one relating directly to Natalee personally.

## Lighthouse: Symbol of Natalee

"*so on my my to the **lighthouse** there was music playing and noone talking for a while when i looked in the backmirror my friend and natalee were kissing and touching (his hands etc was in her blouse but nothing nude or against natalees will)*"

You can see how eagerly I anticipated playing with Natalee. Read my slip, "*so on **my my** to the **lighthouse**"* as I watched, "*my friend and* *natalee were kissing and touching (his hands etc was in her blouse but nothing nude."* I watched Joran in the backseat, touching Natalee, having his way with her. He had already arrived at "the lighthouse" ahead of me—a lighthouse named Natalee. You can hear me saying, 'Oh, **my my** can't wait until I get to the lighthouse, to Natalee's little house.' All this *'looking in the back mirror'*! You can see how watching them have sex excited me, and how I was looking forward to duplicating Joran's fun for myself.

*"Lighthouse"* also represented Natalee, a feminine sexual symbol. That's why I used the image five times—to show you it had so many meanings. Think about it—a house with a light on top that attracts the eyes of sailors, men out for a cruise. A house symbolizes a woman, so a *"lighthouse"* would be what? A blonde woman! "Lighthouse" also symbolizes Natalee in particular—the blonde we saw on the dance floor before we started our dance with her, the *"lighthouse"* surrounded by sharks, Natalee's house that all three of us entered against her will. Even my phrase, *"it was by the lighthouse she"* suggests that *"she"* was the lighthouse.

When things are dark, I have to shine a light on them here. Looking in the *"back mirror"* at the sexual stuff again suggests looking at Natalee's back, suggesting sodomy, as did my earlier slip when she got in the *"backseet."*

## Police Interviews: Matching Sexual Stories

A rumor heard often in Aruba since Natalee's disappearance, told to me by an Aruban reporter, asserts that Deepak was partial to blonde tourist girls. Satish seemed to confirm this when he described Natalee as "the blonde American girl" who he first saw while she was dancing in Carlos'n Charlie's. Deepak's email description of what he saw happening in the backseat of his Honda is the most explicitly sexual scene in the email, but also its revelations continue to match similar hidden confessions which run between the lines through all of the suspects' statements. Since they concocted the cover-up together, in their statements to police the three guys would use the same type of sexual thoughtprints as those found in Deepak's email, but they each do it in their own unique way.

Joran's interviews reveal a plethora of sexual ideas. Besides his stories about Deepak putting on a porn video in the car after Natalee gets in, and group voyeurism involving a girl having sex in the backseat of another Honda, which also hints at group sex, Joran claims that Natalee wanted "fleshly intercourse"– perhaps awkwardly phrased due to translation, but we get the picture. Mirroring Deepak's email, Joran recalls that Natalee wanted to see the sharks and so the three guys took her as mentioned on a *sightseeing tour*. Read that to mean that they all looked upon her and engaged in voyeurism, one of their favorite sexcapades.

Think back to Joran's story about a sex act in the backseat of a Honda, in which he supplied the condom, and we would expect that, in his email, Deepak would hint that the three guys each used a condom with Natalee. And what better place than in The Explicit Email Sex Scene? Looking closely we find a disguised condom reference here, set off by Deepak's special parentheses marker in *"(his hands etc was in her blouse but nothing nude or against natalees will)."* Note *"his hands etc was in her—blouse"* suggests phallic penetration followed by *"blouse"* or a covering—then followed clearly by images of Natalee being nude and sex completely against her will. Together the images suggest the picture of a condom. One reason the boys did in fact use condoms was precisely because they'd be committing rape, sex totally against Natalee's will, and they wanted the evidence against them to show *"nothing."*

## Lesson for Police: Read Every Story Symbolically

This shows us again how we must see every story as symbolic, even another sex story from police interviews such as the time Joran described fingering Natalee in the backseat. He reported first that he pushed her panties aside—read pushed *her* aside, or violated her. Then he said he inserted two fingers. Symbolically, with "finger" representing "penis" (not difficult decoding), he suggests two different penises meaning a gang rape. In completing his story, Joran "thinks Natalee has had a shave in the pubic area and is hairless" which is yet another confession that Natalee was exposed, her covering (her clothes) having been stripped off.

In thoughtprint decoding we take every word as potentially symbolic, and especially so for highly charged sexual language. If police had learned how to do the same thing they could have seen the same consistent story being told over and over again between the lines. Consciously, Joran would have us think Natalee cooperated sexually, while unconsciously he informs us in shocking, symbolic images that this was one brutal assault carried out by these three monsters, as they pushed everything aside in their selfish, predatory pursuit of power.

Continuing to reveal his shadow side, and continuing to confess with virtually every new tale, Joran mentions another story about fingering Natalee in the backseat while riding in Deepak's car. But he stopped, he said, not because it was improper sexual behavior with a young, innocent stranger but because it was showing disrespect to Deepak and Satish. We then have yet another confession of the intense disrespect the boys showed to Natalee.

The search continues and we find another powerful sexual image—Joran told the authorities that Natalee spoke of having slaves on her plantation. But Natalee would never have said any such thing! The alleged comment was awkwardly contrived by the Arubans and drawn from their own naïve stereotype of the Southern United States, but they were about 150 years out-of-date. Nobody in the South talks like that anymore.

Yet here lies the truth in another one of their attempted lies: Natalee *was* their sex slave. They intruded on her plantation, into her house, onto her private property, repeatedly planting themselves there. And in their statements and emails they scream at the authorities an entire litany of potent sexual innuendos. Joran really couldn't have said it any more forcefully—Natalee *was their slave*.

On another occasion, Joran described Natalee awakening, startled from sleep, in Deepak's backseat. Immediately she starts to kiss Joran. Such a scenario suggests that the suspects' sudden sexual attack on Natalee caught her completely off guard. In his interviews with police, Joran provided many details about his promiscuity, describing repeated sexual activity. One night, he said, he was engaged in sexual activity with a girl beneath a blanket in his apartment—with two of his male friends close by. The girl was offered the opportunity to engage in sex with all of them but refused. His hidden message, strongly symbolized by the blanket, is actually a confession that he and his friends are covering up a group assault—and a blanket involved in sexual activity mirrors Deepak's email slip *"backseet,"* which suggested that the boys covered the backseat while raping Natalee.

Taking absolutely nothing for granted, we find another brief yet revealing sexual image in one of Deepak's stories. In his initial police interview Deepak said that as he drove by an "old Hooters building" Joran started to kiss Natalee, soon followed by his touching her breasts. Of course "Hooters building or restaurant" symbolizes "women's breasts" as everyone knows. Despite the restaurant chain's owl logo, its marketing has strongly emphasized its Hooters Girl waitresses wearing white, tight T-shirts. So at the exact moment Deepak begins describing Joran specifically touching Natalee's breasts he immediately refers to an empty Hooters building, meaning that, right off, he's telling us that Natalee ended up dead, that her building was soon empty, that she had died and turned to stone.

With one sexual escapade after another the three boys are shouting at the police, "How many times do we have to tell you what we've done?" Maybe one day they'll catch on. All that's at stake is justice. Nothing more, nothing less.

## Lighthouses Warn

Back to Deepak's story:

Remember I'm telling a story with ideas, with pictures, with a clue here, a clue there. So now, Beth, what do sharks do with their victims? They destroy them. And that's what we did to Natalee.

Think about lighthouses in another way. What do they do? They warn ships of impending danger, try to prevent shipwrecks. When I use *"lighthouse"* as a warning light, you can see we paid no attention— and so, yeah, there was a huge shipwreck. We destroyed Natalee's boat, her life, and our own lives as well.

## The Lighthouse Shines on Deepak's Car—and Joran's House

*"we were just talking etc, in the car and then she said she wanted to see sharks ,it was by the lighthouse she saw them before that can we go , my friend said ok,deepak lets go. so on my my to the lighthouse"*

Don't think for a minute that we ever really went to the lighthouse. First *"just talking"* in the car, Natalee wants to see the sharks. Well that's where she saw them all right, in my car. The entire time I'm talking about the lighthouse we're all in my car. See? I'm shining the light on that house, the house of ill-repute, my Honda.

I immediately repeat myself in *"by the lighthouse— she saw them before that (—can we go)"* meaning that she saw the sharks before ever arriving at the fantasized lighthouse. Another meaning for *"lighthouse"* is secluded place, and again that's what I'm trying to tell you. We stopped on a secluded side road where we attacked her in my car.

Next we have the question, *"can we go,"* implying that Natalee was dead so we needed to do something. Now read the sentence all together, *"it was by the lighthouse she saw them before that can we go"* and you'll see a different message. We had to take Natalee to a house where she *"saw us"* before we could go, before we could leave her. We're under pressure to go somewhere but must first take care of business. Here I'm speaking for a deceased Natalee as though she's a witness, telling you she saw us at a house before we could go and dispose of her body—implying we took her to a house after she died. Now whose house might that be?

Look where I suggest we went, *"my friend said **ok ,deepak lets go. . . . my my** to the lighthouse . . . ."* Joran, speaking in the first-person implies, "OK, Deepak let's go to my house." Right after this Satish will say "let's return," also suggesting that we go back to where we were earlier before all this happened, to Joran's house in Noord. I'm shining the light on going to Joran's house after Natalee died.

Police have considered the possibility that the three boys assaulted Natalee at Joran's house. In police interviews, Joran said he did go to his house with Natalee but that they didn't go in (which might also be seen as a screen to deflect attention from Deepak's car). Deepak and Satish have denied going to Joran's house with Natalee. Nonetheless, vividly and repeatedly, Deepak's thoughtprints strongly point toward the assault's taking place in the car.

In the next scene Deepak again makes it plain that Natalee died in the car, a fact supported by convincing circumstantial evidence, such as the two brothers obsessively cleaning the car. They had some significant DNA of Natalee's to remove—almost certainly her vomitus, probably vaginal fluids, possibly including blood due to the brutal sexual assault, and possibly their own sperm. A car would be far easier to clean than Joran's room. If some non-specific DNA of Natalee's was found in Deepak's backseat, that could be explained away since she was a passenger in his car. It would not be so easy to explain Natalee's DNA should it be found in Joran's room, and it would be even more difficult to explain if her DNA was discovered in the house, along with Deepak's or Satish's DNA.

The overwhelming likelihood is that the assaults took place in Deepak's Honda. And that's the scenario mostly strongly supported by each of the suspects' thoughtprints.

## Order of Assault

*"so on my my to the lighthouse there was music playing and noone talk-ing . . . <u>my friend and natalee</u> were kissing and . . . his hands etc was in her blouse . . . nude . . . against natalees will . . . my brother <u>siad</u> just leave them for a while **untill** <u>we get to the lighthouse</u>, when i arrived at the lighthouse i said well here is the lighthouse they did not pay attention to me , so my brother said lets return (i did not stop anywhere not for a min only **trafficlights**) so after like 10 min my friend is telling me that natalee fell asleep i said you kidding"*

Again I relate the order of our assaults. On the way to the lighthouse Joran and Natalee are engaging in sexual activity in the backseat, which my brother and I observe, with Satish telling me to leave them alone, give them time. Joran, who orchestrated the group dance, went first. Satish added, *"just leave them for a while untill **we** get to the lighthouse,"* meaning that we'd get our turn next with the blonde lighthouse, Natalee, *'oh my my'* remember. Another small slip, *"**untill** we get to the lighthouse"*—meaning two 'tills,' tells you that my broth-er and I were both going to till the ground at Natalee's house. Obviously Satish went second because here comes my turn and I went last—with the crisis occurring on my shift, *"when i arrived at the **lighthouse** i said well here is the **lighthouse** they [ Joran and Satish] did not pay attention to me , so my brother said lets return (i did not stop anywhere not for a min only **trafficlights**)."*

In other words, when my turn with Natalee came the others were not paying attention. My brother has said, *"let's return,"* meaning my turn following his. So I returned to assaulting Natalee and, putting it in parentheses again to highlight the message, I keep driving, meaning I had sex with her for 10 minutes. How many times have I described that specific amount of time? And I can tell you, 10 minutes isn't long for sex.

### Death Quick—Ignored Warning, Running Red Lights

*"(i did not stop anywhere not for a min only **trafficlights**)"*

But you can see what happened. I failed to read the signals of her distress, didn't see the warning signs, and ran the red light. Read through my denial that I stopped at traffic lights. Really, none of us saw the red light coming. That's why I made it plural, *"trafficlights."* I also blame Joran and my brother for not paying closer attention when things went wrong. They should have known that sex distracts you, particularly the power-trip abusive type that makes you completely insensitive. I kept driving sexually, not stopping *"except for trafficlights"*—back to that in a minute—and suddenly Joran informed me *"that natalee fell asleep,"* meaning that she died. You can hear my utter shock in my words: *"you kidding just wake her up."*

That attention-grabber—*"trafficlights"*—is a message for you too, Beth, to slow down and stop, look around, and see the messages I have for you. I've just described in non-stop fashion, without a period in sight, my driving sexual assault, which culminated in the worst outcome imaginable, your daughter's death.

However, I lied when I said I stopped. You can see the truth, *"I did not stop anywhere,"* repeated *"not for a min"*—my abbreviation even tells you I still can't slow down in making my confession. Read the same message, *"I did not stop . . . not for a min only . . . "* implying 'I didn't control myself, not for being a man—I was only being a phony macho man.'

I'm using *"trafficlights"* to shine the light on what I didn't do. I failed to stop with Natalee when I should have. Look, I never should have taken Natalee for a ride at all. I had no business sexually assaulting her. I'm telling you secretly that I ran a huge red light and completely ignored the warning in the back of my mind. I told you the same thing earlier. What do lighthouses do? They warn about danger. We all knew better but we kept on going.

Like I said, another crucial meaning for *"lighthouse"* is my conscience, my deeper intelligence, my soul. I should be arrested. Isn't that what happens when you blatantly run red lights? I know how badly I behaved. I even know the sentence I deserve. Remember, this is a confession. I am the beacon of light. I am the lighthouse; I am the traffic light.

Taking on the role of a prosecuting attorney, at the end of his story with Natalee, Deepak Kalpoe paints a clear picture of his own criminal behavior—he ran a red, red light, big time. Shrewdly, his deeper mind saved the single most powerful image of an overt violation until the absolute end of his presentation. And he tells us exactly how long his assault lasted and how quickly Natalee died. Without a doubt, Deepak unconsciously sees himself as a prosecutor.

With "traffic light" the same thing as "red light," Deepak makes yet another subtle suggestion that Natalee was a virgin. In short he implies a confession that the boys realized she was a virgin and that it momentarily got their attention but in the end they continued raping her. At a minimum it certainly suggests vaginal bleeding as a result of the assault.

## Lighthouse: Shining the Light on the Body—Quick Trip to Ocean Floor

> *"when i arrived at the lighthouse i said well here is the lighthouse they did not pay attention to me , so my brother said lets return (i did not stop anywhere not for a min only trafficlights) so after like 10 min my friend is telling me that natalee fell asleep i said you kidding"*

At the end of the "lighthouse trip" I've told you in several more ways that Natalee has died. First, Natalee wanted to see sharks, predators that destroy their victims. Natalee is not responding when we arrive at the alleged lighthouse, and on the return trip to the Holiday Inn she has fallen asleep—both disguised death references.

But I'm still not through being the lighthouse. I have to shine the light on three more events. After my confession that Natalee died, where do I now need to shine the brightest light in the case? On the body, of course. So read my word pictures. First of all, where are sharks and where are their victims? In the ocean, of course, and there the victims disappear, completely consumed by the sharks.

But to get to the ocean you have to have a vehicle, right Beth? I tell several connecting stories at the same time, but now I'm talking about the body. Look back at the story. Not long after I arrive at the lighthouse, during my turn with Natalee, no one is responding to me. Natalee has just died. Immediately I repeat myself—I connect driving directly to our destination, not stopping anywhere, with Natalee's sudden death, her having "fallen asleep." Our ultimate destination will be the Holiday Inn—code for ocean. See what I'm telling you now? Pretty quickly we took her body to the ocean on a boat that moved pretty fast. Sharks who swim fast, taking their prey with them, symbolize the same thoughtprint.

But before you think Natalee's body has completely disappeared, think back to what I've told you before. The puzzle comes together— same picture, different angle. Remember a *"lighthouse"* shines its light on the ocean and on boats. That's another indication that Natalee's body is 'in the drink,' the ocean. Lighthouses bring to mind ship-wrecks—storms that devour boats that crash against the rocks when you can't see the lighthouse, or you ignore it. Well, our night with Natalee was a colossal shipwreck for us. We destroyed the ship "Natalee"(boats are often named for women, by the way), and where do shipwrecks end up? At the bottom of the ocean. Keep that in mind.

Likewise, after consuming their prey close to the surface, sharks often swim down deep. Here, I'm suggesting that we took Natalee's body to the floor of the ocean. But notice how I stress waiting to get to the (light) house, arriving at the house, and then total silence in response to an announcement of the arrival at the house—all the while the trip is taking place in a car. Silence at the end of a long journey is linked to the water/lighthouse. Can you see the picture of Natalee's final trip—her dead body making its silent journey on its way to her ulti-mate home at the bottom of the ocean, to her horror hotel, 'The Holloway End/Inn'?

How did she get there? We used some type of a vehicle or a contain-er for both silent journeys. First a boat to get her out to the ocean, then a container-type "vehicle" in which we disposed of her. Natalee's body sank to the bottom of the ocean floor—and quickly—because it had been placed in a heavy container of some type. We not only weighted down Natalee's body,  we made sure it would stay in her final home because of the container's own weight and construction. Which means that you can find it. That's what I'm announcing if any-one can hear me. I'm speaking for a silent Natalee. Think of the search for the Titanic with the lights shining on the ocean floor—that's exactly what my mind is doing by shouting at you, 'Lighthouse, light-house, ocean, ocean floor.'

On that boat trip we were anxious to get out there and back, so we didn't fool around. We also didn't want to be seen out and about by fishermen. We wanted as fast a boat as we could get, and not a real big one. We certainly didn't want to get caught with her body in the boat, or even to be seen in a boat. Now think about sharks again, which can move incredibly fast in the water, and you can envision us traveling along speedily in our boat 'by the name of Shark,' on its way to do even more damage to you by hiding your daughter's body. We were sharks of the highest order.

## Container Images: The Trunk of the Car and Deepak's Sadness

The bright light from my *"lighthouse"* also confirms one other familiar part of the story; namely, that we placed her body in a container before dropping it into the ocean. Lighthouses also are surrounded by water, a picture of a house in the water. That's one thing about houses; they are fixed and don't move. Above all a lighthouse is extremely sturdy, made of stone to withstand the ocean's relentless waves and super powerful winds. This is a crucial clue, another matching thoughtprint, reminding you that Natalee's current house, her container at the bottom of the ocean, is anchored and isn't moving. How many times do I have to tell you? Her body is discoverable.

*. . . my friend and natalee were kissing and . . . his hands etc was in her blouse . . . nude . . . against natalees will . . . my brother **siad** just leave them for a while untill we get to the **lighthouse***

There's a hint that we placed Natalee temporarily in another container. With Natalee (and Joran) in the backseat, Satish says basically, "Leave them, leave her, alone until we get to the (light) house." See the picture? Natalee's alone in the back of the car; in other words, we put her body in the trunk while we rode to Joran's house.

Now—right after describing the sex, in the most explicit description in my entire email (*"his hands etc was in her blouse . . . but nothing nude or against natalees will"*)—I make another little slip: *"so my brother **siad** (just leave them for a while)."* Read "so my brother sad"—so Deepak's sad and very depressed over what he's done. Surely I know Satish is depressed as well, and you haven't heard the last of my depression. You will see that I'm very concerned about being left alone, suffering total rejection, maybe taking all the blame.

Strange isn't it, Beth—me depressed when I'm putting on such a good show? But isn't that what a living hell is? My phrase, *"looking in the back mirror"* also tells you I'm constantly looking over my shoulder at the authorities and at my own conscience—my own internal policeman. That would depress anyone, don't you think?

## Lighthouse Sees Big Picture

One last aspect of a lighthouse—it's tall to see above the storms at sea and guide the ships. My email takes you high above the storms, in this case to see what's really going on. The email itself is one big lighthouse. From there you can see the whole story—a dangerous storm, the ship crashing, where it crashed, who survived, and the devastating effect the horrific journey had on them. It also shines its light on exactly where to search for the wreckage.

## Summary of New Information in Scene

- Five times—unlike anywhere else in his email—Deepak uses a vivid message marker, "*lighthouse*," having multiple important meanings and informing us in this scene that we will find crucial revelations and powerful validations of previous thoughtprints.

- "*Lighthouse*"—Deepak shines a powerful light on the case in the vital, next-to-last scene with Natalee, fulfilling his promise. He leaves no doubt that the multiple rapes led to Natalee's death.

- "*Lighthouse*," suggesting secluded place, reveals that the rape occurred on a secluded side road—Natalee never saw the actual "lighthouse."

- Deepak saves the most explicit sexual scene in his entire email for last, with all the details—including how Natalee, the blonde "*lighthouse*"—was stripped nude, overpowered, and continually violated against her will.

- Deepak unquestionably defines his sexual code: Joran put his hands and "*etc*" in a nude Natalee totally against her will with "*lighthouse*"—tall and standing erect—being a clear phallic symbol. Clearly "*etc*" used repeatedly means "rape/sex."

- Strongest sexual predator/violent image in email: they were "*sharks*."

- Deepak connects vivid sexual assault to slip "*noone (talking)*" suggesting "noose" (changing one letter) kept Natalee from talking.

- Deepak elaborates on how the three suspects ignored warnings, "ran a red light" ("*traffic light*")—another major message marker)—and again how he was violating Natalee when she suddenly died.

- Deepak reveals details; he confirms that his rape lasted 10 minutes, and that Natalee died quickly.

- Deep within himself, Deepak is sad and depressed over his actions.

- "*Sharks*" confirm Natalee was consumed, is dead, and is in the ocean.

- Another thoughtprint confirmation of death: Natalee "*fell asleep*"

- As anticipated, Deepak stressed the location of body—the ocean, with "*lighthouse*" and "*sharks*" implying both ocean and shipwrecks at the bottom of the ocean.

- Deepak also stresses that body can be found on the ocean floor in a container, with one last crucial meaning of "*lighthouse*" being a picture of a solid house/container, in the ocean, that does not move.

- All-in-all, Deepak's confession rises to new heights with dynamic imagery—"*lighthouse*," "*sharks*," "*nude*," "*against her will*," not stopping at "*traffic light*," and Natalee "*fell asleep*." We find vivid pictures of confession, rape, destruction/death, and a hidden body, a body held down in a strong and solid cage now resting on the ocean floor.

## Scene 2: Drop-Off at the Holiday Inn

*my friend said* **ok ,deepak lets go. so** *on my my to the lighthouse . . . when i arrived at the lighthouse i said well here is the lighthouse they did not pay attention to me , so my brother said lets return (i did not stop anywhere not for a min only trafficlights)*

*so after like 10 min my friend is telling me that natalee fell asleep i said you kidding just wake her up and tell ask her if its* **holiday inn** *for sure she is staying so my friend woke her up and confirmed with natalee she was staying at the* **holiday inn**, *so i drove to the lobby driveway of* **holiday inn** *and then we woke her up, she got out of the car and fell on the floor my friend said damn she fell and then rushed out of the same door natalee came out and picked her up immediately, after she stood up she pushed my friend and said leave me alone or something like that i can't recall , my friend offered to help het to her room* **she said no. she he** *stepped in the car and while i was driving away i saw natalee walking towards the lobby and a gentleman with a walkie talkie and black clothes approached her and i think they were talking*

## Anticipation

The three guys are now returning to the "Holiday Inn" to take Natalee back to her hotel. Deepak's email story matches the original story they told to authorities. However, just a few days after this email was written, they confessed that this was a lie. As such, this fictional part of the story offers incredible potential for revealing the real story between the lines. In creating this fiction, Deepak's unconscious mind can paint whatever pictures it desires. The pictures it creates, however, will offer striking clues to the truth, to the real story of what happened to Natalee Holloway.

Having emphasized the cause of Natalee's death—the gang rape—in the previous scene, Deepak will likely weave two significant threads together to tie up his story. We can anticipate that he will first remind us again that Natalee died—the outcome of the boys' predatory attack— and will then divulge many more details about the perpetrators' last moments with Natalee. Above all, we can be sure that, in the face of his extraordinary confession, Deepak will specifically highlight the disposal of the body.

## Big Gap Between Periods: Non-Stop Details of Assault and Death

Again Deepak continues his confession.

Step back, Beth, and you can see the enormous pressure I'm under. There are no periods in my email at all, starting with the scene where we're headed to the lighthouse and ending when we've dropped Natalee off at the Holiday Inn. The previous period was inserted in *"my friend said **ok ,deepak lets go. so** on my my to the lighthous,"* and the last period showed up after Natalee's final words to us, *"she said no."*

There's also a rhyme here, which tells the entire story in a nutshell, "Ok Deepak let's go"/ "She said 'no.'" We wanted to be with her and she really didn't want to be with us. Between these two periods, between "go" and "no," is the story of Natalee's assault, her death, and her burial. Sure, I'm speaking for her here about the entire escapade, *"she said no"*—how fitting her last words in this email. Now we're still trying to go, to run, to get out of here without any blame coming our way, and Natalee is still saying, 'No—oh no you won't.'

Of course I can't get away because I've got to keep confessing. The non-stop pressure behind my treatment of these last two scenes tells you how painful yet crucial they are, because I'm shouting at you—I have to get this off my chest as fast as I can. It's continuation of the *"lighthouse"* messages, and yet I never shined the light brighter on what happened. And I haven't turned that light off yet.

I have a particular reason for stressing that here. First, look at all the death images I highlighted:

*(i did not stop anywhere not for a min only trafficlights) so after like 10 min my friend is telling me that* **natalee fell asleep** *i said you kidding just* **wake her up** *and tell ask her if its holiday inn for sure she is staying* **so my friend woke her up** *and confirmed with natalee she was staying at the holiday inn, so i drove to the lobby driveway of holiday inn and then* **we woke her up,** *she got out of the car and* **fell on the floor** *my friend said* **damn she fell** *and then rushed out of the same door natalee came out and picked her up immediately, after she stood up she pushed my friend and said* **leave me alone** *or something like that i can't recall , my friend offered to help het to her room* **she said no.** *[she he stepped]*

## Death and Failed Rescue—'damn she fell'

I treat the crucial moment of Natalee's death with repeated references—falling asleep twice, falling on the floor twice, alone, *'she said no'* (to life), and three desperate urges to *"wake her up."* Joran and I, we talked, he got my attention at that precise moment she fell, the moment of death. Remember, I'm on top of her, out of it, in my own world, and Joran first informs me that she's asleep, not breathing. Like I said before, Joran got my attention and let me know that Natalee was in distress.

But there's more. In shock I tell him to wake her up—*"i said you kidding just wake her up."* Meaning, 'Do something; bring her back!' I couldn't believe what happened; how fast things went south. I still can't! I panicked. In my story Natalee falls back to sleep a second time, we wake her up and she immediately falls on the ground getting out of the car. In a panic, Joran shouts *"Damn she fell"* and rushes out the door to help her, quickly picking her up. Surprisingly Natalee resists any help, pushes Joran away saying, *"Leave me alone."* Then he *"offered to help* **het** *to* **her** *room she said no."*

By now you ought to be able to put this puzzle together by yourself, but let me help you. In my crucial slip (*"my friend offered to help **het** to **her** room"*) I'm pointing out that Joran assaulted Natalee— "*help het*/hit her"—suggesting that he was the one who was controlling Natalee's neck with a noose. Again I use this slip *"het,"* as in first Natalee "*hets*/hits her head," and now Joran "*hets*/hits her"– both times to show how the chokehold led to the aspiration death. And Joran was the one who inflicted the 'head injury,' the strangulation. But at the same time, see, I *"help **het** to **her** room"* too.

That's right—we both helped her to her final room, her final resting place. Also, in my cover-up story I repeat the idea that he was the one controlling her, when Joran alone was the one who picked Natalee up off the ground.

But I'm also describing our rescue efforts again. Natalee suddenly quit breathing air after breathing in her own vomit. So Joran first tried to resuscitate her. He let go of the noose and tried to let her breathe and vomit, but nothing happened. So we—the second time we woke her it was *"we"*—tried together to wake her up and get her to breathe. She was on the ground with Joran, and he was in charge of the rescue, trying to pick her up, to bring her back to life. In the story she fell while getting out of the car—remember? This means that we put her body on the ground. But Natalee never responded, and we really started panicking, all of us. Desperately we attempted a type of CPR.

Three times I tell you about trying to wake her up, pointing out our repeated efforts to resuscitate her. You can still hear our desperate cry: 'Wake up! Wake up! Come back, Natalee.' And notice, three times I tell you that she fell—*"fell asleep," "fell on the floor," "damn she fell."* The last two times happened after three efforts to wake her.

Also, notice in my story the abrupt angry change in her demeanor as she walks off, never speaking to us again. I'm telling you how final the moment was, and how angry I know she would have been with us if she could have spoken. At times during the rape you could see the anger in her eyes, beyond her terror. So all our efforts failed, and Joran, speaking for all of us said, *"Damn she fell"*—**translation:** 'Damn, she died. She's gone for good.'

Natalee fought like a tiger and tried to resist our attack—yeah, she stood up for herself, just as I show her here, standing up and walking off while telling us "no." Notice how painful Natalee's words were to me—*(she . . . said leave me alone **or something like that i can't recall**)*—so much so that I don't want to remember them. I was so out of touch with her at the final moment, no wonder *"I can't recall"* what Natalee said. Last time it was when she was screaming out to her friends; this time it's when she's leaving us. Both times I'm really referring to her stifled voice, when she couldn't breathe or speak because we didn't let her vomit.

Who knew that would lead to her death?

## Slip 'she he' Confession: Natalee Not Dropped Off At Hotel

*my friend offered to help het to her room she said no.* **she he stepped** *in the carand while i was driving away i saw natalee walking towards the lobby*

Next I make a now-familiar but still-revealing slip. In *"she he stepped in the car"* I'm making clear that Natalee didn't stay out of the car but that she got back in it. We never left her at the Holiday Inn. Joran picked her dead body up and put it back into the car—in the trunk, to be transported.

## Flashback: Ordering Natalee Out of Car on Road

*"she got out of the car and **fell on the floor** my friend said **damn she fell** and then rushed out of the same door natalee came out and picked her up immediately, after she stood up she pushed my friend and said **leave me alone** or something like that i can't recall , my friend offered to help* het *to her room **she said no. she he** stepped in the car and while i was driving away i saw natalee walking towards the lobby and a gentleman with a walkie talkie and black clothes approached her and i think they were talking and i had never seen natalee again sinds."*

Beth, you know how I elaborate on two similar scenes with one story. As this scene started, the car stops and Natalee immediately gets out. Sound familiar? See the how important stopping the car is? With Natalee getting out of the car and falling to the ground, I'm not only pointing to her death—she's down—but also harkening back to that moment we suddenly stopped the car on the side road and ordered her out of the car. It would be a natural thing to think about again because that happened not long before she died and it was really the start of it all. This is really a flashback to the moment when we suddenly turned on her.

Now take it step-by-step. First in *"she got out of the car and **fell on the floor"*** think about us first stopping the car, yelling at her, pushing her out, and getting her ready to lie down for us. Joran, the one who shoved her out of the backseat, responded this way, *"my friend said **damn she fell** and then rushed out of the same door natalee came out and picked her up immediately."* As the group assault began, with all of us suddenly turning on her, Joran sarcastically said, *"Damn she fell,"* and immediately followed her out the same door.

You can see what happened next, *"my friend **offered** to help het to her room **she said no**. (**she he** stepped in the car)."* Translation, Joran at first made the shocked Natalee an offer—'go along with us, have some fun with us.'

Natalee responded, *"after she stood up she pushed my friend and said **leave me alone** or something like that i can't recall."* She tried to push us away and fight back. Natalee immediately, *"said no."* Natalee tried to fight back, but notice that Joran, *"picked her up immediately"* meaning he quickly brought her under control *using his hands.* How? Read on: *"my friend offered to help **het** to her room."* Joran quickly got her around the neck as in **"help het her,"** to help overpower her, to bring her under his power, to help force her back to her room, back into the car.

Not only was it quick, it also kept her from screaming. Just as I implied before, she hit her head, only this time she ran into an obstacle while trying to scream out to her friends—meaning Joran's chokehold stopped her from shouting.

By this time we had her surrounded. This is when we stripped her—not only to make her vulnerable and submissive, but because we didn't want any torn clothes, any sign of a struggle. It was a lot easier to control her at first outside the car before she knew what hit her. And that way I could prepare the backseat and cover it with a sheet—we didn't want to leave any evidence of the assault in my backseat, and I like to keep a clean car, a really clean car. It's also a lot easier to have the fun you want in the backseat with a girl who's nude.

It's obvious what happened next: "**she he** *stepped in the car.*" My slip *"she he"* tells you Natalee indeed got back in the car while being controlled by Joran, by all of us. And *"she"* in another way merged with *"he"*—was repeatedly raped by all the "he's." "He" stepped into her car/container. One more subtle picture. She didn't have a chance.

Back in the car now, and skip slightly ahead to "*and while i was driving away i saw natalee walking towards the lobby and a gentleman with a walkie talkie and black clothes approached her and i think they were talking.*" Natalee was forced back into the car where we were all 'dressed in black' and full of evil, where we all approached her, and where I continued "driving away." While taking my turn something happened, "*and i had never seen natalee again sinds.*" She died.

Whenever I have Natalee moving in and out of cars, pay attention. Those episodes tell a big part of the story.

## Wake Up: The Tell—Body on Ground Floor of Holloway Inn

"*so after like 10 min my friend is telling me that natalee fell asleep i said you kidding just wake her up and tell ask her if its **holiday inn** for sure she is staying so my friend woke her up and **confirmed** with natalee she was staying at the **holiday inn**, so i drove to the lobby driveway of **holiday inn** and then we woke her up, . . . and i had never seen natalee again sinds.(**holiday inn** has no cameras in the driveway or lobby) it was around 2.15 am .monday i came to work normally 4- 11 pm)*"

I've told you several ways that, once back in the car, it wasn't long before Natalee died—particularly in "*after like 10 min my friend is telling me that **natalee fell asleep**.*" And since we're in my car when it happened, I'm hinting strongly that's where it occurred. Also, as I said, I was so out of it that Joran had to tell me a crisis had just occurred—"*after like 10 min,*" once more reminding you how long my assault lasted.

Now let's come back to 'The Question'—where is Natalee's body? You can imagine that of all the possible places in the email, this is the scene in which I would shout out the answer to you. That's why I emphasized her death so much here—so I could emphasize where her body is. Well, here's the answer. It's right in front of you. Four times I use *"Holiday Inn"* in rapid succession—it's the key to the code. Look at the sequence of events.

After Joran tells me Natalee has fallen asleep, I reply, *"i said you kidding just wake her up and tell ask her if its **holiday inn** for sure she is staying."* Obviously I'm shocked by this sudden, utterly unexpected turn of events—I'm still in shock. I wanted Joran to magically wake her up but it was too late. And now my guilt is so great that I immediately start telling you where the body is. Notice my slip, *"**tell ask** her if its holiday inn for sure she is staying."* Notice my slip; this is The Tell—I'm not asking you I'm **telling** you and the authorities where she is **"for sure,"** as in *"holiday inn **for sure**."* No question about it. She is in the Holiday Inn—*code for the ocean*. That's where her body is, for sure.

## How to Solve the Case: Four Key Words

I continue to hint about the location of body in four different ways. You want to know how to solve this case in a nutshell, here it is. Four simple words in order: *"fell," "stay," "wake,"* and *"up."*

*"my friend is telling me that natalee **fell** asleep i said you kidding just **wake** her **up** and tell ask her if its holiday inn for sure she is <u>staying</u> so my friend **woke** her **up** and confirmed with natalee she was <u>staying</u> at the holiday inn, so i drove to the lobby driveway of holiday inn and then we **woke** her **up**, she got out of the car and **fell** on the floor my friend said damn she **fell** and then rushed out of the same door natalee came out and picked her **up** immediately, after she stood **up** she pushed my friend and said leave me alone or something like that i can't recall , my friend offered to help het to her room **she said no. she** he stepped"*

Right off, one of those words tells you something crucial about the location of Natalee's body—besides my telling you it's in the ocean. Notice another geographical reference.

## First Key Word: 'fell'

*my friend is telling me that natalee **fell** asleep . . . so i drove to the lobby driveway of <u>holiday inn</u> and then we woke her up, she got out of the car and **fell** <u>on the floor</u> my friend said damn she **fell**."*

As I continue to talk to you in code about Natalee's ocean grave, I point you toward another geographical clue so you'll know where to go from here. The truth is we never took her back to the original *"Holiday Inn,"* but the deeper truth is we took her to another "Holiday Inn" and now you know which one it is—the ocean.

Three times I say it. First after she *"**fell** asleep"* telling you she died but also to alert you to my key word which I proceed to use again twice— *"**fell**"* (on the floor) and the last time, *"Damn she **fell.**"* I'm clarifying exactly where Natalee's body now lies—the ocean floor. As usual I'm saying it over and over until you get it. And indeed, from where she is now she has the potential to damn us, to damn us real good.

## Second Key Word: 'stay/stays'

The next word to look at carefully is *"stay,"* meaning fixed, permanent home, not moving, as in: " . . . *tell ask her if its holiday inn **for sure** she is **staying** so my friend woke her up and **confirmed** with natalee she was **staying** at the holiday inn."* And I connect it to two of the identical, absolutely strongest words I could find—*"for sure"* and *"confirmation"*—doubly underscoring the additional secret, Natalee's body is in the ocean and not moving. That means only one thing: she's in some type of heavy container, and in a minute I will tell you exactly where it's sitting.

Look how clear I make my code. *Once you break the code and determine that "Holiday Inn" means "ocean," everything falls into place.* Then you can compare larger spaces like hotels or oceans to smaller spaces within the larger ones. The container or cage is to the ocean what the hotel room is to the hotel. In essence, I've just confirmed the room number—the container room where her body stays. All that's left is to figure out where the hotel is. That's why you have to pay attention to geographical references to the Holiday Inn, because I'm locating a specific place for you.

## Third and Fourth Keywords: 'Wake' and 'Up'

After all these clues about where her body is, my next instructions to you are cued by two important words: "wake" and "up." First the command "**wake** her **up**" followed by "**woke** her **up**" twice. Listen, not only can you wake Natalee up, she has already awakened, prepared to speak if somebody brings her up—I use "up" five times to tell you exactly what to do. Bring her body up and let her testify against us.

In a real way Natalee is not dead yet. She still has a final word to say—her body itself can speak volumes against us. Ironic, isn't it? We destroyed Natalee, we hid her body, and yet we fear her now in death more than ever. We're afraid somebody will wake her up, but I also can't stop myself from confessing, Beth, from sharing your daughter's fate with you, from pointing you in the right direction

But there's one last thing about that quick trip. In *"[Joran] rushed out of the same door natalee came out"* you can see the stark terror in which we live, the possibility that our greatest fear will overwhelm us in a millisecond. We worry that Natalee will come rushing out of her ocean grave, out of the same ocean door that Joran rushed her to. We live in fear that her body will be discovered.

At the same time I cannot stop myself from speaking again for Natalee from her grave, "*after she stood up she pushed my friend and said leave me alone."* Read first: 'Joran, you left me all alone on the ocean floor, you pushed me into the ocean.' And by standing up in my story, Natalee is also saying, Now I'm prepared to push back with my body, to stand up for myself in a way you least expected, to let the world know with my silent testimony exactly what the three of you did to me.' If somebody can hear my words they will help Natalee stand up by bringing her up—once more that magical word pointing in the magical direction "up." I tell you even more plainly what to do, Beth—somebody needs to pick Natalee up off the floor of the ocean!

*"after she stood up . . . and while i was driving away i saw natalee walking towards . . . ,"*

And by having Natalee stand up, her body erect, just as it is when she's last seen walking off, I'm telling you something specific about how we put her in the water. She's in some type of stand-up container. In the previous scene, when Natalee has just fallen out of the car and Joran rushes out the door to pick her up and take her to her room, you also see a picture of him putting her into that cage. The fact that he picked Natalee up immediately, and she then stood on her own, suggests that he put her in that container sooner rather than later the night she died.

On the other hand, there's still one major clue left. I mean, that's a big ocean out there. I have to get more specific, one last time, so you can be sure.

## Walkie-Talkie—Body in Ocean Lobby

> *"so i drove to the **lobby driveway** of <u>holiday inn</u> and then we woke her up, she got out of the car and fell on the floor my friend said damn she fell and then rushed <u>out of the same door</u> natalee came out and picked her up immediately, after she stood up she pushed my friend and said leave me alone or something like that i can't recall ,my friend offered to help het to her room she said no. she he <u>stepped in the car</u> and while i was driving away i saw natalee walking towards **the lobby** and a gentleman with a walkie talkie and black clothes approached her and i think they were talking (and i had never seen natalee again sinds.(<u>holiday inn</u> has no cameras **in the driveway or lobby**) it was around 2.15 am .monday i came to work normally 4- 11 pm)"*

So here's a third geographic location. Or maybe I should say oceanographic location. This time, in *"i drove to the **lobby driveway** of Holiday Inn (and then we woke her up)"* I reference a particular part of the Holiday Inn: the lobby driveway. I repeat **"lobby"** three times and **"driveway"** twice, obviously one and the same place. Together I mention them five times. Five times. I'm shouting at you, confirming my previous instructions: locating the body in a more specific part of the ocean for you. So where is the lobby driveway part of the ocean? As I said, *"my friend offered to help"* Natalee to her room. I'm taking you to her room in the ocean lobby. That narrows it down.

That's where Natalee stays—in the container where we provided her body a home-away-from-home in the lobby of the ocean. Just like the driveway and the lobby of the hotel is the entrance to a vast space with lots of rooms, "lobby driveway" or "the lobby" translates to the entrance to the ocean. *I'm telling you that her body was dumped not too far from shore,* as in**,** *"i drove to the **lobby driveway** of Holiday Inn (and then we woke her up)."*

Like I said twice before just go "in a ways" into the ocean, but not too far. We drove her out not far from the entrance to the ocean, picked up her dead body and dropped her there. Remember, in my story Natalee fell immediately after getting out of the car as she was entering the Holiday Inn property. Her body then is on the floor not far from the car door, and not far from the front door—both entranceways.

Remember all my references to the bar in the casino of the Holiday Inn, where Natalee and Joran had a drink? Those are all disguised allusions to the nearby sandbar where Joran took Natalee to the "drink," not far out in the ocean. By describing two quick trips—taking Natalee back to her hotel from the lighthouse and Joran's rushing out the door to help Natalee once we arrived—I'm telling you that the trip out into the ocean to dump her body was quick, and we did not go far out.

## Driveway—Search Straight Out from Holiday Inn

Adding *"driveway"* to the equation hints that you can drive right up to it if you follow my directions. *"Driveway"* also suggests "drive away" from the Holiday Inn, using the hotel itself as a marker. In other words, search pretty much straight out from the Holiday Inn. I've already told you that Fisherman's Huts, where we picked the body up, is virtually next door to the Holiday Inn. With my numerous references to the Holiday Inn, which is practically on the edge of the ocean itself, I'm virtually shouting at you that the body-drop was aligned with the Holiday Inn—and not too far out.

Now look back and see the same hints. This would fit with my previous suggestion of getting on the main road, going straight ahead 'in a ways and to the right.' By telling you we went straight to the Holiday Inn once we decided to drop Natalee off, I'm telling you that our night-time cruise was straight out to the ocean.

Experienced fishermen in Aruba told Dave Holloway that—in the dark of night—two miles out to sea seems like five miles feels during the day. This would suggest that the boys, who were clearly in a panic, rushing to get out and get back, would not have gone out nearly as far into the ocean as they might have wanted, to dump the body. Unconsciously Deepak knew that the body wasn't taken out very far—again revealing the vast superiority of the deeper mind. Invariably, perpetrators make mistakes and sabotage themselves at certain points because of deep-seated guilt. Here the suspects did exactly that with the most crucial evidence in the case—yet another reason to believe the body is precisely where Deepak says it is.

In another matching story from Joran, he told of leaving Natalee on the beach and walking a short distance away, off the beach, to the Fisherman's Huts to get out of the wind so that Deepak could hear him on his cell phone telling Deepak to come pick him up. Decoding Joran's story: he is at the Fisherman's Huts area hiding from the elements as he communicates where Natalee is—on the beach/in the ocean, along with the confirming suggestion of using the Fisherman's Huts as another distinct marker for finding Natalee's body. Joran, like Deepak, points to dumping her body in the area between Fisherman's Huts and the Holiday Inn.

## Major Communication: Walkie-Talkie

> *"my friend offered to help het to her room . . . while i was driving away i saw natalee walking towards* **the lobby** *and a gentleman with a walkie talkie and black clothes approached her and i think they were talking . . . and i had never seen natalee again sinds.(holiday inn has no cameras in the driveway or lobby)"*

First I offer to *"help"* you find her room—*"help"* being the magic word. Then she was walking towards: *"a gentleman with a walkie talkie and black clothes . . . and i think they were talking." "Walkie-talkie, talking,"* means 'Hear me out.' I am that gentleman, a gentleman because I'm laying it out for you and the police. I've got my walkie-talkie big time. I'm spilling the beans; heed my directions because I'm the security guard who will take you to Natalee's room, where she now stays.

And where is that room? A man with black clothes approaches Natalee—read Death, the man in black, has come for Natalee-- and as *"i was driving away i saw natalee walking towards the lobby"*, once more the ocean entrance/lobby that's where she is staying. I can still see her going into the water as we drove away in the boat.

But *"security guard"* has more meanings. The guard dressed in black also suggests the three of us, who were functioning as Natalee's security guards to escort her home, were certainly evil.

And maybe I'm also alluding to turning Natalee's body over to one other guard in black, someone who we would totally trust, someone who would take total responsibility for helping us decide what to do with the body—Paulus van der Sloot. Yet strangely enough in the end, part of me—my deeper mind, my soul—is still functioning as the one security guard who, at this late date, still wants to take care of her in the only way now possible: to return her body to you. She is still rightfully yours.

## Deepak's Camera—Plenty of Pictures

*"and i had <u>never seen</u> natalee again sinds.(holiday inn has <u>no cameras</u> in the driveway **or lobby**)"*

I continue to underscore *"lobby"* by putting it in parentheses as I report, *"(holiday inn has no cameras in the driveway or lobby)."* Read through my denial, *"no cameras"* in the Holiday Inn lobby and the message is, 'holiday inn has cameras in the driveway or lobby,' doubly set off by my framing parenthesis. So what am I telling you? Granted, the actual Holiday Inn had no cameras in the lobby, which is why we thought we could get away with a lie, but the more important Holiday Inn in my story—the ocean—*does* have cameras.

Those would be my eyes, which can see her now on the ocean floor near its entrance. We tried to hide her where nobody could see her, deep in the ocean, but my email is the camera, providing a word-picture of precisely where she is, an album filled with pictures of Natalee's last day alive on planet earth. See the pictures—follow the images—and you'll understand what happened.

Look how my slip *"sinds,"* directly connected to *"camera,"* suggests both "sends/ends" and "since." Combining the ideas we have the message that we haven't seen Natalee since we sent her to her end. In my mind I constantly see where Natalee ended up.

Already I've told you in three different ways that the body is in the entrance/lobby to the ocean:

1. First, you can drive up to her and wake her up.
2. Second, you can see the end of her journey, where she walked/ traveled to.
3. Third, you can now see a mental picture of her there.

You must read through both denials—*never* seen Natalee again and *no* camera—and see that location again forever etched like a still photo on my mind's eye. It's the picture on the desktop of my mind when I open my computer, when I wake up every day. Even in my dreams I see Natalee's body, lying there in that container, deep in the ocean lobby on the floor. Believe me, my deeper mind is a twenty-four-hour, nonstop camera that's always on.

To summarize, then, in describing the black uniform of the security guard I'm also picturing the ocean floor without any light, where Natalee's body now lies in the total darkness of death. No light, no life. And yes, that's got to be the blackest of pictures in an album filled with black ones.

But even so, you can still turn all this into the most beautiful, full-color picture of a scuba dive you have ever imagined—if you dive exactly where I've instructed you. See, the final thing I am in this case is a scuba-diving instructor who knows how to take you on a highly specialized dive to find the exact treasure you're looking for. I know where it is, and how to take you there.

## Summary of New Information in Scene

- Again Deepak uses a lack of periods to communicate nonstop his utter desperation as he describes the end of Natalee's life.

- As anticipated, in his final scene with Natalee, Deepak underscored her death with references to: falling *"asleep"* (twice), falling down (twice), plus *"alone."* But most important, he goes into elaborate detail about where to find the body.

- In describing Natalee's falling out of the car on their arrival at Holiday Inn, Deepak's L-2 depicts two scenes involving Natalee leaving the car: first her death in the car and the failed attempted resuscitation on the ground outside the car.

- Simultaneously he is describing a flashback scene to the moment of deceit, when the boys forced Natalee outside the car at the beginning of the rape in order to strip her and prepare the backseat.

- Deepak revisits the specifics in flashback form, of the moment of deceit when the assault began, providing more details—as though he must come even cleaner here.

- For only the second time in his email, Deepak overtly describes an image of Natalee's injury when Joran *"help het her"*—but also confesses that he helped injure her himself.

- Deepak reminds us one last time that he was assaulting Natalee when she died, even describing Joran having to get his attention, *"my friend is telling me that natalee fell asleep i said you kidding just wake her up."*

- Next this is when he points to the unsuccessful resuscitation on the ground—again validating this part of story and reemphasizing that Joran was in charge of the CPR.

- In a major slip, *"she he stepped in the car . . . while i was driving away,"* Deepak confesses that they never left Natalee at the hotel or anywhere else, but put her body back in the car.

- When he describes dropping Natalee off at the hotel, Deepak gives specifics on location of body. These include the code of geographical references to Natalee's hotel: Body located in Holiday Inn, decoded the ocean; on the floor where she *"fell"*; near the entrance or "lobby driveway"; almost straight out from the hotel but slightly to the right.

- Unconsciously, using four keywords, Deepak tells us how to solve the case—(1) body "fell" on ocean floor, (2) "stays" in a fixed container/cage there, (3) "wake" Natalee—discover her body and (4) bring her "up."

- Major validating message markers *"confirmed"* and *"for sure,"* matching perfectly Deepak's earlier *"sure why not"* (drop her at Holiday Inn), verify where Natalee stays—where her body remains at the bottom of the ocean, in a container that makes sure it doesn't move.

- Deepak uses vivid messages markers: the *"Tell,"* *"confirmed,"* *"walkie-talkie,"* and *"camera"* to make his case.

- In review, Deepak's imagery gives us a guided tour of where they dumped the body, including an underwater camera view of the body as it lies in its container, waiting to be brought to the surface.

## Police Interviews

Interrogations of Joran reveal striking thoughtprints of Natalee's body in the ocean. He made reference to the Natalee's "last night <u>on</u> Aruba" suggesting she's no longer on the island of Aruba but in the water. On another occasion he volunteered that he'd had a girlfriend, Elaine, whose nickname, "Fishy," was listed in the memory of his mobile phone. Like Deepak, Joran cannot rid his mind of the image of Natalee buried in the ocean. Twice Joran insisted on talking about two girls, even offering that "I can point out their house to you," suggesting his urge to tell police where Natalee's body currently rests.

He did exactly that when he declared in an interview, " . . . while we were driving past the front of the *container harbor*, Natalee told me that her mother was the sister of Hitler. I laughed . . . she said this to me about five times." In his book *The Natalee Holloway Case*, he takes it a step further, making sure we know who Hitler is, when he tells us that Natalee said, in response to his laughter, "Sorry, I know you are German that is why I had to tell you." Joran laughs even louder because he is not German, and he asks Natalee if she is kidding. But she then insists she wasn't joking.

Briefly but powerfully, Joran links Natalee's body to the startling image of a container in a harbor, and to Hitler, a murderer who tried to hide and dispose of bodies. Joran also points to the same location of the body, as Deepak did—in the harbor/entrance to the ocean

At another point in the book, Joran told about being alone on the beach with Natalee, and how she wanted to change directions. "Let's go to the Jacuzzi, or better yet, let's go this way," he quotes her as saying. And they proceed to walk away from the Holiday Inn towards the Fisherman's Huts.

Decode the full message, context and all, with "Jacuzzi" the single most vivid image of a container in all of Joran's stories, and in a nutshell we have a striking message from Joran about what happened and where to find the body, as he speaks in the first person for Natalee. First Joran portrays Natalee with him in a Jacuzzi: a solid container filled with warm water, a hot tub where couples often completely disrobe to engage in sexual activity, or in wilder scenarios where orgies or group sex occur.

Afterwards, Natalee heads to the beach with Joran, which means a complete change in directions. Now put the whole story together. Read after Natalee died unexpectedly in the "hot tub rape" the three boys had to head in an entirely different direction. They then dumped her body in the ocean, placing it in a strong immovable "underwater Jacuzzi." This has left them, potentially, in unimaginably hot water if the body is discovered, which is clearly possible based on Joran's story. His clue about changing directions also suggests not looking for her body on land, where the hot tub was, but in the water.

In different ways, both boys made hidden confessions, admitting that the body's in water in a container not far from shore, exactly like a container in a harbor. Just as Deepak does repeatedly, Joran—in numerous police interviews—also speaks for Natalee. It's equally clear that the police, untrained in reading Deepak's or Joran's revealing symbolic language, have overlooked these important clues. If they learn the settings on Deepak's mental camera, however, they will then see Natalee's body as clearly as Deepak sees it every waking moment, in his mind's eye.

## Beach Stories

Various additional beach stories have emerged from the three suspects' police interviews, as well as from Joran's book and from his multiple public interviews. These stories continue to provide important validation of Deepak's email profile. Here are brief summaries of several such stories, followed by their decoded versions, all of which continue to shed light on what actually happened that night.

### Sexual Assault

1. Joran took Natalee to his house for sex but she refused to go in with him, instead requesting to go to the beach.
   **Read:** Natalee failed to cooperate sexually with all three suspects and ended up dead, buried in the ocean.

2. Joran told of Natalee stimulating him on the beach, but also how she didn't want him to ejaculate on her hands, so after ejaculating in his own hands he washed the ejaculate off in the water.
   **Read:** Natalee refused to have sex with the three suspects, all of whom reached orgasm and used a condom. In an attempt to wash away their sexual sins they have buried her body in the water.

3. Leaving Natalee on the beach, Joran—breathing heavily—calls Deepak and tells him he is walking home barefoot, because he took his shoes off to go in the water with Natalee and lost them. He also says he left Natalee "passed out" on the beach.
   **Read:** Breathing heavily, shoes/clothes off in order to enter the water with Natalee/enter Natalee all point once again to a sexual assault of Natalee, who died/was lost and is now in the ocean. But all three suspects remain barefoot—vulnerable and exposed, given their paper thin cover-up.

### Death by Aspiration

1. Joran repeatedly references the possibility that Natalee could have drowned after he left her on the beach. Satish repeats the same idea ("I think girl has drowned"), because Joran left her on the

beach one meter from the water where they had been lying down.
**Read:** Natalee indeed died because she drowned/aspirated, and we buried her in the ocean.

2.  After dropping Joran and Natalee off at the beach, Deepak drives off, then stops briefly in front of the Marriott hotel while Satish throws their drink containers out the window.
    **Read:** Deepak presents a clear picture of Natalee aspirating, unable to contain her drink due to their careless behavior. They then throw her away in the ocean, at the same time giving us another clear picture of Natalee in a container. Remember, they treated themselves to a Natalee drink held in a container.

3.  Joran reported various stories linked to seeing stars on the beach with Natalee:
    *   The stars were bright to Joran but not to Natalee.
        **Read:** Natalee couldn't see well as she fell into unconsciousness.
    *   Natalee saw stars.
        **Read:** Natalee suffered a type of head injury, which again led to unconsciousness and death.
    *   While Joran saw the stars, Natalee couldn't see them at all.
        **Read:** Natalee died.

4.  Freddy reported that Joran left Natalee unconscious on the beach.
    **Read:** Natalee died after she became unconscious and is buried in the ocean

### Death and Burial in Ocean

1.  Deepak reported that Joran and Natalee went briefly into the water, sat on the beach, then laid down on the beach where Natalee fell asleep and eventually passed out. Joran left her there, said she was leaving the same day and that someone would find her there. Deepak cursed him for leaving Natalee.
    **Read:** Deepak confesses in multiple ways that Natalee has died—down, asleep, passed out, leaving—and that for sure her body can be found in the ocean.

2.  Most strikingly, the last thing Joran says to Natalee is "Bye." When he last sees her she is sitting facing the ocean.
    **Read:** Natalee died and we put her in the ocean, where she sits in a container on the ocean floor. Look for her there.

# 12
# The Twittys and the Police

We have already developed a definitive profile, but with almost half of Deepak's email yet to go we know that he will continue to confirm his story. He is particularly relaxed now, because consciously he believes he has got his cover-up story in under the wire and he's clean as a whistle. It all sounds believable to him. He's good to go—or so he thinks.

In other words, now that he believes he has covered his tracks, the rest of his email should be a piece of cake for him. But that attitude allows him to ramble on for the longest time and, in so doing he richly validates his hidden confession. His left-brain defenses are down and his right-brain instincts rule. It's time for some serious reflection, as Deepak describes how he's really doing deep down—how he's dealing with the personal, mental and emotional consequences of taking another person's life.

Having extensively decoded the first part of his email, we'll now focus only on the highlights of the balance of the email, decoding crucial references. For the main part, however, all we really have to do is just relax along with Deepak. Sit back and simply let his story come to us as we marvel at the complex machinations of his criminal mind. Rarely will a perpetrator go on and on as Deepak does, both before and after his initial hidden confession.

That verbosity, however, speaks volumes. Despite his outward bravado, young Deepak Kalpoe has a guilty conscience that spurs his deeper intelligence to confess. Although he surely senses his own guilt, he's not aware of how his guilty conscience rules his words. That would truly surprise him, because behind his cocky poker-player demeanor is one guilt-ridden young puppy scared out of his mind—and well he should be.

Another thing he'll likely demonstrate, despite his generally relaxed vibe, is a constant over-the-shoulder look endemic to all criminals. They walk one short step ahead of the law, which is rapidly and relentlessly closing in. Deepak would be shocked to know that, right now, he's the most valuable detective on the case! The clues he's already given us, between the lines of his email, show that he's the one leading the chase, pursuing justice with a passion.

So, how could someone so determined to cover his rear end actually end up spilling the beans on himself, so thoroughly that he leads the police straight to the body? The answer is quite simple—Deepak doesn't know he's doing that. Like most forensic scientists, who remain in the dark about his secret confession, Deepak might well consider himself a sociopath, a criminal with no concern or empathy for his victims. But in fact, his deeper intelligence shows that he does indeed have feelings, feelings so strong that they force him to confess in the symbolic language of his unconscious.

Before this case is solved, Deepak's email confession will make the strongest of arguments for a new breed of investigators to come forward, forensic psycholinguists trained to decode such communications. The field of criminal investigation will be forever transformed.

Meanwhile, let's return to decoding his email. Deepak still has some remarkable things to tell us. Again he returns to the time, which we know immediately is a valuable communication. Investigators invariably establish a timeline for the crime, but now they must stand back and watch the master detective in action.

### 'never seen Natalee again'

"a gentleman with a walkie talkie and black clothes approached her and i think they were talking and i had never seen natalee again sinds.(holiday inn has no cameras in the driveway or lobby) it was around 2.15 am .monday i came to work normally 4- 11 pm after work i called my friend i said whats up he said ok i'm at the raddison casino meet me there , i said ok  so i went there we played poker , we had some drinks and chat and then we had enough and decided that this casino was booring lets go to whyndham hotel casino . so i drove to whyndham and as i was parking my friends dad called him and said the police is at his home with some family members its about the girl you guys went out with yesterday , so my friend said wait there i be there,"

We pick up with "never seen Natalee again sinds," followed by another lack of space with "(holiday inn has no cameras in the driveway or lobby)" in parentheses, setting it off once more with the message "no camera" meaning the exact opposite—that he is looking at Natalee's body in the ocean/Holiday Inn even as he speaks, and is on the verge of giving us a picture of her. Obviously the image of Natalee on the bottom of the ocean rests heavily on his mind.

Indeed, he references sex right off the bat. Deepak tells us " . . . *it was around 2.15 am .monday_ i came.*" Notice how this matches the earlier "*around 12. 10 am so I came.*" Deepak is again locating the time of his climax, and thus the moment of Natalee's death, around 2:15 am. The first thing "Mr. Organized" does is confirm the time of death. This would fit with what Deepak reportedly told investigator Jamie Skeeters, that we would be surprised how easy it was to have sex with Natalee— meaning the assault took place quickly.

To make sure we understand, Deepak brings us back to the sexual scenario that led to Natalee's demise and, follows it with additional sexual innuendos. First "*I came*" was all in a night's work for Deepak. Again Deepak implies he's out of touch and has to call his friend because he's been busy working, busy having a climax. So he asks Joran, "*What's up,*" not only implying an erection but that he's confused about it—hinting again at that moment of Natalee's death that coincided with his climax. Interestingly it is Joran, who is at the "*raddison*"—suggesting "rattison"—that Deepak is indeed ratting out here.

Deepak proceeds with a veritable litany of double entendres. We hear Joran's familiar words, "*Ok i'm at the raddison casino meet me there.*" Once more Joran is encouraging Deepak to enter the same casino Joran had been in; namely, having sex with Natalee, gambling he could get away with it. He wants Deepak to "*meet there*" or "take his meat there." Leaving no doubt, Deepak informs us, "*i said ok   so i went there we played poker , we had some drinks and chat and then we had enough and decided that this casino was booring.*"

The boys played "poke-her" in Natalee's casino, "booring" (as in boring a hole) in her casino, pleasuring themselves at her expense, having another drink of Natalee until "*we had enough,*" again suggesting climaxes all the way around. Deepak's "*camera*" is working overtime, making sure we have a clear snapshot of their crime. And he's chatting us up with his message marker "*chat,*" making sure we hear his confession. Deepak is talking again.

### 'the police is at his home'

"*and as i was parking my friends dad called him and said the **police** is at his home with some family members its about the girl you guys went out* *with yesterday , so my friend said wait there i be there, so we rushed at my friends home and there was **the police** and nataless family and it was a nightmare sinds then. **the police** asked us if we knew this girl showed us a picture we said yes thats her , they said she was missing and eyewitness say she was the last seen with you **guys** . so they asked . . . "*

Suddenly Joran gets a call, and everything changes from this point onward in Deepak's story. This is a turning point: "*the police is at his home.*" Notice the police "*is*" at his home. When it comes to the police, it's always present tense for Deepak. In his mind they're always on their way to his house, constantly about to knock on his door.

But who's actually doing the knocking here? It's Officer Deepak Kalpoe—Deepak's L-2 mind is the police—and, as we will see, it's also the judge and jury. To show just how pressured he is, Deepak repeats "*the police*" three times in rapid-fire succession. And in his mind the police are inseparably connected to Natalee's family because he must answer to both.

Now we come to a series of sentences-within-a-sentence at this key juncture when the police arrive on the scene. We would anticipate significant additions to his confession here.

## 'my friends dad'

First Deepak reminds us just how much Joran's dad was involved in the entire cover-up. Indeed he is "*parking my friends dad*"—parking Paulus—in the center of this case. Also reading his sentence this way, "*my friends dad called him and said . . . at his home . . . about the girl you guys went out with,*" we find the same message as before, namely that at his home that morning Paulus had discussed in detail with the three boys exactly what had happened to Natalee. Deepak in this sentence as previously mentioned subtly but clearly links Natalee to the van der Sloot home with his words "*at his home . . . the girl you guys went out with yesterday.*"

This scene occurs at approximately 3 am on May 31, 2005, when Beth Twitty and others arrived a second time at Joran's home looking for Natalee. At 1 am Paulus had refused to answer the door for them. Two Arubans with the Twittys had looked over the fence surrounding the home, where they saw Deepak's car. It seems that shortly thereafter Deepak and Joran left to stage a phone call from Joran's father to get them to come home.

The phrase, "*at my friends home and there was the police*" also suggests not only that Joran and Deepak were at his home, but also how shocked everyone there was when Beth Twitty and the entourage arrived so quickly. The related slip, *"rushed at my friends home"* suggests that the boys initially panicked when the Twitty group showed up, and left to collect their thoughts—perhaps sent on their way by Paulus with instructions such as, "You boys go off and get your story straight."

In retrospect it seems that Paulus, the shrewd lawyer, wanted the boys eventually to be interrogated at Joran's house where they were most comfortable and as well wanted the boys home first before the police arrived. As this case initially unfolded, Paulus' fingerprints were all over it. Here he was, a well-connected adult with a sharp, legally oriented mind, trying to stay one solid step ahead of the authorities.

## 'A nightmare sinds then'

> *"we rushed at my friends home and there was the police and nataless family and it was a **nightmare sinds then**. the police"*

Deepak has made it plain he is living in a perpetual nightmare, and that it continues to be a nightmare that "sinds/sends" his mind to spinning, especially since he was confronted by police and Natalee's family. Inevitably he connects the two together in his mind. Shortly, when he describes his powerful confrontation with Beth Twitty, he'll explain why meeting Natalee's family was *"a nightmare"* for him. Now we find a series of questions posed by both the police and by Natalee's family. Deepak answers all.

## Question 1

> *"the police is at his home with some family members its about the girl you guys went out with yesterday , so my friend said wait there i be there"*

We must see that the first question actually came through Paulus, *"the police is at his home . . . its about the girl you guys went out with yesterday , so my friend said **wait there i be there**."* In regards to the missing Natalee, Deepak has his friend, Joran, speaking for all of them when he says, *"(wait **there**) I be **there**,"* thus repeating his earlier confession—"The girl we went out with—oh, we were there all right. We were really there!"

## Question 2

*"the police asked us if we knew this girl showed us a picture we said yes thats her"*

Here the real police enter the picture and ask if the three boys knew this girl. First we see a key repeat message marker, "the police **asked**"—we can be sure Deepak has himself under oath to his soul. And his question comes sharply into focus. *"Knew"* is a clear reference to sexual intercourse (harkening back to biblical days), and the real question is "Did you guys assault her?" Deepak is unconsciously leading us to an answer. When he adds the message marker *"showed us a picture"* we know that what follows is important, and Deepak answers, *"yes that's her,"* once again implying that they were with her and indeed knew her sexually.

The message marker *"picture"* fits strikingly with *"camera."* The real question is, "Do you have a picture of sexually assaulting Natalee in your mind?" and Deepak answers for them, "yes, we do." Unmistakably Deepak is showing us the pictures in his mental camera, confessing in yet another way that he can't erase from his mind that vivid picture of Natalee's rape.

## Question 3

*"they said she was missing and eyewitness say she was the last seen with you guys ."*

In response to this question he adds the elite message marker *"eyewitness"* so we can be sure his next message is the unadulterated truth. The police ask a question about Natalee being missing and the *"eyewitness"*—who is none other than Deepak's unconscious mind—says, *"she was the last seen with you guys."* Deepak again puts a period here to make sure we see his message, "This is a definite—she was definitely with us, we were all eyewitnesses." Again Deepak draws on another rich image, "the eye," following "camera" and "picture." These images inform us of his all-seeing L-2 unconscious mind that secretly sees everything. The L-2 is like a fantastic computer with "unconscious vision" so capable that its abilities astound us.

## Question 4

*"so they asked a few more questions and we said we don't understand* **we left her at holiday inn lobby drive way** *how could she dissapear"*

The crucial question again—where is Natalee? Now first read through Deepak's classic denial, *"we don't understand"* decoded "we certainly do understand"—which means we should be all ears at this point. Deepak seems to be insisting that Natalee did not disappear. In a way, his answer is, "She didn't disappear. She's staying in the **holiday inn lobby drive way.**" In response to the key police question, Deepak returns to the key place at the key moment. They left the body at the "Holiday Inn," Deepak says yet again using his code word for the ocean while yet again adding the *"lobby drive way"* detail: the entrance to the ocean.

## Question 5

*"so they asked a few more questions . . . how could she dissapear and then natalees stepfather jumped and said "yes thats because after she went with you assholes she lost" and then my friends father jumped"*

Deepak has not yet finished answering the other part of the question, **how could she disappear** meaning "What happened to her?" Remember, this question is preceded by the crucial message marker *"the police asked,"* followed by another *"because"*—Deepak is unquestionably alerting us to "Listen up because here comes the answer to the question of what happened." To emphasize its truthfulness, he puts the answer in quotes.

Deepak then describes Natalee's stepfather exploding and blurting the answer, *"yes thats because after she went with you assholes she lost."* Deepak is answering that "Natalee disappeared because 'she lost,' she died." In essence, "She went with us and lost her life." That occurred because all three of the boys were, in Deepak's own unconscious words, *"assholes."*

We must keep in mind what Deepak really thinks of himself and his compadres—his scathing self-criticism will continue unabated. Deepak's conscience is bothering him so badly he allows Jug Twitty to speak for him and call them the names he feels they deserve. And, by referring to the three of them as "assholes," Deepak also suggests that the crime against Natalee included anal sodomy. Between the lines Deepak has answered all the key questions posed by the police.

## Summary of Scene

- Immediately after finishing his cover-up story, Deepak begins to reveal his guilt in deeper ways.

- He shows that Natalee's family and the police threaten him greatly, causing him to confess.

- With a litany of sexual innuendos, Deepak demonstrates that he's constantly looking back at their defining sexual misdeed—he cannot get the brutal assault out of his mind.

- Deepak's conscience arrives on the scene and, as a result, he reveals a number of answers to police questions.

- About the girl, Deepak answers, "oh we were there."

- In response to the police question, "did you know her" meaning "Did you have sex with her"—he responds, "yes we knew her."

- "Was she last seen with you guys?"—eyewitness Deepak answers, "absolutely, definitely—period."

- Next question, "To where did she disappear?" Again Deepak leaves no doubt that she's in the *"lobby driveway of the Holiday Inn"* meaning just out a short ways in the ocean.

- To the final question, "What happened?" Deepak says she died, *"she lost"* and we're *"assholes."*

## Joran's Father Jumps In

> *"and then my friends father jumped and said thats enough <u>you can't talk</u> to the kids like that this is not **the us** your out of you **juristiction** this is not the way i want you people out of my yard i know the law (my friends father is **e judge**)"*

The message marker "can't **talk**" suggests another denial with an important message coming up. First, in *"and then my friends father jumped"* Deepak is alluding to how all of them, including Paulus, experienced the knock on the door that night by Beth Twitty and company. But more important, here in Deepak's story, Joran's father jumps in and, as promised, we find another confession between the lines, " *then my friends father jumped and said thats enough you can't talk . . . kids"*—confirming that

Paulus was involved early and told them not to talk, which also fits perfectly with the two boys leaving the home when the Twittys arrived.

Secretly consumed by guilt, Paulus—in Deepak's story—is acutely attuned to young people being verbally mistreated. Do you think this might have something to do with his having learned just how the three suspects, one his own son, actually mistreated Natalee to the point of causing her death? Certainly we can see Paulus' cover-up comment, *"This is not the us [USA] your out your juristiction"* as meaning "You won't be able to prosecute these boys in Aruba because of our connections." By and large this is what has transpired. But by reading through the denial, *"This is not the us [USA] . . . juristiction,"* we find Deepak facing his American accusers as though he's standing before a U.S. Court of justice. We also find the message, *"this is us"*—suggesting a confession.

Instinctively Deepak's unconscious mind wants to tell the truth and he makes a significant, condensed slip *"juristiction"* which speaks volumes. It implies that he fears a "jury stick" (and a "jury strict"), in other words a "jury sticking it to them" for being out of bounds—for what?— "sticking Natalee." Follow the sexual innuendos and we have a message in which Deepak has Paulus speaking for them and for Natalee: *"this is . . . us— your out . . . you stict(s)/sticks— this is not the way I want you people out of my yard I know the law."* "Stic" is not far from "stick," or one and the same with "dick," and the resulting message: the three boys confess, "this is us, our sticks/dicks are out" and—where are they?—but in Natalee's yard, who then replies, *"this is not the way. I want you people out of my yard. I know the law."*

Just before this we can see the same message, *"jumped and said thats enough you can't"*—as though Natalee is instructing the boys to stop jumping her, *"that's enough."*

For this lawless behavior Deepak clearly suggests the verdict: *"The way . . . you people . . . yard I know the law (my friends father is e judge)"* translated, "My friend Natalee's father, the 'e judge' or the 'Nataleeeee judge,' knows the law and the three of us should immediately head to the jail yard." In a moment Deepak will straightforwardly repeat the same verdict leaving no doubt that the three suspects deserve prison sentences.

By placing these slips in Paulus' mouth, Deepak depicts Joran's father as also out of bounds, and as a participant in the cover-up. This is confirmed by the slip *"my friend's father is e judge,"* highlighted by parentheses. Deepak makes another of his revealing patented slips with *"e judge,"* suggesting that Joran's father is not really "a judge" but in this circumstance a false judge. *"E judge"* also suggests "be judged" and that all four of the parties—the three suspects and Paulus—should be held accountable.

## Scene: ID the Security Guard

> *"i know the law (my friends father is e judge) so afterwards another family member of natalee suggested to **the police** if we can **id** the security **gard** we said **ok**. **we** went <u>there there</u> was no **suck** security_working <u>there</u> as we **discribed**. so then we were just **standing in the lobby** there were <u>questions</u> <u>etc.</u> asked by other members ,"*

Immediately after saying he knows the law, Deepak notes the presence of **"the police"** and that another *"family member of Natalee"* wants to know *"if we can **id** the security **gard"**—and *"we said ok [period]."* Understand Judge Deepak's promise. Unmistakably, "id"—one of the strongest message markers imaginable—contains the promise to identify the security guard that was supposedly with Natalee when she was last seen. Judge Deepak (or Officer Deepak) has now basically promised to unconsciously finger the culprits.

Next Deepak takes us straight to the Holiday Inn. Using a major slip, *"We went **there there**,"* repeating *"there,"* followed by *"**there** as we discribed,"* also suggests the body's location, there in the Holloway Inn/End—the ocean. It's as if Deepak can't say it enough, as if he's screaming at us, "Look there, there, there!" He even takes it a step further, delivering the message "that's a definite" with a period at the end of the short sentence, *"there as we **discribed**."* On the heels of these blatant suggestions Deepak then takes us to that familiar place in the Holiday Inn—" *we were standing in the lobby*" reminding us yet again because of the crucial message marker "identify"exactly where Natalee's body is: not very far out into the ocean where she can be found in a container.

## Innuendo upon Innuendo:'no suck security'

Immediately the slip *"id the security **gard"*** suggests that *"gard"* means *"gar"* or a predator-type fish that can attack humans similar to his earlier, more powerful, image of "sharks." The use of *"id"* also suggests the primitive nature of man, a creature of selfish, predatory, self-gratifying instincts. And taken together, the three images of *"sharks,"* *"gar"* and *"id"* imply sexual predators that end up killing their victim. Clearly, "gar" matching *"sharks"* also implies that the body is in the ocean.

Deepak's additional slip *"no **suck** security"* suggests they indeed assaulted Natalee, "f——d" her and were evil—dressed in black—for not protecting her. Indeed, as security, the three suspects "sucked" as in "f—k security." Notice now the slip, *"discribed"* with "dis" suggesting they "dissed" Natalee—with "disc" also suggesting "dic" and how, exactly, they dissed her. With the blatant, *"suck"* we can now see string of embedded crude sexual innuendos, *we went* <u>there there</u> *. . . suck/f__k . . . working* <u>there</u> *as we 'dissed/dicked' so then we were just* <u>standing</u> *in the lobby (entrance to Natalee) . . . by other members.* Remember, Deepak promised a shocking, graphic story befitting the names he gave them, "gar" and *"sharks."*

With those three, Natalee had no security whatsoever. Deepak has answered his promise to "id the security guards" whose names were Joran, Satish, and Deepak. In any number of ways, Deepak is both confessing and guiding us to the body. The fact that a family member prompted this confession reveals how the very mention of Natalee's family stirs up phenomenal guilt—just as we saw in the very first sentence. And we're about to see why.

## Scene: Deepak Encounters Beth Twitty

*"no suck security working there as we discribed. so then we were just standing in the lobby there were questions etc. asked by other members , and then me and my friend walked to the car natalees mom was sitting and we said mam you have to believe us **we did not do anything with you daughter**, she was crying and said i don't believe you 2 , i promise you i will make you life a living hell because of this ."*

In every forensic document there is almost always a center where the peak confession occurs. This is that moment in this email. It's absolutely no coincidence that Deepak placed it here, in this powerful scene in which Joran and Deepak meet Beth Twitty face to face.

He writes, *"then me and my friend walked to the car natalees mom was sitting."* The phrase *"Natalee's mom"* suggests a very personal relationship, and that Deepak felt intensely responsible for taking Natalee from her "mom" in the most personal of ways. That explains why he wrote her so personally, "Dear Beth." His greeting, *"we said mam,"* again reflects Deepak's sensitivity to mother figures, who most assuredly taught him such manners.

Now the more complete sentence, *"we said mam you have to believe us we **did not** do anything with you daughter, **she was crying.**"* First, with

268 — Into the Deep

the blatant denial Deepak admits he's lying and suggests "mam we **did** do something with your daughter." Note that it wasn't "we don't know" what happened to your daughter, it's "*we **did not do anything** with your daughter.*" The real message "we did something with your daughter" suggests, first, the familiar sexual innuendo that they did something sexual with her, and then it suggests that they did something with her body.

## 'I don't believe you 2'

In Deepak's story, Beth wasted not a second before responding, "*and said i don't believe you 2.*" But we must see first how Deepak again employs a blatant phrase to draw attention to his guilt. We must also read through his denial to find his confession again speaking for Natalee, "*you 2*" as in, "*natalee . . . was sitting and we . . . do anything with you . . . she was crying and said i don't believe you 2.*" "I can't believe what you're doing to me, and you too—you're going to continue the assault." Then Deepak makes sure we know first person what he did to Natalee: "*i promise you i will make you life a living hell*"—and indeed he made her life a living hell, the last few minutes she was alive.

What a way to go out—no goodbyes to your mother, your father, your friends—just leaving this world not only in the absolute, stark terror of a brutal assault but in the even more frightening terror that struck her the moment she couldn't breathe. Talk about a living hell—oh, Deepak knows what he did to her! In "*you daughter, she was crying,*" Deepak makes sure we know that Natalee was crying during the vicious assault, which fits exactly with his earlier idea of Natalee begging them to stop. And crying also fits with an uncontrollable liquid oral expression, as in Natalee trying to dispel abdominal tears known as "throwing up." In "*believe you*" Deepak is also crying out unconsciously, "Believe me about my confession—every single image."

Deepak then hears the words from her mother, now in Natalee's place, as if they're coming straight from Natalee's mouth right after the assault, as Beth uttered the terrifying words that still shake Deepak to his core: "*i promise you i will make **you life a living hell** because of this .*" See, once again it's the eternal present for Deepak, as though he's actually living in the very moment of Natalee's speaking from her grave to him about what he's done to her, and indeed Beth pronounced sentence on Deepak for what he did, "***you life a living hell** because of this .*" I sentence you to an ongoing, living, moment-by-moment hell for what you did to me Deepak Kalpoe—and that goes for your two friends—you 2," meaning "you other two."

How just, how right that Natalee's mother got to deliver those words for her. Deepak could sit before a hundred judges, allowing Beth or Dave to tell him how badly he hurt them, and it would never be as powerful as the words he heard that night when he was least expecting them— when he had his guard down, thinking he could put one more over on Beth, as he did with Natalee and only God knows who else.

Speaking of the prison of the mind—we're looking dead-on at it.

Deepak then clarifies, in vivid terms, just how much he has been suffering from that sentence. He will never forget two things—the image of Natalee when she died and those ominous words of Beth Twitty. Deepak's slip, *"you life a living hell,"* is as if he is speaking personally to life itself and what it has continually done to him.

When you help take someone else's life, however accidentally and especially in a brutal sexual assault, you instinctively know to whom you must ultimately answer, a force beyond the family and even beyond the police. It's no accident that at this moment Deepak invokes these images of judgment. *"Hell"* also matches his reference to The Judge and The Law, revealing his powerful guilt and explaining why he's now suffering a *"living hell"*—period. Shortly, he will close his email with the single most frightening word in the English language—or any other— that gives *"hell," "the law,"* and *"judge"* their terrifying power—*"God."*

## 'we will help in any way possible'

> [*"i don't believe you 2 , i promise you i will make you life a living hell because of this .]* **anwyas** *we said we were sorry again ans that we will help in any way possible."*

His significant misspelling **"anwyas"** reveals how shell-shocked Deepak was by Beth's confrontation. It also suggests "and yes," as in "and, yes, you have made my life a living hell, shocking me so badly I can't even spell." But in Deepak's stammering we find a hidden pearl of wisdom in his repeat slip *"anwyas,"* the suggestion "go in a ways— "yes"—pointing us back to his familiar directions to the body. Never underestimate the ability of the unconscious mind, even in a stammer, to utter pure wisdom.

We also have another car with another woman on the seat in the car crying, the mother of the very girl whose life Deepak helped end less than 24 hours earlier. We can only imagine how powerful a moment this was for young Deepak. Beth's weeping would have reminded Deepak of

Natalee in every way. Here we find further confirmation, within the body of the email itself, that Deepak unconsciously wrote this letter to Beth. It's no wonder that Deepak responds in such a dramatic and striking way—"*we will help you in any way possible.*" Notice, also, how Deepak seals his promise by surrounding the short sentence with definitive periods, revealing unconsciously how badly he wants to confess. We can anticipate great help from Deepak at this point, in many ways.

How would Deepak help Beth Twitty—"*in any way possible*"? The best way Deepak can help, the maximum way—and really, the only possible way at this point—would be by telling the truth, via a confession that includes the whole story, including the body's location. You want to help us now, Deepak, then tell us where the body is and seal your fate!

One day Deepak and/or the other two guys may make an open, conscious confession, including an apology. But for now, this email is without question Deepak's *unconscious* apology to Beth Twitty and to Dave Holloway and to the rest of Natalee's family. That's why he has written such an epic story, even in the terse format of an email. And he's not through yet. We will pay particularly close attention here, assured that Deepak has some surprises for us. Deepak's promise of maximum help means maximum confession. Indeed, he now takes his confession to another level. (Along these lines, Joran's comments in his book that whoever was involved with Natalee's disappearance would one day break is a striking prediction and reflects how like Deepak that guilt consumes him.)

### 'I was a witness'

> " . . . *we will help in any way possible.i went home 7 pm tuesday, i was then called 2 pm by the* **police for questioning** *i went* **gave a statement** *they said i* **was a witness** . . . *the same went for my brother and my friend . . . and had to* **sign their statement** *also ,*

His idea of "*i went home*" immediately after his dramatic promise seems to confirm a key cover-up stratagem, for Deepak to go home and establish an alibi. Note also the message marker "*police questioning*" and how Deepak fulfills the prediction that he will help police and help Beth Twitty by confessing. Deepak says, "*i* **went gave a** *statement . . . (they said) i was a witness,*"—telling us again between the lines that he was indeed a witness to Natalee's demise. He was there. In "*the same went for my brother and my friend . . . and had to* **sign their statement also,**"

Deepak is not only confessing for his two compadres in crime, but he also suggests that Joran and Satish will confess unconsciously if we pay attention to their words as well. He is hinting to the police that valuable confessions could be culled from all three suspects, by thoroughly examining the thoughtprints in their police interviews.

Deepak has suggested in the strongest of terms that he considers this email, his hidden confession, as good as a signed statement to the police. And indeed we will see that Deepak signs this email by setting his name clearly apart, at the end, for all to see.

## Two More Innuendos

> "wednesday i was called again to show them how <u>i drove the route</u> that day ( i could refuse was my right i still decided to go , as did my brother and friend ) the <u>drove us one by one</u> and then we were free to"

Next we find another blatant sentence containing a sexual innuendo describing the assault: "Wednesday I was called again to show them how I drove the route ["root"] that day." He follows this with "drove us one by one," suggesting "one-by-one we drove into Natalee"—yet another striking innuendo. Deepak simply appears to be putting this down as a reminder, for the record. Yet these innuendos point us toward a far more vivid message—when he puts the heart of this case in all caps. If you held the email up, ten feet away where you couldn't read any of the regular print, this message would still leap out.

### 'GIRL KIDNAPPED ASK JORAN VANDER SLOOT'

> "thursday morning my friend called me (he goes to aruba international school and his mother is a teacher there and he is a straight A student ) in panic and said there a re family members here at school and they are sharing **flyers** and the **flyers** said : GIRL KIDNAPPED ASK JORAN VANDER SLOOT (thats my friends name ) the **principle** asked them to leave and they did."

Now Deepak reports that Joran called him in a panic, suggesting that, in truth, they are both in a panic. With repeated major educational "slow down: entering school zone" message markers (Aruba International School, mother a teacher, friend a straight-A student), Deepak now takes us to the heart of the case and the centerpiece of this email, urging us in the strongest of ways to pay close attention here. Using yet another major message marker, *"flyers,"* and repeating it for emphasis, Deepak tells us—in the all caps I highlighted above—that Natalee's friends were posting a flyer at his school and elsewhere; to repeat: "GIRL KIDNAPPED ASK JORAN VANDER SLOOT." Simply and powerfully, Deepak confesses to the crime using Joran as a representative of them all. He could not say it any more plainly except to add, "AND THE KALPOE BROTHERS."

Deepak is saying in no uncertain terms that Joran van der Sloot was involved in the kidnapping—and, indirectly, so were he and Satish. Unconsciously he could have not said it any better. This is the straight-A version of the story and fully fits with why the three of them are panicked. This is also just one of three times when Deepak capitalizes a name in the entire email, and here he caps the whole thing using the largest caps possible.

Why would Deepak be so blatant? He answers that question with another striking slip, misspelling *"principle"* and thus assuring us that he has it right—he's operating on principles. He's a principled person who ultimately seeks justice. That's why he's confessing, unconsciously, uncontrollably, between the lines.

## Scene: Deepak's Reflections at Home—Overwhelming Guilt

### *'treathen phonecall'* and *'crazythings'*

> *"so thats my part of the story yesterday and today it was quiet no* **treathen** *phoncalls what we got before and i won't mention the crazythings the newspapers etc. writes about us its to much to mention. at home"*

Deepak continues to confess. Again he reminds us that the email is a secret story: *"so that's my part of the story yesterday and today,"* and he still has more to say as he now moves to the aftereffects of his crime. First he confesses in a striking message marker *"phone call"* combined with a key slip, *"treathen phone calls,"* which can be translated as "we treated ourselves to a 'hen' (a female/Natalee) and should be threatened/judged."

Perhaps most important, in *"treathen"* Deepak gives us another subtle clue as to what happened to Natalee, how they were a fatal threat to her. When people kill hens or chickens they ring their necks, suggesting that Natalee died because someone had her bound around the neck during the assault.

The sexual innuendos along with him next mentioning Joran's father trying to remain cool sheds more light on the striking slip *"quiet no **treathen** phoncalls"* suggesting "threat"—"then"—"phonecall when someone is greatly threatened." Deepak's slip underscores that indeed the three boys called Paulus when they were feeling tremendously threatened after the assault.

By emphasizing *"story,"* Deepak the reporter alerts us that he has more "news" for us. In *"Won't mention crazythings the newspapers etc writes about us its too much to mention"* we find first another denial *"won't mention"* which we read right through to find *"crazythings"*—so crazy two words were merged into one—along with that magic word *"etc"* again. By now we know beyond a shadow of a doubt that *"etc"* is code for sexual assault/rape. Deepak is once again reporting how crazy they all were when, with an absolute lack of boundaries, they all assaulted Natalee. Furthermore, he's revealing how the murder is driving him so crazy that he runs his words together. The newspaper, also known as "The Deepak Email Special," is accurately reporting from deep inside of him. Soon he will shift and begin reporting on the inner worlds of those around him.

## 'losing it she is crying constantly . . . hands are red"

> *"at home my mom is losing it she is <u>crying constantly</u> , my dad blood-pressure got high also his hands are <u>red</u>"*

Next Deepak describes the enormous pressure his deeper, unconscious guilt has created for him: his mom is *"losing it"* and crying constantly; his father's blood pressure is so high his hands are red. **Translation:** Deepak is about to explode inside because he has Natalee's blood on his hands. Also, *"losing it she is crying constantly"* becomes one more disguised image of an uncontrollable liquid and oral discharge— *"losing it"* fits perfectly with Natalee throwing up, causing her to lose her life. Deepak also implies that he's really close to breaking—certainly investigators can keep this in mind.

## 'I'm pretty worried also'

> *"my friends home is a disaster also ,his mom is <u>crying constantly</u> also his dad is pretty cool he calmes us down and talks to us also not to worry , my brother is preety cool but on his face you see he is worried , my friend is pretty worried also. i'm pretty worried also"*

Deepak shifts to the pressure he detects in Joran's home, which is also a disaster with Joran's mother *"crying constantly"* just like his—again reflecting that, deep inside, Deepak is drowning in tears. He provides another clue about how much the three guys had been talking to Paulus van der Sloot: *"he calmes us down and talks to us also not to worry."* Deepak's slip "calmes" suggests "clams" and ocean as does "down." The entire phrase *"calmes us down"* suggests the message: "Paulus tried to calm us down by telling us to dump the body down in the ocean, where the water moves toward the U.S."

## Scene: Legal Representation

> *"we have 2 lawyers one for my friend and one for me in case we get arrested and **charched** with something his dad can't defend **hin** he is a judge and he is too emotional attached ."*

Deepak now moves to the law. He mentions two lawyers for two people, reflecting his own battle—his conscious mind's L-1 lawyer is trying to get him off and his L-2 lawyer obviously confesses. With the run-on sentence *"in case we get arrested and charched* (slip suggesting "churched"—indeed men know the law, while God ultimately metes out justice) *with something his dad can't defend hin* [sic] *he is a judge and he is too emotional attached"* Deepak delivers several messages. First Deepak implies that God is The Judge and that Deepak has no legal defense for his actions, nor do any of the suspects, including Paulus. Second, Deepak suggests that Joran's father is too involved in the case and stepped over the boundaries. Then Deepak unconsciously instructs the authorities what to do now, "arrest and charge them" since he has told them enough. In *"arrested and charched with something his dad can't defend"* he obviously thinks the same thing should happen to their accomplice, Paulus.

We notice one more revealing (as always) slip from Deepak, *"can't defend **hin**,"* with *"hin"* suggesting "hen" or female. He is clearly linking all the guilty parties' mistreatment of Natalee—"didn't defend the hen," didn't defend her, to their lack of defense. Now his matching recent slip *"treathen"* takes on even stronger meaning.

Judge Deepak continues to issue his verdict in *"judge . . . he is too emotional attached,"* suggesting "He lost control emotionally and attacked her." Finally, in the message marker *"too emotional,"* which matches his recently preceding comment about *"losing it,"* Deepak implies that he is about to reveal something very powerful, something that is deeply bothering him emotionally.

# 13
# Final Confessions

*The earth is the LORD's, and all its fullness,*
*The world and those who dwell therein.*
*For He has founded it upon the seas,*
*And established it upon the waters.*
(PSALM 24:1–2 NKJV)

## Scene: Post-Graduate Work—a Boat Trip to Dump the Body

*"he is too emotional attached .my friend has his graduation this thursday*
*he has to go to the states in july he has a* **full scholarship. i had to go**
*to vacation also end of this month.many politicians find we should be*
*locked up rightnow.We"*

In *"my friend has his graduation this Thursday he has to go to the states
in july he has a full scholarship,"* we find a brief sentence suggesting "study
this closely, like a scholar," with a subtle clue as to Natalee's whereabouts and how she got there. Study the word "scholarship." Deepak is
saying, "be a scholar and see the embedded image of a '**ship**'"—the
email's most overt reference to a boat. The run-on sentence "(*scholar*)
*ship . . . had to go"* confirms the message.

Deepak doesn't just leave the two subtle images/thoughtprints suggesting "ship" hanging out there by themselves, but immediately confirms the same idea with two more references to ocean trips.
Significantly, he again points specifically to traveling west toward the
United States.

"*Full (scholar) ship"* suggests that the boat they used to dispose of
Natalee was full on the night in question. Deepak depicts a small boat
filled with a few guys and the girl's body. That's exactly the size of the
boat to which Joran had access. Deepak's run-on sentence *"Full (scholar)
ship. I had to go to . . . end of this"* also suggests that he was physically in
the boat that took Natalee's body out to sea, and that he was involved

275

the whole way, until the "*end*." Those two noticeably short sentences, one involving Joran's trip over the ocean to college in Holland and the other Deepak's ocean trip vacation, strongly suggest the same thing. The purposeful periods confirm the information as definite. (With Deepak in the boat, he also strongly endorses the cover-up of Satish being home on his computer if in fact the computer timeline is accurate.)

"Full boat" implies more rather than fewer people in the boat, which includes the possibility that Joran, Deepak, and even two accomplices were all along for the ride. Deepak possibly confirms this by mentioning that both he and Joran had plans for ocean travel.

Next, in his third brief sentence in a row, including another run-on sentence, Deepak again depicts his verdict: "*end of this . . . many politicians find we should be locked up rigthnow*." His super-sharp L-2 mind does two things at once by simultaneously clarifying that, not only do the three boys deserve to be "*locked up right now*," but that Natalee's body is locked up in a container.

Notice the powerful suggestion in the sequence, "*has to go to the states . . . (scholar) ship . . . had to go . . . end of this . . . find . . . locked up rightnow*"—telling us that Natalee's body had to go on a ship, where they put the body in the water on the western side of the island toward the states. Furthermore, he instructs us that investigators can end this whole thing if they search the ocean where they will find her "*locked up rightnow*." Yet again he makes an invaluable slip in "*rightnow*," reflecting his urgent message, "Search now"— "find her now." Deepak desperately seeks relief from his oppressive "life is now a living hell" guilt.

## Scene: '*alarms*'—Deepak's PowerPoint Presentation About the Body

> "*We heard a lot of false **alarms** that she was dead , she was seen with 2 guys , her hair is cut and is red now ,she was in a crackhouse etc, we were arrested and , my car is by the police we confessed to murder and rape,  she went in a restaurant to buy food but none of those were true.*"

Now Deepak begins "*We heard a lot of false alarms*" and takes us to a number of alleged rumors about Natalee. In so doing his L-2 mind is screening a quick PowerPoint presentation about her body's whereabouts. First, the vivid message marker, "*alarm*," takes us back to the previous sentence and the message, "In case you've been sleeping go back and read the vital clues I just gave you about her body." Next he will confirm and elaborate on his story, and as he lists the *"false alarms"* we read through his classic denials for the truth.

- *"she was dead"* = Natalee is dead.

- *"last seen with two guys"* = only two out of the three suspects, Joran and Deepak, took Natalee's body out in the small boat to dump it, and not Satish. It's also possible but very doubtful that he's referring to Joran, accompanied by one boat driver.

- *"hair is cut and red"* = suggests moment of death: "air is cut and her face is red," validating flushed face from strangulation/asphyxiation. This is one of the most striking references to Natalee's strangulation. That's the one moment above all that Deepak can't forget, which is why he underscores it with *"alarm."*

- *"she was in crackhouse"* = Natalee was on drugs, but more important, Deepak suggests "I have just cracked and told you where her body is—in a container (a type of house) in the ocean." He is trying to tell us where Natalee "lives now."

- *"we were arrested"*/ *"we confessed to murder and rape"* = email is a hidden confession of murder and rape for which they should be arrested.

- *"she went in a restaurant to buy food"* = she is restaurant food (like fish), she's at rest in the ocean. Also the subtle message that she went into the restaurant Carlos'n Charlie's (a bar and grille) and was bought food—drug food. Clearly, Deepak believes that Natalee's drugging had a lot to do with her dying, with her vomiting and aspirating.

- *"none of those true"* = all of these statements are true.

## Scene: Deepak reminds Beth—Also a Confession to the Police

*"So betty that was my part of the story what i said here is the same in* **my statement to police"**

Next *"So Betty/Beth that was my part of the story—what I said here is the same in my statement to police"* has Deepak reminding us once again, as he returns to the key message marker *"story,"* that this email is a

278 — Into the Deep

hidden story, first for Beth Twitty's eyes only. Then he makes it plain in *"what I said here is the same in my statement to police"* that he is also talking to the police.

*"My part of the story"* again alerts the authorities that Joran and Satish have also revealed important information between the lines of their police interviews. "Part of story" also suggests a key way to decode Deepak's email—read his incredibly lengthy sentences part by part, and recognize his revealing hidden sentences within the wordier sentences.

## Scene: Judge Deepak's Verdict and the Call for Other Victims

> *"what i said here is the same in my statement,people are saying they are bad guys lock them up , the family is going thru a lot righnow , but what they don't know how the other families feel and how they also have a reputation and carreers **etc**."*

We find Deepak's own inner judge continuing to render a harsh verdict in *"My statement . . . they are bad guys lock them up."* Once more Deepak insists they should be locked up, adding yet another label, this time "bad guys." He goes on to write, *"they don't know how other families feel"* as if the Judge is sentencing him.

On the other hand, reading through his denial, we can see that unconsciously Deepak now has all-too-much awareness of what he's done to Natalee's family, so much so that it's driving him crazy. Note that the thoughtprint *"bad guys lock them up"* is again in the context of speaking to Betty about family. Deepak confirms that he wrote Beth because of his guilt.

In *"they also have a reputation and carreers etc."* he suggests, particularly with his familiar code word *"etc.,"* that the three boys had a reputation of backseat sexual assaults (slip *"carreers"* = "car rears") and possibly sodomy. Observe how smoothly Deepak connects two striking sexual images.

## Scene: Major Confession—We *'were the 3 guys'*

> *"how they also have a reputation and carreers etc. because when this all is over they will still be talks that **were** the 3 guys that had something to do with the **kidnap** of natalee **its a small island**.they don't understand the pressure we are having also, if this girl turns up dead we have a <u>problem</u> **we were the last seen with her** . **I lost** a lot of friends who*

*think we had to do something with this, many of my friends supported us also brought food etc. for us at home and know we are innocent, we are innocent"*

Deepak suggests a possible conclusion to the case *"when this all is over,"* then he proceeds to give the authorities the answer for which they are searching. We find the message marker *"talks"* followed by the crucial slip *"**were** the 3 guys that had something to do with the **kidnap** of natalee its a small island."* His slip *"were"* instead of *"we're"* dramatically changes his meaning and again reads like an overt confession, as his unconscious mind intended it. To further his confession he mentions *"the kidnap of natalee"* as though it was a foregone conclusion when, even two years later, it isn't. Deepak has just provided a sterling example of a phenomenon police interrogators know well— many suspects volunteer too much information, inadvertently revealing their guilt.

Like a lawyer making a closing argument, Deepak points out the undeniable strength of the circumstantial evidence. He notes that Aruba is a tiny island and it's highly unlikely that Natalee would have gone off with anyone else after they'd been with her or even stayed at the beach alone. It's very unlikely that a young girl who has been drinking would go off with three strangers in a car on their home base—an island that runs on pleasure, with these three having questionable pasts and an affinity for tourists—and someone else committed the crime. No way. Remember, Deepak's legal counsel here suggesting "3 players, one tourist girl, small island" as one counter-statement to Paulus' "no body, no case."

Along the lines of volunteering too much information to do with Natalee's body, Satish in a police interview related that Paulus had informed them, "no **corpse**, no case" –a hint that Deepak knows Natalee is dead because he saw her corpse, indeed a strong revealing unusual word at that point in the investigation.

## 'something to do with kidnap'

*"When this is over they will still be talks that were three guys that had something to do with kidnap"* suggest that other people know about their crime. This also subtly encourages victims who experienced previous assaults to come forward, again as if he's a district attorney calling for other witnesses to testify against the three guys.

In the blatant hidden sentence *"had something to do* (read: "had to do something") *with the kidnap of natalee it's a small island . . . the pressure"*

Deepak also suggests they were desperate to get the body off the island, fully recognizing how hard it would have been to hide it on the small island. Only six days after Natalee's disappearance and Deepak is labeling it *"the kidnap of Natalee"*—no one else knows what happened, but he does. His specific reference to kidnapping is just one more in an incredible litany of revealing slips.

In *"if this girl turns up dead we have a problem we were last seen with her"* we see Deepak summarizing the case against them. Already the circumstantial evidence is piling up but, if the body surfaces, it would be overwhelming. Reading between the lines we again can hear Paulus van der Sloot's counsel, "no body, no case" which some have suggested he never said. Deepak's thoughtprints strongly suggest otherwise, including the clear messages throughout his email that Paulus was involved early on and lectured the boys on what to do. Likewise again Satish in his police interviews made plain Paulus unquestionably advised them that without the "corpse" the authorities lacked evidence.

Here Deepak repeats an earlier thoughtprint to make sure we know that, indeed, Natalee was *"last seen"* with them. He takes us back to his comments to police in another brief sentence in which he clearly establishes this idea/thoughtprint. Note, " . . . *a nightmare sinds then. the police asked us if we knew this girl showed us a picture we said yes thats her , they said she was missing and eyewitness say she was the **last seen with you guys** ."*

Also reading through the period in *"we were the last seen with her . I lost,"* Deepak reflects his awareness that indeed everything has backfired on him, and he could potentially lose out in a more major way if the body is discovered. Deepak shows he knows that Natalee's body would prove their guilt—which is precisely why his L-2 mind has told us where it is. The phrase *"if Natalee turns up dead"* clearly suggests that the body can be discovered. *"Turns up"* also resonates with his earlier repetitive keyword *"up,"* suggesting again both an ocean burial and that her body can be brought "up." It is also Deepak's only direct reference to Natalee's *"death,"* suggesting again an attorney's closing argument emphasizing that Natalee is definitely gone for good.

In *"if this girl turns up dead we have a problem,"* notice that Deepak doesn't abbreviate *"problem"* as he did before. Because he fails to abbreviate the word here, he affirms that his previous slip of *"prob"* suggested "probe" and "rape" when describing activity with Natalee in the backseat of his Honda.

"*Many of my friends supported us and brought food **etc** for us at home*" suggests first that certain friends—more than one—were involved in the entire escapade with Natalee. A friend who brought them "*food etc*" read **"etc food"** suggests someone who helped feed Natalee drugs to turn her into sexual/"etc" food. Deepak suggests another friend helped dispose of Natalee's body—pointed her toward (the) "*us at home*"; that is, dumped her on the western side of the island facing her home, the U.S.A., turning her into ocean food matching the idea above that Natalee was last seen in a restaurant. We even find the embedded statement "*friends brought us home,*" suggesting the distant possibility that, after dumping Natalee's body, friends took Joran and Deepak to their homes. Certainly the idea of "*friends who think we had to do something with this*" makes a distinctive reference to friends who know what happened because they were involved to some degree. Deepak continues to hint that at any point a witness could come forward to testify against them.

## Scene: Blatant Denial Confession in Caps—I HURT Natalee

"*know we are innocent, we are innocent also we promise i would **NEVER hurt** anyone in anyway, i would do every everything to help find her thats what we told eveyone also  , i would take a bullet to save her and bring her back to her family if i had to so would my friend also.i would **never never hurt** anyone i'm a very happy and social person who likes to make  friends with people and **not hurting** them*"

We come again to one of the three all-caps "shout-outs" in Deepak's email. If ever we needed a major lesson in forensic decoding—read through denials—we have it here. "*Know we are innocent, we are innocent*"—repeating the keyword "innocent"—sets up a blatant denial in caps, "*we promise I would NEVER hurt anyone in any way . . . I would never never hurt anyone.*" Deepak is clearly protesting his innocence far too much. Along the way, his L-2 mind insists that we should remove "NEVER" and instead emphasize "We HURT her—in fact, yes, we killed her." His denial also underscores that this email is part of his staging and secretly underscores that—on the conscious L-1 level—the entire letter is a lie, a contrived work of fiction.

In the sentence "*I would do **every everything** to help find her that's what we told everyone also*" Deepak strongly reminds us just how much he has delivered on his L-2 promise to Beth Twitty to help her, to admit what happened to Natalee and to point the way to the body. This is a strong summary reminder that, indeed, Natalee's body is discoverable.

With the words *"I would take a bullet to save her and bring her back to her family"* Deepak suggests the punishment he deserves and that, deep down, he harbors suicidal wishes because of what he has done. He now reveals that behind his repeated commands, "lock them up right now," are even stronger wishes to be punished. He also reveals how powerful an effect his confrontation with Beth had on him by suggesting he deserves to take a bullet to repay Natalee's family. This confession is the only way Deepak can bring back Natalee, if only for a moment—by speaking for her, by reporting all the gory details. "Taking a bullet" also suggests her sudden, violent death, and that Deepak views Natalee "taking" the spiked drink (which led to her aspiration death) as equivalent to a fatal shot.

When he writes *"I'm a very happy and social person who likes to make friends,"* Deepak suggests both his cover-up face as seen by his grandmother figure, Betty, and also his m.o. as a sexual predator. With another sexual innuendo, Deepak depicts himself as someone "who likes to put the make on 'friends' like Natalee."

## Scene: Deepak's Prayer

> *"and i **pray** to god that they **find** natalee **soon** and **find** her <u>well</u> so that this nightmare ends for all of us and they we <u>prove</u> we had nothing to do with this, i hope you **pray** for all of us say hi to everyone there hope to <u>hear from you</u> **soon** and may god bless.........."*

When Deepak writes, *"I pray to god that they find natalee soon and find her well so that this nightmare ends for all of us and we prove that we had nothing to do with this,"* we find several key messages. Most obviously we read through his denial in *"we prove that we had nothing to do with this"* to see his message: "we had everything to do with this." His slip *"**they we** prove we had nothing to do with this"* suggests his continual unconscious wish that *"they"*—meaning the authorities—indeed prove the guilt of all three perpetrators. Importantly, with *"prove"* Deepak again suggests that his email could eventually be accepted in court as legal proof of the crime they committed.

Again in *"**find** Natalee soon and **find** her"* he directly instructs Beth (and Dave Holloway) to search for the body. Deepak feels that the discovery of the body will lead to the end of everyone's nightmares. When he hopes that we will *"find her well"* he again informs us in his possiblity that she might not be well, along with the keyword *"well"*, that Natalee is indeed deceased. He closes his email exactly as he opened it expressing to Beth, *"hope your family is fine* (well).*"*

Addressing Beth again in *"I hope you pray for all of us . . . hope to hear from you soon,"* Deepak first seeks her forgiveness. Deepak is truly pleading with Beth for forgiveness. Now we know why judges make murderers face their victims' survivors in court—and Deepak is presiding over his own courtroom here.

Prayer is a special kind of message marker—Deepak uses it twice—suggesting that his conscience is in overdrive. He follows this not only with *"hope to hear from you soon"* but also with *"say hi to everyone"*—two message markers implying someone being receptive to communication. This is his reminder that in this email he has communicated with everyone—Beth Twitty, Dave Holloway, Natalee's broader family, the police, his own grandmother, and his surrogate grandmother. One last time he reminds the police they can hear his confession *"soon"*—"now" in fact, if they pay attention.

## Peace with His Maker

*"hope to hear from you soon and* **may god bless**......... *bye bye Deepak"*

In the name of God, because his conscience is bothering him so badly, Deepak capitalizes his own name, indicating he was a major participant in Natalee's death just as Joran was. He also ends the letter with one last, unmistakable key to the code when he closes the body of his letter with the longest pause and thus a number of periods to guide us to go back and follow his periods as key punctuation guides and messages of definite conclusions. This pause also implies that the rest of the story is yet to be told. If his confession is properly heard, indeed it's *"bye bye Deepak"* as he will end up in jail.

Finally he turns to his only hope for forgiveness, his very last words " *. . . and may god bless . . .* " His signature and final words, *"bye bye Deepak"* with his own name alone, far apart, down on the page, suggest "Bye Bye Deepak—you should be going to jail, you're going to have to face God all alone and when Natalee died at your hands you went down as well. You died too." No wonder prosecutors say that when a guilty man goes free, he's sentenced to the prison of the mind, one of the most brutal lock-ups imaginable.

In the back of his mind Deepak is still thinking about hell. He'd like to find a way around it. Remember, *"living hell"* were Beth Twitty's magic words—that she would make his *"life a living hell"* were the words that pushed Deepak into this confession. All along, deep down he has been continuously dealing with God. This is where lie-detector tests come from—because people naturally tend to tell the truth. We must not miss Deepak's final request, to hear from God—referring to him twice and repeating "soon" to show us how desperate his need is.

Only one message will do, because at this awful, horrible, miserable point in his life there is only one answer that will truly help him. He must hear God tell him "You're forgiven." In the final analysis, that's what Deepak's deeper mind has been trying to show him, and us, from the beginning to the end of his email. Thus the question remains: not only can the authorities hear his hidden messages but can Deepak himself? That's what the brilliant, nurturing, deeper mind is all about—taking ownership of oneself, warts and all. Confession is just another name for truth.

## Conclusion

As we come to the end of Deepak's hidden story, we must ask ourselves some questions. Was it cohesive? Was it powerful and shockingly graphic? Does it ring true? Did Deepak deliver on his promise?

Indeed, we find an incredibly believable, powerful coalescing story of exactly the type Deepak promised Beth. He has shown a remarkable capacity to lead us to understand the story through punctuation messages (e.g. periods, quotes, parentheses, and all-caps), and other key message markers. With his thoughtprint images he has told us a punishing story filled with disturbing news about Natalee's death, including violence and sex. He has described a brutal rape, Natalee resisting and begging for her life, the moment she died amidst the assault. He identified specifically who was sexually assaulting her and who was choking her at that moment.

Deepak has also told us what happened to the body, how it was placed in a container and taken out to sea in a boat but dumped where it might be discovered. He made plain how terribly guilty all three suspects are, declaring that they should be jailed. He has strongly suggested that Joran's father was involved in the cover-up. In the end, Deepak has answered almost all the personal questions Beth or Dave or the authorities would have about Natalee's last night—and he has done it all between the lines.

# Afterword

In his extensive confession, Deepak Kalpoe has much to teach forensic science. This is by far the longest and richest verbatim communication, or forensic document, I have personally examined. In Deepak's closing statement, *"So Betty I will say goodbye now hope you believe me,"* he is not only appealing to Beth/Betty, but also to law enforcement, hoping they will hear him. He introduces the crucial matter of "belief," which really means "hope you have the knowledge to understand me, the knowledge of L-2 unconscious communication." While "belief" too often carries the connotation of "blind faith," this is the furthest thing from Deepak's mind.

Understanding how unconscious communication works is exactly what it takes to decode it. If you don't believe it's possible, if you don't believe the mind communicates in a second language, you won't see the messages in a thousand years. Indirectly, Deepak is addressing the authorities in forensic science who, by and large, don't presently believe in unconscious communication nor understand that everyone possesses a brilliant deeper intelligence, as Deepak has demonstrated in spades. We see then how close "belief" is connected to "knowledge." Along these lines, Augustine once said, "Faith is knowledge seeking understanding."

Clearly, modern science developed because it believed there was secret knowledge waiting to be revealed in the universe, and that nature didn't give up its secrets easily. As the ancient philosopher Heraclitus noted in 500 B.C., "Nature loves to hide things." Would we expect the most complex creation of nature—the human mind—to be any different?

Because the unconscious mind always communicates indirectly in its own symbolic language, it must constantly be decoded. It can never speak directly. This has presented huge problems to law enforcement, which has traditionally adopted a direct question-and-answer approach. But the human mind is the human mind is the human mind. Decoding requires arduous work. Comprehending symbolically coded communication is no easy task. We can either do the hard work and take advantage of the knowledge it reveals, or we can ignore it.

Currently, law enforcement and traditional profilers would not even consider Deepak's phenomenal confession a forensic document. Forensic science has much to learn about expanding its approaches. Thoughtprint decoding offers great promise to forensic science when forensic documents are available—and indeed, how many such overlooked already documents exist? Verbatim productions such as journals, letters, emails, and poems are often overlooked. This new profiling approach not only creates an entirely new type of document examiner, but also an entirely new type of profiler even as it shows how interrogations can be profiled in fruitful new ways.

## Court Admissibility

Deepak also underscores that his hidden confession is as good in court as a signed confession to the police. He continually links his email to a "statement to the police." In so doing he speaks in favor of the legal admissibility of thoughtprint decoding and unconscious confessions into the court. Given the phenomenal brilliance of the deeper intelligence, lawyers and judges must now pay attention and also consider that this paradigm shift in knowledge speaks to their discipline as well.

To put it as plainly as possible, if a panel of judges asked my professional opinion if Deepak was unconsciously communicating, beyond a shadow of doubt, that his email should be considered a confession he wanted admitted into evidence, I would answer, "Yes—and furthermore he validated that message in numerous ways," which I would then list. If they asked me whether the unconscious mind spoke in its own unique language, and that we can now understand that language I would again answer, "Yes." Certainly thoughtprint decoding with its inbuilt method of validating messages moves the psychological side of forensic science toward a hard science.

Everything comes down to how the human mind works, and the question, if indeed, we have discovered a brilliant deeper intelligence lurking below the surface of our conscious minds—a deeper consciousness that waits to guide us, especially in matters of right and wrong. For the record, the same issue of knowledge regarding the unconscious mind confronts the entire field of psychology and academics in general. When a breakthrough of this magnitude takes place—a discovery of a vastly superior intelligence within each person—it shakes the whole world.

Breakthroughs always bring about changes, sooner or later, which brings us back to Deepak's admonition: "Believe that I am speaking clearly though in an indirect language to you." What law enforcement and forensic science does with that knowledge will determine how soon the wave of the future becomes standard practice, a living, functional reality. Given the history of breakthroughs in knowledge in any field, the process of implementing it takes longer rather than shorter. If we listen we can speed up that process.

# Appendix A
# Two Types of Listeners

I understand how it seems strange at first that our L-2 mind communicates so extensively, and that it can actually solve murders. But the idea that unseen bacteria surrounded us once shocked surgeons, who previously refused to scrub before surgery and did not use surgical gloves. As a medical doctor I have watched as major advances have initially been ridiculed, including the idea of microsurgery—whereas now, laproscopic or arthroscopic surgery is state of the art.

As we learn how to look deeper into the human mind—or I should say listen more deeply—we are on a similar cutting edge of knowledge. We can be sure that the ever-present skeptics are around, but when it comes to the mind they take it to another level entirely because, quite frankly, we have never had a breakthrough such as this. This breakthrough takes us to a level at which our soul itself puts each of us under our own personal microscope—psychoscope, actually, since "psyche" in Greek means "soul".

That's where all our deeper secrets reside, the secrets that we keep from ourselves. Nobody really wants to face the integrity of the deeper intelligence until they learn that the truth really does set them free. Initially we operate by a secret code—don't go near the right brain/unconscious, and the more pain that's down there for someone the more that's true.

Murder cases take us to incredibly powerful places in our psyches because they touch on the powerful emotions we most want to avoid: the capacity to be really hurt by another person, or to really hurt someone else. Quite simply, when you've been terribly hurt you feel as if someone has just murdered you, has just killed your soul. There's not one of us who doesn't know real emotional pain, but some folks have been hurt so badly they don't want to know how bad. So they hide it and too often hurt other people, often by vicious personal attacks.

That's where the two types of listeners—"right-brain" and "left-brain"—come from, and they are worlds apart. (In my model, left brain means conscious mind, right brain means unconscious, as I explained in chapter 3.) These left-brainers have a huge split in themselves—

between their conscious and their unconscious—and intend to keep it that way. The purely left-brain folks want nothing to do with the unconscious mind and have a vested interest in denying unconscious communication. They would hope and pray that a deeper intelligence doesn't exist and will do everything in their power to avoid such a reality. Typically, these people often mock the unconscious and most things psychological, except for their version of reality—meaning "Stay in my left brain or I'll get nasty!" They will label explorers of the unconscious "Freudian," which should be translated either as "disturbed, sexually preoccupied psychologists" or as just plain weird.

Others have the same basic attitude about the unconscious, only they hide it better, calling themselves "skeptics," which often is just another name for being close-minded. Sadly I have encountered more than enough such people, even in journalism. In the JonBenét Ramsey case one reporter who interviewed me wrote one of the most slanted newspaper pieces I've ever seen, informing me before his first question he didn't like the idea of my "reading minds." All I could say was that the unconscious L-2 mind begs to be heard—it's the part of the mind doing almost all of the communicating. I simply decode the language. I said the same thing to Wichita profilers in the BTK case who took issue with my work (which eventually proved to be accurate). I had the same experience with certain commentators on *Court TV* in the Holloway case, even though their lead investigative reporter, Diane Diamond, actually embraced my work.

There is also a type of listener who espouses an understanding of unconscious communication but in the end really can't hear it. The major distinction between listeners is ultimately this: those who believe a superior deeper intelligence brilliantly communicates unconsciously, and those who believe the unconscious either isn't all that bright or doesn't communicate at all.

One last thing. For some the Holloway case evolved on the Internet into the emergence of pro-Joran/anti-Natalee posters who viewed Joran as the case's real victim. Certainly Joran's own blame-the-victim mentality makes sense for the phenomenally self-indulgent sexual predator who wrote his book to please that audience.

What I say to those defenders of Joran van der Sloot is simply this. Now allow Deepak Kalpoe to speak truth from his soul, his deeper intelligence. But I have no illusions that those intent on degrading and attacking Natalee Holloway will listen. They haven't the slightest interest in unconscious communication. For them it's most convenient to simply deny that the unconscious mind exists, or at least to deny its relevance. To these people, this book will mean nothing because they refuse to hear the messages delivered by the deeper intelligence. They're simply not listening.

What I have seen in these high-profile cases is that people often make up their own minds early, and generally stick to their opinion—it's just human nature. Beyond that, because of their resistance to ideas that they don't readily understand, some people's reactions are downright mean-spirited. And the story of a young American girl from a somewhat privileged family, going off to a Caribbean island for several days of partying, clearly evokes all kinds of nasty emotions. Natalee, sadly, became a perfect foil upon which these people could dump all of their own foibles.

Even so, despite what I call "deeper intelligence phobia," many other people now recognize this intuitive, superior, deeper intelligence as the repository of the phenomenal brilliance which exists within each of us, and we either use it or we don't. This book is about my efforts to listen to the messages from the deeper minds of the three suspects, particularly those revealed so dynamically by Deepak Kalpoe.

# Appendix B
# More About Message Markers

Nonverbal markers include punctuation and spacing—the "body language" of the document. This body language helps organize the hidden messages; it also highlights conclusions and validates the verbal messages.

Punctuation message markers, or "punctuation messaging," includes periods, commas, colons, caps/headlines, quotation marks, parentheses and spacing, all of which Deepak uses to highlight his story.

In forensic documents such markers always reflect much L-2/unconscious thought. The following are a summary of nonverbal message markers.

## Periods

Periods are used in two ways, first as a simple L-1 punctuation mark used at "face value" and second as L-2 message markers that say "Stop here and focus." In a lengthy email such as Deepak's, we can look at the periods as traffic lights, which he flashes to make sure we really stop and look around for clues. Since the issue at hand here is Natalee Holloway's fate, periods carry unusual potential for linking and highlighting important messages to be associated with her fatal endpoint. Periods also have another L-2 meaning, suggesting *final, end of story,* and *all she wrote.* They can also introduce a closing declaration or conclusion.

In his email Deepak uses periods in two characteristic, unique ways. First he writes *at extreme length without any period at all,* suggesting that he's anxious to get that part of the story off his chest and thus underscoring a crucial part of the narrative. Also, by failing to put periods in a number of run-on sentences, Deepak reveals parts of his confession that would otherwise be hidden by encouraging the reader to combine phrases and sentences in different ways. In fact, Deepak does this on the very first page, revealing vital information that explains some of the events leading up to Natalee's disappearance.

Deepak also uses *extremely brief sentences* when he wants to stress one particular point, or to emphasize a particular conclusion with respect to Natalee's fate.

## Caps

As everyone on the Internet knows, when you want to shout you put your words in all-caps. Deepak does the same thing in three places, to underscore his confession. And, because most of his email is in continuous lowercase, when Deepak uses all caps he's clearly shouting a significant L-2/ unconscious message. For example, *"Natalee was "VERY drunk"* and *"NEVER (would Deepak hurt anyone)"* along with the blatant *"GIRL KIDNAPPED ASK JORAN VANDER SLOOT."* In these three places alone, Deepak tells the entire story in a nutshell.

### Quotes and Parentheses

Deepak uses quotes to highlight messages that speak for his victim. This is the same thing other perpetrators are also prone to do, unconsciously. He will use quotation marks correctly on only four occasions, three of which involve key statements by Natalee while the fourth one is part of his description of Jug Twitty's angry confrontation with the suspects. In other places Deepak will use implied quotes via "she said" statements.

On ten occasions we will also see Deepak make important observations, and further underscore information, by using parentheses. For example, he once combines a parenthesis with an all caps message to doubly underscore the crucial information he's providing, *"(by then Natalee was VERY drunk)."*

### Spacing and Positioning—More Body Language

Spacing and positioning allow a writer to emphasize messages by setting them apart in prominent locations in the document—for example, in greetings, signatures, beginnings of paragraphs, ends of sentences and left- or right-hand columns. Spacing and positioning can be thought of as "key-location messaging." Deepak will begin his email and one of the most important messages in his letter by setting apart his opening, *"Dear Betty."*

### Central Message

The goal in criminal investigation is to get to the heart of the matter. In forensic documents, perpetrators invariably guide you to the center of the document, to the heart of the case. This often involves "body language," meaning some extremely valuable, nonverbal clue. Deepak demonstrates this clearly—when we get there, the clue just leaps out at us.

## Follow the Period Strategy

As we examine these message markers, we will adopt an initial strategy that will keep us on track throughout the profile. It amounts to "Follow the periods" or "follow the conclusions." We will also keep all these nonverbal message markers in our minds as we focus on the verbal message markers explained below.

## Verbal Message Markers

Nonverbal markers work hand-in-hand with verbal message markers to guide the profiler to a perpetrator's confession, and that's what happens in Deepak's email.

Verbal message markers are thoughtprints that primarily refer to communication per se—communication images. These include everyday words such as "called," "talked," "said," "questioned" or "answered." Such words become even more important when connected to powerful qualifiers, such as "police questioned," which Deepak will use on two key occasions.

Such references to communication are red flags indicating that key messages are being delivered. In these ways the writer say, "I'm telling you or I'm about to tell you something really important." Specifically, when he uses "police questioned" it tells us his internal policeman, his conscience, is operating in overdrive and he's providing extremely crucial information.

Many times a writer will use more dramatic message markers for emphasis. We can think of these as *different types of "messaging" similar to "text-messaging"* on cell phones. Here are some other common specialized types of verbal L-2 message markers that Deepak uses:

1. Elite *"flashing light"* markers are references to vivid, attention-getting types of communication. Deepak uses these repeatedly—lighthouse, alarm going off, traffic light, screamed, news, dancing and police questioned are all good examples.

2. Education *"school zone"* markers, which include Deepak's references to school, classes, scholar, learning, telling a story and "why we did this," all urge the profiler to "go to school here." A particularly key message marker is "story," signifying that the writer is telling the hidden story of the crime. When we see the word "story" it's as though we're entering a school zone with flashing lights.

3. *Keyword or repeat messaging* occurs when a writer uses the same word two or more times, thus suggesting "don't miss this." Deepak repeats several keywords, including "Betty," "natalee" and "Holiday Inn." Keywords can also simultaneously be educational or elite flashing light markers—in Deepak's case repeating both "lighthouse" and "news," doubly underscoring their importance.

   Interestingly, despite using "natalee" multiple times in his email, never once does Deepak capitalize her name.

4. *Denial messaging* or "thou doth protest too much" (for example "I didn't do this crime") all suggest exactly the opposite message. Denial is one of the most common forms of unconscious L-2 confession, and often it's a major key to a hidden confession—a red flag, signaling that a person's deeper intelligence is pressuring him to tell the truth. Deepak resorts to this device time and time again, particularly at one of the three moments he puts in all caps the word, *"NEVER."*

5. *"Slips"* or *"slip messaging"* includes misspellings or omissions that the L-1 mind overlooks, which describe what the perpetrator has done. I refer to slip messages as *command performances* or *direct-access messages*, in which the L-2 mind briefly takes over and says, in effect, "Let me say it directly and unmistakably so you'll be sure to read the message the way I really intended it." Deepak's unconscious mind repeatedly makes revealing slips. It's one of the most common ways in which he tells the truth.

6. *"Blatant phrases"* are special slips that Deepak makes—an overlooked "blatant phrase" which tells the real story. Early in his email, Deepak puts a blatant phrase in quotes and speaks for his victim, using the phrase *"last day,"* indicating that his victim died on *that day.*

   Other message markers that Deepak uses include *"sounds like"* messaging, similar to the way the parlor game Charades is played. He also demonstrates *"linkage messaging"* in which he unknowingly links two key ideas to show they're related. For example he links "lighthouse" to a key idea which explains what he and his accomplices did with Natalee. A variant of this is *"vertical messaging"* in which Deepak communicates vertically—think crossword puzzles. Remember, the L-2 mind is a creative genius at communicating.

We also find *"audience markers"* in which a perpetrator will reference police authorities, as well as others to whom he's secretly confessing—and indeed Deepak confesses to several different people, including the police. And last of all a writer will often use *"document markers,"* overt or disguised references to the forensic document itself, which he makes to draw attention to its relevance, even suggesting that it should be used in court. Deepak links his email to a signed statement he gave to police.

Verbal message markers work hand-in-hand with nonverbal markers—and with key images—to guide profilers to the truth. Deep down a perpetrator's unconscious is actually profiling the case. The message markers all point to the full "thoughtprint story," a completely true and accurate account of what actually happened. Every word has a double meaning. But rather than the first, superficial meaning, the second meaning—the thoughtprint meaning—tells the true story.

# Bibliography

Beattie, Robert. (2005). *Nightmare in Wichita: The Hunt for the BTK Strangler*. New York: Penquin Books.

Burrough, Bryan. (January 2006). "Missing White Female," *Vanity Fair*.

Douglas, John. (1997). *Mind Hunters*. New York: Pocket Books.

Foster, Don. (2000). *Author Unknown*. New York: Henry Holt and Co.

Geberth, Vernon J. (2007). *Practical Homicide*, 4th Edition. London/New York: Taylor & Frances.

Hodges, Andrew G. (1994). *The Deeper Intelligence*. Nashville: Thomas Nelson.

___ (1998). *A Mother Gone Bad*. Birmingham, AL: Village House Publishers.

___ (2000). *Who Will Speak for JonBenét?* Birmingham, AL: Village House Publishers, 1998.

___ (2002). "Suicidal Threats: Listening Between the Lines," *Suicide and Law Enforcement*, Quantico, VA: FBI Behavioral Science Unit.

Langs, Robert J. (2004). *Fundamentals of Adaptive Psychotherapy and Counselling*. New York: Palgrave McMillan.

___ (1988). *A Primer of Psychotherapy*. New York: Gardner Press.

___ (1973). *Technique of Psychoanalytic Psychotherapy*. Volume 1. New York: Jason Aaron Publishers.

Van der Sloot, Joran & Vokejevic, Z. (2007). *The Natalee Holloway Case*. Netherlands: Sijthoff.

# About the Author

ANDREW G. HODGES, MD, is a board-certified psychiatrist in Birmingham, Alabama and has been in private practice for more than twenty-five years. Previously he was an assistant clinical professor of psychiatry at the University of Alabama at Birmingham School of Medicine. A published author of several books, he has also written for a major FBI publication.

Dr. Hodges is a gifted communicator and has been interviewed extensively in both print and electronic media, on such programs as *Anderson Cooper 360–CNN*, *Fox National News*, *Primetime CNN*, *MSNBC Morning Show*, *Hannity-Colmes*, *The Catherine Crier Report*, *The CBS Morning Show*, *Court TV Investigation* (*Holloway Case*), *The View*, *A Word on Words* (syndicated PBS), and in various newspapers including *USA Today*, *The Chicago Tribune* and *The San Francisco Chronicle*.

For more than a quarter-century, Dr. Hodges has helped pioneer a breakthrough to the unconscious mind, which he explained in his groundbreaking book *The Deeper Intelligence* (Thomas Nelson, 1994). His first book, *Jesus: An Interview Across Time—A Psychiatrist Looks at His Humanity* (Bantam, 1988) utilized decoding techniques on Scripture to explore the human personality of the Son of God.

Dr. Hodges has further developed the technique of forensic document decoding by accessing the unconscious mind of a suspect in criminal investigations. For example, as a result of applying this technique to the JonBenét Ramsey ransom note, Dr. Hodges wrote two highly acclaimed books on the case, *A Mother Gone Bad* (Village House, 1998) and *Who Will Speak for JonBenét?* (Village House, 2000).

Hodges is currently being consulted in a number of unsolved murders. He was on the verge of being brought into the BTK case at the encouragement of former Wichita Police Chief Richard LaMunyon (and various forensic professionals) when BTK was captured.

Forensic experts, including highly qualified criminologists and FBI agents, believe that the techniques developed by Dr. Hodges will soon become a significant weapon in the criminal investigator's arsenal. They have proven themselves to be both accurate and consistently reliable.

(For more information, please visit www.forensicthoughtprints.com)

# What Others Say . . .

*Once again in the Natalee Holloway case Dr. Hodges has written a fascinating account and profile of the hidden meaning behind a suspect's own words. Probing the deeper intelligence, Dr. Hodges offers law enforcement a new and promising technique in solving crimes".*

> Charles Donald Byron
> Special Agent, Federal Bureau of Investigation
> (Retired)

*With his latest book* Into the Deep, *Dr Hodges advances forensic psychiatry and forensic profiling—both lacking new tools particularly in solving puzzling cases. With "thoughtprint decoding" Hodges offers a solid way of getting at crucial overlooked clues. Based on clinical and mathematical work, "thoughtprints" is completely consistent with the notion that every criminal leaves behind clues about their crime. In this gem, Hodges deals with little known workings of the mind that reveal vital information in a disguised form. For the reader who wants the best look imaginable at the criminal mind, this will be a fascinating read.*

> Harold S. Schaus, Jr., M.S., DAPA
> Past President
> The Society for Communicative
> Psychoanalysis and Psychotherapy

*Andrew Hodges is the ultimate "mind hunter." In this book he retells the Natalee Holloway story from inside the mind of a major suspect—one of the last people to see the victim alive, and one of only three who know what really happened. Dr. Hodges has been the courageous reader of the mind from the JonBenet Ramsey ransom note to the search for BTK. Several times I have been along for the ride, listening to him think about forensic cases. Hodges is a practicing psychiatrist who knows how to read the forensic roadmaps to the unconscious. Read this book and go along for a new ride.*

> Patrick J Callahan, PhD, FAPA, ABPS
> Fellow, American College of Forensic Examiners

*As a former district attorney, I am convinced that Dr. Hodges makes a compelling case for 'thoughtprints' in solving criminal cases and their potential for forensic evaluations. Practicing as a trial lawyer for years in the county in California where a judge first allowed DNA to be admitted into evidence, I am particularly attuned to innovative new methods of forensic investigation. Recently, our branch of the national educational legal society (Inns of Court) consisting of eighty lawyer/ judge members featured the 'thoughtprint decoding' method as the central presentation.*

Richard A. Regnier, Attorney
Diplomate National Board of Trial Advocacy

*During the last six years I have consulted with Dr. Hodges several times regarding cases where written notes were involved. As a retired FBI agent and active chief of police I have found his unconscious communication technique to be useful. I think his study of the ransom note in the JonBenét Ramsey case was insightful and found his book to be fascinating.*

Donald Dixon, Chief of Police
Lake Charles, Louisiana
Special Agent, FBI, retired

*I have followed with interest the use of thoughtprint decoding developed by Dr. Hodges to identify suspects in criminal cases. My support of his techniques also stems from my background as a prosecutor and district attorney.*

Parham Williams
Dean, Chapman University School of Law
Los Angeles, California

*Indeed a new type of investigator is on the forensic scene. The discovery of the deeper intelligence is like the discovery of DNA. Hodges' profiling method offers us hidden confessions and chilling explanations as to motives when forensic documents or oral interrogations are available.*

Irving Weisberg, Ph.D., psychologist
Faculty member, Adelphi University
Garden City, New York

*Dr. Hodges has successfully applied a sound and validated method of decoding the unconscious mind to the world of criminal investigation. This exciting work demands serious consideration.*

M. Mark McKee, Psy.D.
Associate Professor of Psychology
Illinois School of Professional Psychology

*Following this well-validated new forensic method of psycholinguistic decoding sometimes makes one feel like Dr. Watson, hurtling along behind Hodges' Sherlock Holmes.*

Arthur R. Jacobs, MD
Clinical Instructor in Psychiatry
Albert Einstein College of Medicine
Bronx, New York

*Hodges' thoughtprint forensic approach represents a significant validation of cutting-edge awareness in hidden communication.*

Duncan J. J. Magoon, MD
Clinical Instructor in Psychiatry
Wayne State University Medical School
Detroit, Michigan

*A remarkable application of a new psychological technique.*

Marc Lubin, Ph.D.
Professor of Psychology
Illinois School of Professional Psychology
Chicago, Illinois

*Dr. Hodges demonstrates well the understanding from in-depth therapy that we cannot keep secrets; our unconscious mind speaks volumes.*

Marc Kessler, Ph.D.
Associate Professor of Psychology
University of Vermont
Burlington, Vermont